COMPLETE POEMS
AND SELECTED LETTERS OF
MICHELANGELO

COMPLETE POEMS
AND SELECTED LETTERS OF
MICHELANGELO

TRANSLATED, WITH A FOREWORD AND
NOTES, BY CREIGHTON GILBERT
EDITED, WITH A BIOGRAPHICAL INTRODUCTION,
BY ROBERT N. LINSCOTT

RANDOM HOUSE · NEW YORK

Acknowledgment is gratefully made to Yale University Press for permission to reprint Creighton Gilbert's translation of two madrigals, "Lady, up to Your High and Shining Crown" and "Led on through Many Years," which appeared in *Lyric Poetry of the Italian Renaissance*, edited by L. R. Lind.

DESIGNED BY VINCENT TORRE

TRANSLATOR'S FOREWORD

The Poems and the Personality

MANY WRITERS are known to us through poems and letters. When we like the poems, we often turn eagerly to the letters in order to get behind the scenes; the letters are an intimate, private communication, in contrast with the poems, which are universalized in result, however intense and personal their origin.

With Michelangelo we almost have to reverse this view. The surviving letters of Michelangelo have a distinctly public character; they show us the external man. Many of them are business letters and are thus offshoots from his art of sculpture; they are useful to the historian in fixing the dates of his activities and showing the sequence of his works. Many are to his family, but these, too, deal to a large extent with business matters, and it is typical that to learn of his emotional attachment to his family we have to turn to some of the poems.

We can, to be sure, infer a good deal about Michelangelo's personality from the letters, though the most facile inferences are not the most accurate. The long series of letters to his nephew browbeats the young man cruelly. The other letters are full of complaints and could make us think that Michelangelo was continually whining. Certainly he never ceased to complain of unfair treatment and of being cheated. From the letters alone we might be led to believe that Michelangelo was unbearably selfish. We can be rescued from this improbable idea of a short-sighted complacency by the poems. These show, with far greater acuteness, that he complained of his own shortcomings and failure with even more bitter rage. Putting these two observations together, we reach, I suggest, a meaningful deduction: all his life Michelangelo set before himself goals of achievement which were impossible. He applied these standards to everyone, first to himself, to his outrageously put-upon patrons, to his merely ordinary nephew. Never having experienced a failure of nerve that would lead him to admit compromise as the only plausible outcome of effort, he maintained the stress of his goals all his life. Perhaps this is what great men do. The fact that many of Michelangelo's works are unfinished is clearly part of the same situation: it has been realized by many observers that he was discouraged by the failure of his own carving to match his original idea. (He was the first artist to leave unfinished works that appeal to modern aesthetic feelings as completely expressive forms, and his art is infinitely more personal than that of any other artist of his time.) The unfinished has often been discussed as a factor in Michelangelo's art, but it has not perhaps been emphasized that, it is at the heart of his expression.

The poems, then, reveal the private person whose public

self we know in his sculpture and painting. Their role corresponds to that of other people's letters. It was a social convention of Michelangelo's time to write letters in verse, especially in the sonnet form, and especially by way of paying compliments. Michelangelo's poems, like those of many other amateur poets of his time, were first produced this way. These early poems are few, and it may be that many others were not kept. Later, Michelangelo developed as a poet. Many are still addressed to his few closest friends, others to God, and in some he is evidently talking to himself.

The poems are difficult, for several reasons. One is that Michelangelo was an amateur writer and did not smooth things out. Some of these difficulties are impossible to resolve; for instance, antecedents are sometimes ambiguous. Other difficulties come from the shorthand presentation of very involved ideas; since readers of poetry today are used to that problem, the very long, prosy, and ultimately unsatisfying running expositions used by older editors are excluded here.

On the other hand, a main difficulty today was no problem at all in Michelangelo's time, that is his constant employment of a particular philosophical attitude, Neo-Platonism, which was as prevailing then as Freudianism today. The following may help the reader to understand some terms that recur over and over.

Platonic love today seems a diluted, sometimes absurd thing, as in the phrase "their affection was purely Platonic." For the Renaissance, on the contrary, Platonic love was a very difficult ideal, a constant wrestling with the unceasing temptation of sexual love, but desirable for reasons of religion and tranquil self-realization. That it was so for Michelangelo is first suggested by the very sensual early poems.

Furthermore, Platonic love cannot be simply decided upon, but must be reached by stages, beginning with its opposite, physical love, its only possible point of origin. The very object physically desired must be what is purified into spiritual desire. Many of the poems are about the process of this struggle. The beloved object may, if she will, help the lover to turn his love Platonic. According to a convention, the most spiritual element in the object of love is her eyes, and therefore the poems make constant references to them. A frequent point is that her eyes draw his heart to them. If, according to a figure of speech common in the love poetry of all ages, she captures his heart, then its route of travel is imagined as passing through her eyes to her heart where both hearts are merged into one. Michelangelo's sense of the physical, the vivid force of his imagination, and his love of carrying things out to their conclusions, all make him present this image with startling physical literalness, and draw further implications from it.

Paradox is one of his favorite devices, and one of the things that makes the poems difficult. Paradox is involved fundamentally in Neo-Platonism when the lover must first be attracted to the beloved object in order to rise above love. The relation of love and death is a favorite paradox. If the lady refuses to pay attention to him, he says conventionally, he will die; but if she is kind, then he will die in the sense of being damned as a sinner. Conversely, only by cruelty can she save him. This is a simplification of a theme treated in many of the poems with intense and subtle variations.

Ice and fire are among the favorite figures of speech. Michelangelo had a strong sense of becoming aged, which he first expressed in a letter written when he was forty-three. The ice of old age can paradoxically extinguish the fire of passion, a contradiction underlined by the fact that these figures retain their literal attributes and are not treated as mere metaphors. Ice may also be the beloved object's rejecting attitude, and both figures may appear together.

The sense of aging is connected with Michelangelo's acute sense of his own body as something vulnerable. Images of flaying, wounding with arrows (sometimes fire darts), and decay recur and remind us of Michelangelo's one self-portrait, which appears in his *Last Judgment*. There the saints hold up signs of their martyrdom in the traditional way. St. Bartholomew, who was flayed to death, holds his skin, and the crumpled face on the skin is Michelangelo's. The image of the hurt body is related to the relatively few images drawn from the technique of sculpture, such as hammering stone and melting metal. Michelangelo presents himself as the hammered or melted object, the "artist" being his beloved object who creates him but, in the typical case, does not finish him. A characteristic Neo-Platonic idea is used in the sonnet in which the artist is shown chipping the stone to reveal the statue already inside, but failing to do it properly.

The frustrating difficulty of reaching spiritual calm through excitement over beautiful women can be circumvented in one way. This is by loving a man, since sexual excitement is there not involved. This solution is offered explicitly in poem 258. "Violent passion for tremendous beauty" is free of sin if it aspires to Heaven. Love for a woman is "too much unlike" and should be avoided.

> One draws to Heaven and to earth the other,
> One in the soul, one living in the sense,
> Drawing its bow on what is base and vile.

Since this was a solution to Michelangelo's most urgent problem, the expression of such love for men is frequent. Rejecting "the sense," it does not involve homosexuality. A single poem taken in isolation from the writer's personality (which would be justified in a "public" poet) could of course seem to have that implication. Michelangelo actually faces this problem of misunderstanding in an early poem, 56, crabbed in style but unambiguous, where he laments that his feeling is wrongly judged not only by "those who always see themselves in others" but by the beloved object himself. But "in fact, the unbelievers are the liars." Michelangelo's fears that people would apply their own standards to him were all too justified. The matter has been the center of sensationalizing gossip, which is why this documentation seems necessary in a relatively thorough form. In part, it is encouraged by the sort of people who are mainly interested in Van Gogh because he cut off his ear; they do not stop to think that even that fact would not be notorious had Van Gogh not been a genius, and that only thus has it come to their attention—yet they pay heed to it and not to his genius. In part, it is due to more pardonable difficulties, such as the use of the same vocabulary in all ages for sensual and Platonic love, although it is worth noticing that the poems to men never use the detailed physical imagery of the early ones to women, like 4 and 20. But the chief reason is probably that in the Victorian period Platonic love-poetry was tacitly understood to be a shamefaced euphemism for sexual yearnings, and "those who always see themselves in others" refused to believe that Michelangelo had different interests. Michelangelo once openly refers to another man's homosexuality; his tone seems to say that it is a rather ridiculous foible. The reader may find this easier to understand if he reminds himself once again that Michelangelo's Platonic love is not the timid, bloodless thing that we usually associate with it, but an agonized defense against the temptations of women. A curious corollary of all this is that when speaking of a completely spiritual woman like Vittoria Colonna he quite naturally refers to her in the masculine gender.

Michelangelo's dissatisfaction with people led him to live much alone, with little social activity, concentrating on his work and apparently surrounded by litter which he usually ignored but sometimes found depressing. As he grew older, he withdrew even further because of his horror of celebrity hunters, who clustered around one who was apparently the first person to be publicly regarded as a genius in the modern sense while still alive. When the celebrity hunters could not be ignored, he treated them with veiled irony, as in the letters to Varchi and the King of France (65, 78). On the other hand, he had a few close friends—perhaps as "compensation"—with whom his relationships were intense. He revealed himself to them absolutely and passionately and praised them with complete disregard for their human inadequacies. These included the handsome and accomplished young man Tommaso Cavalieri, the banker and amateur writer Luigi del Riccio, and the pious widow Vittoria Colonna, Marchioness of Pescara, whom he regarded as his teacher in religion. Many of the poems are addressed to these and others though it is rarely possible to be sure just which, and it is usually not important to know.

Among these people, Luigi del Riccio has a special importance for us, because, in addition to handling Michelangelo's financial affairs, he took a lively interest in the poems and proposed that they should be published. Michelangelo, who could not take the trouble to organize them himself, was agreeable, and as a result there are many fair copies in Luigi's handwriting, some of which show revisions. These were probably agreed upon in their conversations, since it is known that Michelangelo asked Luigi's advice. After Luigi's death (or perhaps after a preceding quarrel) the project was abandoned.

Luigi del Riccio is also responsible for a group of poems distinct from the pattern of all the others—the forty-eight epitaphs for Cecchino Bracci. Cecchino died at the age of fifteen, and Luigi, who had been his tutor and relative and had had, at least in Michelangelo's opinion, a homosexual interest in him, begged for a tomb design and for an epitaph. The result was forty-eight quatrains, many of them more like epigrams than epitaphs, in which Michelangelo explores the paradoxes of death and youth in an exhaustive range of variations and logical conclusions, including those in which the tomb is the speaker. Michelangelo had hardly even seen Cecchino, and the feeling expressed is not at all personal. It is an exploration of the idea, to see how many possible answers there are to the same question. The effect of reading all forty-eight is hardly moving, but cold and even comic. The comedy was quite clear to Michelangelo, who sent the epitaphs to Luigi in batches with notes like: "I didn't want to send this one, because it is very awkward, but the trout and truffles would force Heaven itself," or "For the salted mushrooms, since you will have nothing else," or "This the trout say, not I; so, if you don't like the verses, don't marinate them again without pepper."

As endless variations on a theme, the epitaphs do help the reader to understand Michelangelo's method of composition. This could also be shown, if it were not so intricate and bulky, by printing the rough drafts of the other poems, sometimes mounting to ten. They show the same changes of thought, exploring what follows logically if the writer rejects the hypothesis he had made and tries another, even an opposite one. One simple example is 144. It originally began with the same two lines as at present, but the third was: "It is theft not to give what is yours." When he started to revise, Michelangelo did not write down the first two lines, but the third as we now read it, making the opposite statement. And the whole poem then moves off in such a different direction that one might be justified in considering it another poem altogether. Here then, as in the epitaphs, the triggering of the intricate idea, and its variation of logical conclusion and paradox, are essential.

The "trout and truffles" bring up a curious quirk in Michelangelo's personality—his violent reaction to gifts. He went to absurd lengths to avoid receiving them, as his letters to his nephew show. When accepting them, he gave thanks in a way which showed why he did not want them: he felt himself under extreme obligation, impossible to repay. Several of the poems are such thank-you notes. A few others were written on some special occasion, and thus are more like the letter-poems of his contemporaries. They range from the youthful complaint to Pope Julius II to the late compliment to Vasari on the publication of his *Lives of the Artists*, another present. To understand such poems, it is necessary to have some knowledge of the circumstances. Fortunately, this is largely supplied by the letters. In his old age Michelangelo hoped to retire to Florence, and since he thought Vasari controlled the favors of the Duke, he was pathetically obsequious to him. But the change from the bold complainer to the "humble servant" is in great part a matter of the times. During the first half of the sixteenth century the change from republican and

representative institutions to absolute monarchy and its so-
cial forms was conspicuous all over Europe, from England
to Florence.

Most of the above remarks apply to the poems of the
middle years (there being very few extant from the early
period) which are intricate in form and need comment.
The late poems are simpler and more open in style, a
change which also occurs in the letters. They are easier as
well because the figures of speech survive in our own cul-
ture; the approach to God, the hope and fear of death. It
is sometimes said that these poems show a spirit of resigna-
tion. That is only partly true. Michelangelo does not ex-
pect to be able to match his ideas in his work, but he is no
less concerned about them. The common comparison of
Michelangelo's sonnets to Donne's holy sonnets can only
be made if the theme of Michelangelo's late religious
poems is imposed on the gnarled, intricate conceptual style
of his middle period.

Michelangelo used a number of poetic forms, but the
chief ones were the sonnet and the madrigal. The epitaph
appears only in the Cecchino Bracci series; the use of the
eight-line stanza, the long poem in terza-rima like the
Divine Comedy, and a few other forms, appears only in a
dozen cases all told. The sonnets and madrigals are about
equal in number. The madrigal is not a form used today
and does not correspond to the fal-la-la form of old Eng-
lish music. Its distinctive character is the irregular rhyme
scheme and the indefinite number of lines, generally be-
tween ten and twenty. Michelangelo's sonnets are far bet-
ter known than his madrigals, probably because the sonnet
form is familiar to us. Indeed, people who refer to Michel-
angelo's poetic work often use the phrase "Michelangelo's
sonnets," and it is one of the easiest ways of telling whether

someone has looked seriously at the poems. In Michelangelo's lifetime the sonnets were already more interesting to literary people, but the madrigals attracted musicians. It can be shown that Michelangelo was more comfortable with the irregular madrigal. Although his sonnets and madrigals exist in equal numbers, a considerable number of sonnets were abandoned unfinished but hardly any madrigals. In several cases a poem begun and abandoned in another form, capitolo or sonnet, was rewritten and completed as a madrigal.

The text of the poems comes down to us first of all as a large body of manuscripts. There are probably more holograph manuscripts of Michelangelo in existence than of any other poet of his age or earlier; they were kept partly because he was a celebrity, as mementos, and partly because they had not been published. The publication went through several stages. The first edition in 1623, by a grandnephew, was heavily revised and bowdlerized, and fragments were completed. Yet it made the poems famous, and was used for the beautiful translations of Wordsworth. The original texts were published in 1863 and were used by Symonds for his translation of the eighty complete sonnets, which has been often reprinted. In 1897 Karl Frey published a superb and elaborate edition making all the variants available. It has been the source of many smaller, popular editions, produced without checking the manuscripts, and for all the recent translations.

In 1960 Enzo Noe Girardi published in Italy a new edition, the first since Frey's to survey the manuscripts. Although this translation has been in the making for twenty years, it has been rechecked in the light of Girardi's improvements. He has added about twenty fragments which had come to light since Frey's edition and been published in various books from 1909 on, but inserted neither in the popular editions that used Frey without further research nor in a recent "complete" English translation. Girardi has also added the two sestinas. On the other hand, he has omitted three or four poems from Frey's list which, as he shows, are clearly early drafts of other poems and have no place in an edition unless it is also to contain several hundred others in the same category. These had also appeared without criticism in the smaller editions and translations based on Frey.

Girardi has relegated to an appendix some fifteen poems which exist in Michelangelo's handwriting but which are not by him; they are poems by others, mainly Petrarch, that he copied down. These, including eight lines of a sonnet, are printed with a warning by Frey, but some of his hastier copyists and translators present them as Michelangelo's work. I assume that Girardi considered that they should be eliminated, but needed to be accounted for in case those familiar with Frey's edition should look for them. Accordingly, I have omitted them here. I have also omitted four other items. Two of these are well-known statements in prose, in an elevated style, which Frey had inserted among the poems. Though they have a rhythmic quality, they are written in prose form in lines all the way across the page and cannot be justified as poems. These appear in Girardi's text as numbers 13 and 14, so that in following his order, this book gives each poem after the first twelve a number less than his by 2. The two others appear in his appendix. One is a page on which Michelangelo drew a figure of David and wrote on different parts of the paper three things: "David with sling and I with bow / Michelangelo / The high column is broken, and the green . . ." The last of these is a line from Petrarch; the first is rhythmic, but being associated with the drawing and isolated from any other writing, it seems excessive to call it a poem. The fourth omission, a single line (Girardi, appendix 26) is one that, as he says, may be a draft of a line which appears in another poem, number 79 in this book, but is even closer to the last line of number 256. This shows how difficult these decisions are. All this means that I have reduced Girardi's appendix of forty-one items to twenty-seven; these twenty-seven follow his order. Besides the Petrarch quotations, Girardi used his appendix very rightly for fragments too brief to contain a single complete thought.

The main contribution of Girardi's edition, however, is its greatly altered order of presentation, based on a much more thorough study of chronology. Girardi notably disproved Frey's idea that all the poems referring to God must be late. The use of this order will, I believe, help in the pleasure of reading as the author's thought is seen shifting and growing. All the above is perhaps over-detailed, but seems called for since Girardi's edition is so new that even those familiar with the poems may welcome such notes.

Little needs to be said about the procedures used in this translation. The principle has been complete fidelity. In form, the original rhyme scheme and lengths of lines are retained. In sense, every phrase in the original is to be found in the translation, and no additional ones, not even the translator's favorite fake, the second synonymous adjective, are included. I cannot say every word is kept, since idioms must be respected; phrase by phrase seems the best. Word order is altered for the same reason, as well as for the meter.

Some friends have urged a simple declarative word order

so as to adhere to the ideal of modern English prose-like poetry. Inverted word order has bad associations with Victorian versifiers and with translations pushing for a rhyme. But that is a bad use of such inversion, not the fault of the inversion itself. It appears in Elizabethan English poetry, which is the cousin of Michelangelo's, in much modern English poetry since Dylan Thomas, and in Michelangelo, where I believe it departs from the standards of his time.

Michelangelo's rhythmic beat is very irregular and sometimes makes us stumble. I have used many reversed feet, allowed by the original, and encouraged by the greater scope they give for capturing the sense. There is a temptation to smooth the meter, but I believe it vitiates the poetic effect of roughness and strain, even of amateurishness, like a plaster cast that eliminates chisel marks. I know I have not always escaped the pitfall of unclear rhythm.

The most "special" device of these translations is the systematic use of assonance instead of rhyme. It is forced upon me, since faithful rhyme and faithful meaning are impossible to combine in one translation. It has the support of modern English poetry and even of some distinguished past translators of Michelangelo, beginning with Emerson. But its best justification is found in observing the Elizabethan poets. Italian sonnets always base their first eight lines on two rhyme sounds only, abba abba. When the sonnet was adapted into English, the Elizabethans, with a right instinct, at once altered this to four rhyme sounds, abba cddc. English will not bear so much repetitive rhyme except in comic verse. Thus a translator of Italian poetry should reduce the repeated sound; yet if he uses the form abba cddc, he breaks the two stanzas apart and destroys the formal structure. To use the original structure abba abba, but with assonance, is the solution to the problem. This applies to madrigals as well, which also repeat the rhyme sound four times. The difficulty is that when there are two somewhat similar rhyme sounds, they may become muddled together in assonance, and I fear I have not always escaped this. But I hope I have produced versions which illustrate the chief point, the quality of having rhyme, and that in this and other ways I have been faithful to Michelangelo.

A similar method has been used in translating the letters. They are often as snarled and as difficult as the poems —in fact, they parallel the poems of the same dates, being most complicated in the middle years. Since there is no problem of formal structure to be considered here, it has been suggested to me that the sense should be made simpler, especially by breaking up the long sentences. I do not believe that this justification for change has merit. In clarifying, it is almost inevitable to interpret an ambiguous phrase in one way and exclude other ways, thus imposing an interpretation on the reader and limiting his scope for making independent interpretations. In a narrow sense, the only reason for publishing the letters is as documents, since they are not works of art. And documents lose all value if they are not available with the most literal precision one can manage.

In a wider sense, however, the letters have value as spontaneous expressions of Michelangelo's character, as distinguished from the highly wrought expressions of the poems. This leads to the same result, for the crabbed involution of clauses is a manifestation of his personality. Even though some of the more important letters were rewritten before being sent, they (like the poems) remain just as gnarled as at first. Their author knew this when he wrote: "If I shouldn't write as correctly as one ought, and if I don't hit upon the main verb sometimes, please excuse me," and later, "If I don't know how to write what you will know how to understand, don't be surprised, for I have lost my brains completely."

Had Michelangelo been a polished stylist in his letters, the proper translation would be as polished, even if it had to depart from his phrasing.

The standard edition of the letters in Italian was produced in 1875. It has been amended in many details since, but there has been no new systematic edition bringing these alterations together, or what is more important, checking them against each other. For that reason it is used here, as it generally is, with the warning to the reader that there are errors, especially in the suggested dates of the undated letters.

Since 1943 some thirty of my translations of the poems have appeared in various magazines and anthologies. All of them have been revised in the final drafting of this book, except two, first published in *Lyric Poetry of the Italian Renaissance*, edited by L. R. Lind, published by the Yale University Press and reprinted with its permission. More recently, about twenty poems have been published in the present final version in *Arts Yearbook*, 1961, and in the 1962 revision of *A Documentary History of Art*, edited by Elizabeth Gilmore Holt and published by Doubleday Anchor Books.

It is my hope that the very large number of people who have encouraged this work over a long period know of my thanks to them and the impossibility of mentioning them all.

CREIGHTON GILBERT

Brandeis University

CONTENTS

ILLUSTRATIONS

FOLLOWING PAGE 132

1. Manuscript page of the sonnet on the Sistine Chapel, 1510
   Archivio Buonarroti, Florence
   The tiny sketch by Michelangelo on the right illustrates the verse that describes his stance while painting the ceiling. It is a self-portrait and also includes a head from the ceiling, but briefly and sharply satirized in a way that does not appear in any other drawing by him.

2. *Medici Tomb,* about 1521
   British Museum, London
   This design shows the project nearly in its final phase, including the River Gods (below), which were never carved, as well as the Times of Day (above). A sonnet is written on the back of this sheet.

3. *Phaeton,* 1533
   Windsor Castle
   The third drawing for Cavalieri (see also illustrations 6 and 7) shows the presumptuous Phaeton, who thought he could drive the sun horses as well as his father Apollo, falling down to earth where his frightened sisters watch, driven by a thunderbolt of Zeus. The story is told by

Ovid, and some of the poses are developed from ancient sculpture. The similarity of the fall from the sun to images in Michelangelo's poems is striking.

4. Sheet of sketches, about 1525
   Ashmolean Museum, Oxford
   The two wrestling groups are quick ideas for a sculpture of Hercules and Anteus which was never executed. The other sketches are thought by most specialists to be by an assistant in the workshop, but reflect a number of Michelangelo's interests: the caricatured heads, the owl (for the figure of Night in the Medici Chapel), the anatomy of the leg and its skeletal form, and the lines from an eye showing the scope of its vision.

5. *Resurrection*, about 1532
   Windsor Castle
   Nothing is known of any project for which this composition might have been intended. It exists in three drawings, of which this is the most finished. The astonishingly original approach to the traditional subject recalls the poems that explore the difficult movement from earth to heaven.

6. *Tityos*, 1532
   Windsor Castle
   Tityos, as described in Virgil's *Aeneid*, was a giant punished for his presumptuous love for Latona by being tied to a rock in hell, where a vulture continuously ate his liver but never consumed it. The drawing was one of a group made as a gift for Tommaso Cavalieri, and many copies of it exist.

7. *Children's Bacchanal*, 1533
   Windsor Castle
   Also a gift for Cavalieri, this uniquely rich composition has no precedent, and the themes seem to be Michel-

angelo's invention. In general they are interpreted as the physical aspects of life, in which the soul does not participate.

8. Projects, about 1540–45
   Casa Buonarroti, Florence
   This drawing is typical of many in having half a dozen sketches for several different purposes. It is included here because the tomb at the lower left (and perhaps some of the others) was the one designed for Cecchino Bracci. There can be little doubt of this, since it includes a portrait bust which was demanded here, but which Michelangelo otherwise never used.

9. *Annunciation,* about 1545–50
   British Museum, London
   Michelangelo provided designs about this time for two paintings of this subject. In works of these years like the *Pietà* in Florence Cathedral, he withdrew from his earlier heroic sweep; the bulky figures are static, and their limbs are as if caught in an awkward twisted position, yet they retain and even increase their majestic dignity.

10. *Crucifixion,* 1550's
    British Museum, London
    A group of Crucifixion drawings belongs to the end of Michelangelo's life. They are exceedingly sculptural, while they are also nearly dematerialized, a merger of opposites that is less hard to accept after reading the sonnets written at the same time. They show Mary and John in varying positions; the Mary here, almost nestling against the body, is especially moving.

11. *Crucifixion,* 1550's
    Windsor Castle
    Among the late Crucifixion drawings this is the one most concerned with bodily strain in the figure of Christ. It

also shows a series of revisions, each of which pushes the arms higher.

12. *Madonna,* about 1560
    British Museum, London
    This figure, statuesque and trembling, may be the latest surviving drawing by Michelangelo.

BIOGRAPHICAL
INTRODUCTION

I

> He passed most of his life in
> the midst of tragic disasters
> . . . In his most creative
> years he found himself alone,
> perhaps the greatest but, alas,
> also the last of the giants born
> so plentifully during the fif-
> teenth century.
>
> BERNARD BERENSON

FRUSTRATION is a commonplace of the artist's life, but
Michelangelo's was a rare case of frustration by power
politics. For it was his misfortune to become too famous
too soon, at a time when the prestige of a ruler was en-
hanced by the reputations of the artists who served him.

As a result, he was torn between powerful patrons competing for his services, and seldom had the satisfaction of finishing a project before he was snatched away for another.

He was born during the golden age of the Renaissance in an Italy of petty states combining and recombining in a ritual dance of intrigue and double dealing. His adult life was spent in a time of calamity when Italy was the battleground for the armies of France and Spain. He died in a period of slow decay, in an Italy enslaved and exhausted; the buoyant energy of the Renaissance drained away; the age of reaction at the door.

The fountainhead of the Renaissance was Florence, city of the Medici. Here Cosimo (1389–1464) had used the fortune inherited from his father, the richest banker in Italy, to augment the power of his family and the prestige of his city. Here the foremost artists of Italy experimented with the new techniques of painting, sculpture, and architecture; the most eminent scholars studied the masterpieces of sacred and profane literature, especially the newly discovered works of Greek and Roman writers. In Florence, earlier than in any other city, the stimulus of these new techniques and cultures freed and fertilized creative minds.

This ferment rose to its highest point under Cosimo's grandson, Lorenzo the Magnificent (1449–1492), who made his court the intellectual and artistic center of the Western world; meanwhile, by an adroit system of alliances, keeping the peace, and extending the power of his city-state.

II

Michelangelo lives forever as the type and symbol of a man, much suffering, continually laboring, gifted with keen but rarely indulged passions, whose energies from boyhood to extreme old age were dedicated with unswerving purpose to the service of one master, plastic art.

JOHN ADDINGTON SYMONDS

During the time of Lorenzo, an undistinguished citizen of Florence, Lodovico di Lionardo Buonarrota, served briefly as magistrate in the nearby village of Caprese. Here a son was born to him on March 6, 1475, whom he named Michelangelo. Soon afterward, the family was back in Florence, living in the crowded household of Lodovico's brother. Michelangelo was put to nurse with a stonecutter's wife, which led him to say in later life, "From my foster mother's milk I drew the skill to make figures with chisel and hammer."

When Michelangelo was three years old, Florence was shaken by one of those paroxysms of violence characteristic of the period. The Pazzi family, long jealous of the Medici, attempted to murder Lorenzo and his brother Giuliano during High Mass in the cathedral. Giuliano was killed; Lorenzo wounded. The assassins were hunted down and caught, and Botticelli was ordered to commemorate the affair by sketching their corpses, hung by the heels for greater shame.

For a few years Michelangelo attended school, though even as a child his bent was all toward art. His father, who preferred genteel poverty to demeaning labor, urged a more gentlemanly profession, since to him an artist was only a craftsman, a man who worked with his hands and not his head. But in the clash of wills the child's was stronger, and

at the age of thirteen he was apprenticed to the illustrious
Florentine painter, Domenico Ghirlandaio.

In the Medici gardens Lorenzo had thrown open his col-
lection of ancient and modern statues as a training ground
for young artists. Ghirlandaio, asked by its custodian to
choose two of his apprentices to study in this informal
academy, chose Michelangelo as one. Many years later his
biographer and self-styled friend, Giorgio Vasari, told the
story, or legend, of how the boy was singled out by Lorenzo
for the skill with which he had carved the head of a marble
faun. This much at least is true; at the age of fourteen
Michelangelo was invited to live in the Medici palace as a
member of Lorenzo's household.

Here was the perfect forcing bed for young genius. Lo-
renzo was more than a shrewd politician; he was a man of
taste and intelligence who had surrounded himself with
the foremost painters, sculptors, poets, and scholars of the
age. It was a time of transition, and at the Medici dinner
table Michelangelo must have heard much talk of the new
Humanism that had burst the bonds of medieval philoso-
phy by divorcing learning and religion, and turned men's
minds toward the pagan culture of Greece and Rome; of
Plato and Platonism (still imperfectly understood); and of
the exciting new techniques that had extended the bound-
aries of the arts as Humanism had extended the boundaries
of the mind.

Into this worldly and pleasure-loving society a somber
note was now injected. Savonarola (1452–1498), a Domini-
can priest, a reincarnation of the Hebrew prophets and a
forerunner of the great Puritan divines, began to preach
the sermons that were to shake Florence to its foundations;
sermons castigating luxury and vice, and prophesying di-
vine wrath to come.

During his most impressionable years Michelangelo was ~~thus~~ buffeted on one side by the pagan doctrine of the worship of the senses, and on the other by the dread of an angry God—a conflict that was to find supreme expression many years later in the frescoes of the Sistine Chapel. Meanwhile, Greek and Christian themes gave him the subjects for his first important works of sculpture: the *Madonna of the Steps* (in low relief) and the *Battle of the Centaurs* (in high relief). Then in 1492 Lorenzo the Magnificent died, and the golden age began its slow decline into an age of chaos.

For the next two years Michelangelo lived with his own family, mastered, by many dissections, the mechanisms of the human body, and planned a statue of Hercules. During this time Florence seethed with unrest under the incompetent rule of Lorenzo's son, Pietro (1471–1503), and the fiery preaching of Savonarola. These were the last of the good years. To settle a dynastic squabble between Naples and Milan, the intervention of Charles VIII of France had been solicited. In 1495 a French army poured over the Alps, and during the remainder of Michelangelo's life Italy was fought over and ransacked by rapacious foreigners, to whom her weakness and her wealth were an irresistible invitation.

In Florence the prestige of Savonarola was inflated by the French invasion, which appeared to bear out his prophecies of doom. When Pietro signed a humiliating treaty with the French, the citizens rose in anger, cast out the Medici, and proclaimed a republic. Michelangelo, seized by one of those sudden panics of which he was the lifelong victim, fled from the city and sought refuge in Bologna. There he found a noble patron who took him into his household and procured him commissions to carve two half life-size saints in marble and a kneeling angel for the church of St. Dominic. After a year in Bologna he returned in 1495 to a penitential Florence, now ruled in fact, if not in name, by Savonarola.

At first the exhortations of the priest had been directed against vice, luxury, and sin—subjects without power of reprisal. Now he took the fatal step of moving into the political arena. During the long years of Medici rule the citizens of Florence had forgotten even the principles of self-government. In a series of flaming political sermons, Savonarola led the way step by step to the establishment of republican laws and institutions. But the strain of excessive and unnatural virtue had begun to weary the pleasure-loving Florentines; Savonarola's political reforms had alienated the rich; his charges of ecclesiastical corruption had infuriated the Borgia Pope, Alexander VI. In 1498 he was accused of heresy and treason, arrested, tortured into a false confession, and hideously executed.

Two years before Savonarola's downfall Michelangelo had left Florence. Vasari says that he had fashioned a sleeping Cupid which he sold to a dealer for thirty ducats. Stained to appear antique, either by Michelangelo or by the dealer, it was sold in Rome for two hundred ducats. The purchaser, Cardinal Riario, discovering the deceit, demanded a refund and sent a messenger to Florence to identify and bring to Rome the sculptor capable of so exquisite a work. The story is of dubious authenticity, but either for this reason or fearful of the growing tensions in Florence, Michelangelo set out for Rome, arriving in June 1496.

Here he was lucky enough to find a rich and cultured patron, Jacopo Galli, for whom he carved a statue of Bacchus, symbol of pagan delight in the sensual life. And in the summer of 1498, soon after he received news of the degradation and death of the great preacher he had deeply admired, he was offered four hundred and fifty gold ducats by a French cardinal to carve, for a chapel of St. Peter's in Rome, a life-size *Pietà* of marble, the Virgin holding across her knees the dead body of Christ. Though only twenty-three years of age, Michelangelo created a *Pietà* of such supreme loveliness and flawless execution that, as Vasari says, "It is a miracle that a stone without shape should have been reduced to such perfection." By this work Michelangelo's reputation was made. Solicited by friends, he returned in 1501 to Florence, now under a republican government headed by the weak but well-intentioned Piero Soderini.

Soon after Michelangelo arrived in Florence, he agreed to make fifteen small statues for the tomb of Cardinal Piccolomini in Siena. This contract was soon set aside—the first of many broken contracts that mark Michelangelo's career and the only one in which the initiative was his—when Soderini offered him a more challenging project. For nearly forty years dust had been gathering on a block of marble eighteen feet high from which a Sienese sculptor had agreed—and failed—to make a statue of Hercules. Greatly daring, Michelangelo now contracted to carve a colossal statue of David from this same misshapen block. With his usual passion for secrecy he surrounded the marble with a wooden enclosure and hewed at it with such fury that he slept in his clothes and munched his meals of bread as he worked. When completed, the statue was suspended in a sling within a framework of planks and, with windlass and rollers and the help of forty men, was moved in four days to the site selected beside the entrance to City Hall where all Florence flocked to gaze and to admire. "This work," wrote Vasari, "has carried off the palm from all other statues, modern and ancient." In payment for it Michelangelo received four hundred crowns, and it was set in place in the year 1504.

According to Vasari, Soderini praised the statue except for the nose, which seemed to him too thick. Thereupon Michelangelo, taking his chisel in one hand and scooping up marble dust in the other, climbed the staging and pretended to chip away at the nose, letting the dust sift from his hand as he did so. Then he climbed down and asked his critic how he liked it now. "I like it better," Soderini said. "You have given it life."

During these four years in Florence Michelangelo found time for other works, notably a life-size *Madonna and Child*, now in Bruges; an unfinished circular relief known as the *Pitti Madonna*, after the Florentine family for whom it was made; another circular relief (also unfinished) of the *Madonna and Child* for Taddeo Taddei; and for his friend, Agnolo Doni, as a wedding gift to his wife, a circular painting in tempera of the Holy Family known as the *Doni Madonna*. During this same crowded period he found time as well to study Italian poetry and to write his first sonnets.

The success of the *David* led to an even more ambitious project. For the Cathedral of Florence Michelangelo contracted to carve statues, larger than life, of the twelve apostles. But this contract, too, was set aside when Soderini offered him a wall of the council room of the Palazzo Vecchio on which to paint a scene from the history of Florence in competition with Leonardo da Vinci, who was already at work on his *Battle of Anghiari* for another wall of the same chamber. Characteristically, Michelangelo selected an incident of the war with Pisa when Florentine soldiers were surprised while bathing in the Arno; characteristically, because it enabled him to deal with a subject that already obsessed him: the naked male in many postures.

In fresco painting designs were drawn and enlarged on paper to full-size cartoons—an earlier and different meaning of the word from our present one. These cartoons were then pasted onto the smooth surface of a newly plastered wall and the outlines of the figures were marked by charcoal dusted through small holes or slashes. Finally, the paper was removed, and the artist applied his colors to the plaster. Michelangelo's cartoon created an even greater furor than his *David*. Before he could transfer it to the wall or make more than a beginning on the statues, he was summoned to Rome to accept a commission from Pope Julius II. His cartoon, like Leonardo's, was a victim of its own success. Both were studied, copied, and handled by so many artists that they were finally reduced to fragments.

III

> *I already have a wife who is too much for me; one who keeps me unceasingly struggling on. It is my art, and my works are my children.*
>
> MICHELANGELO

Rome in the sixteenth century was an anomaly among Italian cities. She did not breed artists; she requisitioned them. To the artists it meant larger commissions, more money, wider fame; to the Papacy, the luster of being the cultural as well as the religious center of Christendom. Of all the Popes of the Renaissance none equaled in energy and arrogance the Pope who had summoned Michelangelo to Rome. In Bramante, Julius had found an architect whose ambition and daring matched his own; in Michelangelo, an artist of equal audacity. To Michelangelo was assigned the project of designing for the Pope a tomb of unexampled splendor. Bramante was to create a new St. Peter's, the most magnificent church in Christendom, in which to place the tomb.

First, marble had to be provided in great quantity, and so for nearly a year Michelangelo was in Carrara urging on the excavation and shipment of marble blocks. Then, back in Rome, he applied to the Pope for money to pay the shippers. But Julius, preoccupied with plans for war, refused to see him. Anger at the rebuff and a panic fear that jealous rivals sought his life led Michelangelo to take flight. Selling all his furniture, he set out for Florence with such speed that the Pope's emissaries, dispatched with orders to bring him back to Rome, were unable to overtake him before he reached the safety of Florentine territory. But Julius was not to be denied. To the government of Florence came three papal briefs demanding the runaway's immediate return. Michelangelo toyed with the idea of leaving Italy and taking service with the Turks, from whom had come flattering offers. But Soderini, dreading the wrath of Julius, persuaded him by the promise of safe-conduct to return to the Pope's service.

Meanwhile, the Pope had left Rome at the head of five hundred soldiers and twenty-five cardinals, determined to add Perugia and Bologna to the papal dominions. Michelangelo met the Pope at Bologna and threw himself at his feet with a noose about his neck in token of submission. A bishop who was present attempted to intercede, saying that artists were ignorant creatures who knew no better, whereupon the terrible-tempered Pope beat the bishop with his staff, crying out, "It is you who are ignorant." His anger thus deflected, the Pope restored Michelangelo to favor and commissioned a bronze statue of himself, ten feet high. In eighteen months Michelangelo completed the statue, which was set in place over the door of the church of San Petronio in Bologna. Three years later the citizens rose in revolt against the Pope, tore down the statue, and melted it into cannon for use against its subject.

Returning to Rome at the Pope's command, Michelangelo was again ordered to suspend work on the tomb and told instead to paint a series of frescoes for the Sistine Chapel. Suspicious as always of rivals, he saw the request as inspired by Bramante and Raphael in the hope of discrediting his skill, since sculpture, not painting, was his chosen profession. But the Pope insisted, and filled with misgivings, Michelangelo agreed to undertake what was to become his most famous work.

In the same year, 1508, Italy took another decisive step toward ruin. By the League of Cambrai, Julius united the powers of Europe to assist him in his vendetta with Venice. When that proud city was humbled, he joined with Spain under the slogan *Fuori i Barbari* (Out with the Barbarians) to rid Italy of the French. The battle of Ravenna accomplished this purpose, but King Log had been exchanged for King Stork. Amid the turmoil Florence was occupied by the Spanish, heavily fined, and compelled to accept the return of the Medici.

During the four and a half years of these disastrous events, Michelangelo was working in extreme discomfort,

painting the great vaulted ceiling of the Sistine Chapel.*
At first he had thought to have assistance and had hired
Florentine painters to work under his direction. But his
standards were too high to be met by anyone but himself.
One by one the assistants were thrown out by the irascible
perfectionist, who then locked the doors and carried on
the whole vast project almost single-handed, depicting,
through the medium of hundreds of figures, the story of
Genesis from the Creation to the Flood, with accessories
of prophets and sibyls and the forefathers of Christ.

When the work was half finished, the impatient Pope
demanded that the Chapel should be thrown open to the
public, and all Rome thronged to see the paintings. So de-
lighted was the Pope that he ordered Michelangelo to
complete the second half with all possible speed. This he
did in twenty months without the help of anyone even to
grind his colors, expedited, says Vasari, by the Pope's threat
to have him thrown from the scaffolding if he did not
hurry. On October 31, 1512, the work was completed.
"The giant task was over," writes Charles H. Morgan in
his biography of Michelangelo, "and the development of
painting in the Western world achieved a new dimension."

This task behind him, Michelangelo once more took up
his chisel and attacked the Pope's tomb. Then in 1513
Julius died and was succeeded by the pleasure-loving Gio-
vanni de' Medici (1475–1521), Pope Leo X. Leo was a
friend of the Duke of Urbino, the chief heir of Julius, and
at his suggestion a new contract was signed, moving the
site of the tomb from St. Peter's and promising its comple-
tion within seven years. This marked the beginning of the

* For Michelangelo's own description of his discomfort, see his fifth
sonnet.

second phase in what is known as the "Tragedy of the Tomb." Hereafter, the tomb was to be a pawn on the political chessboard.

Two years later Leo changed partners, allying himself with the new French King, Francis I, partly to offset the growing power of Spain and partly to wrest from his former friend the Dukedom of Urbino, an object which he achieved with dazzling speed. At this point Leo must have said to himself that it made little sense for the greatest artist of the age to be engaged in glorifying the family of his enemy instead of his own. And so, in 1516, the humbled Urbino was forced to sign a third contract with Michelangelo, whereby the splendor of the Julian tomb was to be greatly reduced and the time extended in order to leave the sculptor free to accept other commissions, an opportunity of which the Pope promptly took advantage.

In the interval between the signing of the second and third contracts, Michelangelo had completed three statues for the tomb: the gigantic *Moses,* embodiment of strength and electric energy, and two *Slaves,* or *Captives;* also, for three Roman patrons, a life-size *Christ Risen* which was finished (and botched) by another sculptor after Michelangelo left Rome. Then, following the signing of the third contract, the Pope ordered him to abandon the Julian tomb and design a new façade for San Lorenzo, the family church of the Medici in Florence.

For two years Michelangelo flitted between Florence, Carrara, and Rome, drawing up plans and arranging for the necessary marble. Then new difficulties arose. Cardinal Giulio de' Medici (1478–1534), cousin of Leo X and the Pope's man of business, ordered Michelangelo to abandon work at Carrara and open up quarries within the territory of Florence. The consequent difficulties and delays so disheartened Michelangelo that he asked to have the contract canceled, a request that was promptly granted, since the rebuilding of St. Peter's was draining the papal treasury, which needed replenishing to meet new threats of war. And so another vast project was set aside; more years of Michelangelo's life were wasted. But the Pope decided that the prestige of having Michelangelo in his employ was not lightly to be lost. And so, in 1520, he ordered him to build a fitting tomb for the Medici family in San Lorenzo. For thirteen months Michelangelo worked on this new project. Then in 1521 Leo X died, and an aged cardinal of Utrecht was elected as Adrian VI (1459–1523).

With the Medici out of power, the heirs of Julius came to life, demanding that the harassed sculptor complete the tomb or return the money that had been paid to him. But in the following year Adrian died and another Medici, Cardinal Giulio, ascended the papal throne as Clement VII. Negotiations with the heirs were broken off, and Michelangelo was sent back to Florence to resume work on the Medici tomb. For two years he pressed forward, his work interrupted at one point by a request from the restless Pope that he turn architect and design a Medici Library, and at another, that he add statues of Leo and Clement to the tomb. A more serious interruption was a new demand from the heirs of Julius for an accounting, and for completion of their project. But the controversy was temporarily resolved by catastrophe.

By the year 1527 the political tragicomedy of double-dealing had taken a grimmer turn, the change of partners a more frenzied pace. Following the defeat of his ally, Francis I, at Pavia in 1525, Clement had joined forces with the victorious Charles V, Spanish King and Hapsburg Emperor. The following year, changing sides once more, he formed the "Holy League" to drive the Spanish from Italy. Never was double-dealing more mercilessly avenged. An army of mercenaries, let loose by the Emperor in retaliation, entered Rome in May 1527. The Pope took refuge in the castle of Sant' Angelo (once Hadrian's Tomb), and the soldiers plundered and murdered at their leisure. Disguised as a peddler, Clement escaped from the city. Then the plague struck, spread by the rotting bodies. The soldiers, and the few thousand inhabitants left alive, fled from the city, leaving Rome an empty ruin.

In Florence the citizens had taken advantage of Clement's plight to cast off the Medici yoke once more and proclaim a republic. Michelangelo seized the opportunity to abandon work on the tomb of the Medici and to attempt to finish the tomb of Julius. But Clement again changed partners, allying himself with the Emperor and borrowing his army to recapture Florence. Recognizing their peril, the citizens of Florence speeded preparations for a siege and put Michelangelo in charge of strengthening the fortifications. He spent the summer of 1529 remaking the city's defenses. Then, in fear of the enemy without and traitors within, he left Florence in a panic, as he had thirty-five years before, and took refuge in Venice. Repenting of his flight and solicited by friends to return, he slipped through the enemy lines and resumed his post in the besieged city. It was probably at this time and as a relief from the tensions of war that he painted his *Leda and the Swan*. Then, forewarned of the city's impending surrender and anticipating the vengeance the Pope was planning to take on the leaders of the uprising, he went into hiding. But Clement, ever practical, offered him a full pardon provided he would complete his work on the Medici tomb, an offer that Michelangelo thankfully accepted.

The following year the heirs of Julius once again clamored for their money or their tomb. After months of wearying negotiations, with Clement as intermediary, a fourth contract was signed whereby Michelangelo agreed to complete six figures and to delegate five more to other sculptors.

During these years in Florence, Michelangelo continued to work on the figures for the Medici tomb: Giuliano, Duke of Nemours, animated and vigilant, and in contrast, Lorenzo, Duke of Urbino, lost in contemplation, his somber face half hidden by his helmet. Stretched at their feet were the recumbent figures of Day and Night, Evening and Morning. These statues carved, he turned over to his assistants the completion of the tomb, and thankfully departed from Florence, now ruled by Alessandro (1510–1537), a particularly hateful Medici. The year was 1534. Hereafter Rome was to be his home.

IV

The Last Judgment remains a stupendous miracle . . . The note is of sustained menace and terror . . . a sense-deafening solo on a trombone.

JOHN ADDINGTON SYMONDS

Michelangelo was an excellent man; a pity that he did not know how to paint.

EL GRECO

Two days after Michelangelo arrived in Rome, Clement died. During the eleven years of his papacy Rome had been sacked, Italy had been enslaved, England had been alienated, and the Lutheran schism had widened beyond healing. His successor was Paul III (1468–1549), and one of the first acts of the new Pope was to pre-empt the services of Michelangelo. When the sculptor pleaded for time so that he might finish the tomb of Julius, the Pope refused, crying out in anger, "I have had this desire for thirty years, and now that I am Pope, do you think I shall not satisfy it? I shall tear up the contract." The assignment given Michelangelo was to complete the decoration of the Sistine Chapel by repainting the end wall above the altar, then covered with frescoes by Perugino. His title was to be "Chief Architect, Sculptor, and Painter of the Apostolic Palace."

And so, in his sixtieth year, Michelangelo again took up the brush and set to work on his second great fresco, *The Last Judgment*. Of this painting Vasari says, "The intention of this extraordinary man has been to refuse to paint anything but the human body in its best proportioned and most perfect forms and in the greatest variety of attitudes, and not only this, but likewise the play of the passions and contentments of the soul, being satisfied with justifying himself in that field in which he was superior to all his fellow craftsmen." Bernard Berenson more acutely points out the exaggerations of power and the brutality of tactile values showing the scorn and bitterness that Michelangelo now felt toward the world.

In the more prudish age that followed, some attempt was made to cover up the nakedness of the figures. Indeed, during Michelangelo's lifetime there was criticism, the

Pope's chamberlain protesting to Paul that the work was more fitting for a brothel than for a chapel—a remark that the artist is said to have repaid by portraying the chamberlain among the devils in Hell.

As soon as *The Last Judgment* was completed, the Pope commissioned two frescoes for the Pauline Chapel: *The Conversion of Paul* and *The Martyrdom of Peter*. These were to be the last of Michelangelo's paintings, but before they could be undertaken something had to be done about the tomb of Julius. After several more months of negotiations the heirs reluctantly agreed to what proved to be the last of all the contracts. Michelangelo was to furnish the majestic statue of Moses (carved thirty years before) and two lesser statues (which he did with haste and indifference), and all other work was to be done by his assistants. This was the final act in the "Tragedy of the Tomb," which for thirty-seven years had enmeshed Michelangelo in negotiations, recriminations, and threats of lawsuits. "In bondage to this tomb," he once said, "I lost all my youth."

The last nine years of Michelangelo's life were spent, for the most part, in the practice of architecture. He had survived Bramante, who had conceived the new St. Peter's, and his successors, Raphael and Sangallo, who had carried it forward. Now, in 1546, he was put in charge of its construction. He threw himself into this new task with his accustomed fire, little dimmed by age, changing plans and designing the great dome—an amazing feat of architecture and engineering, especially for one without training and with little practice in this highly technical field. For this Pope and his successors he also designed and supervised the construction of other great projects.

In 1564, in the midst of these vast enterprises, death struck Michelangelo at the age of eighty-nine. He was first buried in Rome; then, according to Vasari, his body was wrapped in a bale as though merchandise, "lest there be a tumult in Rome," and carried secretly to Florence. There Michelangelo was buried with pomp and ceremony that would have thoroughly annoyed the old sculptor, and a catafalque was erected, heavy with florid ornamentation.

V

The genius of Michelangelo was recognized in his lifetime, for it has been seen that Julius II, Leo X, Clement VII, Paul III, Julius III, Paul IV, and Pius IV, all supreme pontiffs, always wished to have him near them; also Suleiman, Emperor of the Turks, Francis of Valois, King of France, the Emperor Charles V, the Signoria of Venice, and Duke Cosimo de' Medici; all offering him honorable salaries, for no other reason but to avail themselves of his great genius.

GIORGIO VASARI

What manner of man was this who was hailed in his lifetime as "almost divine," and for whose services popes and princes competed?

Condivi, a friend and disciple, describes Michelangelo as of medium height, lean and broad-shouldered, with a

wide forehead, flat nose (it had been broken in boyhood by
a fellow student), yellow-brown eyes, thick black hair and
a forked beard. He was of robust health, content with
little food and sleep, enduring hardships without com-
plaint, caring nothing for comfort, living like a poor man
even when rich, and never accepting favors for fear of be-
ing obligated.

Vasari says that at night, when Michelangelo was un-
able to sleep, he would rise and work with chisel and ham-
mer, a candle stuck in his cap for a light. He adds that
once when he visited him after midnight and found him
thus engaged, Michelangelo, unwilling that Vasari should
spy on his work, dropped the candle, saying, "I am so old
that death often pulls me by the cloak, that I may go with
him, and one day this body of mine will fall like the lamp,
and the light of my life will be spent."

Of his character Condivi says, "While still young, he
gave himself, not only to sculpture and painting, but to all
kindred arts, with such devotion that, for a time, he almost
withdrew from the fellowship of men, so that by some he
was held to be proud, by others eccentric. As he greatly
delighted in the conversation of the learned, so he took
pleasure in the study of writers of both prose and poetry.
He had a special admiration for Dante. Likewise, with
great study, he read the Holy Scriptures; also the writings
of Savonarola. He loved not only human beauty, but every
beautiful thing, admiring them all with a marvelous love."

Unlike his great contemporary, Leonardo da Vinci,
whose immense creative energy was dispersed in many di-
rections, Michelangelo's was always channeled toward art;
sculpture if he could; painting and architecture if he must;
poetry for what could not be expressed by chisel or brush.

Living in a time of exalted villainy, he conceived the

world as evil and man as existing in the shadow of a just and angry God. Steeped in the philosophy of Plato, the poetry of Dante, and the teachings of the Bible, he was a unique synthesis of the new Humanism and the old Christianity.

Michelangelo was never married except, as he said, to his art. The extravagant sentiments of some of his poems reflect the conventions of the period which Michelangelo developed in his own personal and emotional way. They show a tender and sensitive side to his nature, a bondage to beauty of mind and body; but they show nothing more. By contrast, the letters to his family denote a man crotchety and solicitous, generous, difficult, and suspicious; a character of great integrity and of formidable thorniness.

The word most often used by his contemporaries in describing Michelangelo's art was *terribilità*. This sense of passionate fury sums up not only his art, but equally his life and personality.

ROBERT N. LINSCOTT

Two recent books on Michelangelo can be highly recommended: for the general reader, *The Life of Michelangelo* by Charles H. Morgan; for the serious student, Tolnay's five-volume biography.

BIOGRAPHICAL DATES

1475 March 6, born in the village of Caprese in Tuscany, second son of Lodovico (1444–1531) and Francesca. Lodovico, grandson of a successful banker and son of an unsuccessful banker in Florence, lived on a small income from land and occasional government posts; at this time he was Podesta (governor) of Caprese. March 31, Lodovico's term expired; the family doubtless returned to Florence. The oldest son, Lionardo (1473–1510) entered the Dominican order in Pisa in 1491 and played virtually no part in Michelangelo's life.

1477 May 26, brother Buonarroto born.

1479 March 11, brother Giovansimone born.

1481 January 22, brother Gismondo born. About this time the family was living in an apartment rented from Lodovico's brother-in-law, a dyer. December 6, mother died.

1485 Father's second marriage to Lucrezia Ubaldini (d. 1497).

1488 April 8, Michelangelo left grammar school and was apprenticed for three years to the painter Domenico Ghirlandaio.

1489   Left Ghirlandaio and studied sculpture in the garden of Lorenzo de' Medici the Magnificent.

1492   Lorenzo the Magnificent died, succeeded by his oldest son Piero.

1494   Rising against Piero de' Medici, who fled (d. 1503). Republic re-established under Savonarola. October, Michelangelo fled and after a brief stay in Venice went to Bologna.

1495   In Bologna, carved three small statues which brought to completion the tomb of St. Dominic. Returned to Florence, carved the *Cupid*, sold to Baldassare del Milanese, a dealer.

1496   June, went to Rome. Carved the *Bacchus* for the banker Jacopo Galli.

1497   November, went to Carrara to obtain marble.

1498   August, in Rome, commissioned by Cardinal Groslaye to carve the *Pietà*. In Florence, Savonarola burned at the stake; Florence organized traditional republican government.

1501   May–June, in Rome. Cardinal Piccolomini of Siena commissioned fifteen statues. (This project had progressed in 1504, but went no further after that.) August, in Florence. Cathedral Board commissioned the marble *David*, which was installed in 1504.

1502   August, Town Council of Florence commissioned the small bronze *David* as a gift for a French diplomat (finished in 1508 by another sculptor).

1503   April, Cathedral Board commissioned the *Twelve Apostles* (only the *Matthew* was begun).

1504   August, the Gonfaloniere (chief executive) Soderini commissioned the fresco of the *Battle of Cascina* for the Town Hall, to accompany the *Battle of*

Anghiari being painted by Leonardo da Vinci (only the cartoon was executed).

1505   March, Pope Julius II called Michelangelo to Rome to work on his tomb, which was to have forty life-size sculptures. Michelangelo spent the following months in Carrara to arrange for marble-quarrying.

1506   April, fled from Rome to Florence, gathering that the Pope had abandoned his interest in the tomb. Bought a farm, the first of many. August, the small *Madonna of Bruges*, carved a few years before, shipped to Flanders. November, went to Bologna to ask pardon from the Pope, who had reconquered that city. Worked on the colossal bronze statue of the Pope, installed there in February 1508.

1508   March–April, in Florence. May, Rome; began the Sistine Ceiling.

1510   September and December, brief trips to Bologna to obtain money for the ceiling from the Pope.

1512   October, ceiling finished. Return to Florence of the Medici, assisted by the army of the Emperor, which sacked the town of Prato. Fall of the republic.

1513   February, Pope Julius II died. May, new contract with his heirs for the tomb, which was to be less ambitious in structure, but to have even more sculptures. Work on the *Moses* and the *Slaves*. Election as Pope of Leo X, second son of Lorenzo de' Medici the Magnificent. Florence was informally ruled on his behalf by his younger brother the Duke of Nemours, his nephew (son of Piero) the Duke of Urbino (a title taken away from Pope Julius' family), his brother-in-law Jacopo Salviati, and his cousin Cardinal de' Medici.

1514 Contract for the *Risen Christ*. Occasional visits to Florence in 1514, 1515, and 1516.

1516 July, third contract for the Julius tomb, with fewer figures and more time. Trip to Carrara. Autumn, the Medici planned a façade for their parish church of San Lorenzo in Florence and obtained a drawing from Michelangelo. He made a model which provided for ten statues.

1517 Mainly in Carrara. April, bought a house from the Cathedral Board to use in carving the statues for the San Lorenzo façade.

1518 January, in Rome. Contract for the façade with twenty-two statues. February, Cardinal de' Medici told him to obtain marble not at Carrara but at nearby Pietrasanta, which was under Florentine control. Spent most of the year in Pietrasanta, with visits to Florence. October, reassured the heirs of Pope Julius.

1519 Mainly in Pietrasanta and Florence. The Pope and Cardinal forced the heirs of Julius to permit him to work in Florence only. He therefore spent thirteen months in Carrara to get fresh marble for the Julius tomb, replacing that sent earlier to Rome.

1520 Contract for the façade of San Lorenzo canceled; it was to be done by others in a simple form. Cardinal de' Medici planned instead the Medici tombs, for the Duke of Nemours (d. 1516), the Duke of Urbino (d. 1519), and other members of the family, to be placed in a special chapel of San Lorenzo.

1521 Began work on the Medici chapel. Trip to Carrara. The *Risen Christ*, finished by others, installed in S. Maria sopra Minerva, Rome. Death of Pope Leo X;

his book collection sent to Florence. The Dutch Pope Adrian VI elected.

1522–23   In Florence, working on the Julius tomb, though urged by Cardinal de' Medici to work on the Medici chapel.

1523   November 19, Cardinal de' Medici elected Pope Clement VII. Project to build the Medici Library in Florence.

1524   The building of the Medici Chapel finished. Work on the statues for the tombs of the Dukes. Project to add tombs for Popes Leo and Clement. Work on the Medici Library.

1525   Arguments over the Julius tomb. Steady work on the Medici tombs and Library continued through 1526.

1527   Sack of Rome by troops of the Emperor; the Pope a refugee. Florence exiled the Medici and re-established the republic.

1528   July 8, death of brother Buonarroto, leaving a widow, daughter Francesca, and son Lionardo (b. 1518). (None of Michelangelo's other brothers had any family.) The Pope and Emperor, reconciled, planned to attack the republic. Michelangelo named a member of the committee of nine to fortify the city.

1529   April 8, chief of fortifications. Visits to various cities on military business. September 25, fled to Venice. September 30, declared a rebel. November 30, returned with safe-conduct and resumed work on the fortifications.

1530   August 12, the republic fell and the Medici resumed power (permanently).

1530–31 Work on the Medici tombs; two of the statues finished. The Pope issued a brief permitting him to do no other work.

1531 Death of his father.* November, his assistant Antonio Mini left for France. Michelangelo gave him drawings and models.

1532 Planned to renegotiate the contract for the Julius tomb. April, visit to Rome. June, contract ratified, with only six figures, and a penalty against Michelangelo. July, to Rome; met Tommaso Cavalieri.

1533 June, to Florence; work on the Medici tombs and Library. Sent drawings to Cavalieri. November, to Rome.

1534 June, to Florence; met Febo di Poggio. September, to Rome, permanently. September 25, Pope Clement VII died; Paul III (Farnese) elected. Began work on *The Last Judgment*.

1536 Met Vittoria Colonna.

1537 December 11, the Pope issued a *motu proprio* to prevent the heirs of Julius from disturbing the work on *The Last Judgment*.

1541 Vittoria Colonna retired into a convent at Viterbo. October 31, *The Last Judgment* finished.

1542 Became friendly with Luigi del Riccio. February 27, arranged for Raffaello da Montelupo to carve three statues for the Julius tomb. March 6, agreement with the Duke of Urbino (heir of Julius) that Michelangelo would complete the other three. August

---

* Until recent study, Michelangelo's father was always thought to have died in 1534, solely on the basis of the lines in Michelangelo's poem on his death, referring to him as ninety. For that reason the poem appears out of order in all editions including the latest, which is followed here to avoid inconvenience.

20, formal (and last) contract, in which Michelangelo was to finish the *Moses* and Raffaello was to complete the other two statues nearly finished by Michelangelo.

1542 October–November, the Duke delayed ratifying the contract, while Michelangelo worked on his three statues and delayed beginning the Pauline Chapel for the Pope. December, contract ratified.

1543 Began painting the Pauline Chapel.

1544 January, sketch for the tomb of Cecchino Bracci. June–July, illness; stayed with Luigi del Riccio in the Strozzi Palace. Vittoria Colonna returned to Rome.

1545 Julius tomb installed. Crucifix for Vittoria Colonna. December, illness, again with Riccio in the Strozzi Palace.

1546 Gave the *Slaves* (left over from the early Julius projects) to Roberto Strozzi. Designed cornice for the Farnese Palace (of the Pope's family). Luigi del Riccio died.

1547 January 1, named architect of St. Peter's. February 25, Vittoria Colonna died.

1548 January 9, brother Giovansimone died.

1549 November 10, Pope Paul III died. His successor Julius III confirmed Michelangelo as architect of St. Peter's. Pauline Chapel finished.

1550 Benedetto Varchi in Florence published his explication of a sonnet by Michelangelo. Vasari published his *Lives of the Artists.*

1553 Nephew Lionardo married. Condivi's life of Michelangelo published.

1555 Pope Julius III died. Marcellus II, his successor, unfavorable to Michelangelo, died in a month; Paul

IV then confirmed Michelangelo as architect of St. Peter's. November 13, brother Gismondo died. December 3, servant Urbino died. Exchanged sonnets with Bishop Beccadelli, one of the overseers of St. Peter's.

1556 Work on St. Peter's continued in this and following years.

1559 Design for the church of S. Giovanni dei Fiorentini. Paul IV died and Pius IV reappointed Michelangelo.

1560 Design for Porta Pia and other city gates. Completed wooden model for the dome of St. Peter's.

1564 February, working on the Rondanini *Pietà* for himself. February 18, died.

POEMS

1

UNFINISHED ROUGH DRAFT
OF A SONNET

After being happy many years, one short
Hour may make a man lament and mourn,
Or one whose ancient famous family line
Illumined him, will fade out in a moment.

Under the sun there's not a thing that's transient
Not overcome by death and changed by fortune.

2

STANZA, PERHAPS FOR AN
UNWRITTEN SONNET

I alone burning keep within the shade,
After the sun has stripped his rays from earth;
Everyone else from pleasure, I from grief,
Lament and weep, stretched out upon the ground.

3

SONNET

Till now I was allowed, happy and grateful,
To avoid and beat off your fierce abuse,
But now, alas, must often beat my breast,
And know how strong you are, against my will.

And if no predecessor harmful missile
Toward the mark of my breast ever came close,
Now you can take revenge with all the blows
From beautiful eyes, and all of them are mortal.

From how many snares and meshes too,
By evil lot, a lovely little bird
Long years escapes, to die more evilly.

And love as well, Ladies, it's clear to you,
Has saved me many years, and when I'm old
Gives me a crueller death, it's clear to me.

4

SONNET (1507–08)

A wreath with flowers, happy and well braided
On someone's golden brow, is so rejoiced,
One's by the other past another thrust,
As if to be the first to kiss her head.

All through the day that dress is well contented
That binds her breast, and then seems to be stretched,

And what they call the filigreed gold has touched
Her neck and cheeks, and cannot make an end.

But happier still, that ribbon seems delighted,
Having a golden tip made in a manner
To press and touch the breast that it has yoked.

And I believe the simple sash that's knotted
Says to itself, I'd fasten here forever!
How would it be then that my arms would act?

5

SONNET TO JOHN OF PISTOIA
ON THE SISTINE CEILING (1509–12)

I've got myself a goiter from this strain,
As water gives the cats in Lombardy
Or maybe it is in some other country;
My belly's pushed by force beneath my chin.

My beard toward Heaven, I feel the back of my brain
Upon my neck, I grow the breast of a Harpy;
My brush, above my face continually,
Makes it a splendid floor by dripping down.

My loins have penetrated to my paunch,
My rump's a crupper, as a counterweight,
And pointless the unseeing steps I go.

In front of me my skin is being stretched
While it folds up behind and forms a knot,
And I am bending like a Syrian bow.

And judgment, hence, must grow,
Borne in the mind, peculiar and untrue;
You cannot shoot well when the gun's askew.

John, come to the rescue
Of my dead painting now, and of my honor;
I'm not in a good place, and I'm no painter.

6

SONNET TO POPE JULIUS II

If any ancient proverb's true, my Lord,
This is the one, that those who can, don't wish.
You have believed what's fabulous and false,
And let truth's enemy have your reward.

I am your faithful servant, as of old;
I am to you as the sun's rays are his.
My time does not disturb you or distress,
I've pleased you less the more that I have labored.

At first I hoped your height would let me rise;
The just balance and the powerful sword,
Not echo's voice, are fitted to our want.

But virtue's what the Heavens must despise,
Setting it on the earth, seeing they would
Give us a dry tree to pluck our fruit.

7

MADRIGAL

Who is it bringing me to you by pressure,
Alas, alas, alas,
Though I am loose and free, bound up so tightly?
If you can fetter us without a fetter,
And without using hands or arms have caught me,
Against your beautiful face who will protect me?

8

MADRIGAL

How can it be I am no longer mine?
O Heaven, Heaven, Heaven!
Who's robbed me of myself
Who's closer to myself
Or can do more with me than I can even?
O Heaven, Heaven, Heaven!
Who through my heart can move,
But seem to touch me not?
What is this thing, O Love,
Through the eyes invades the heart,
And seems to swell in the small space inside?
And what if it burst out?

9

STANZA, PERHAPS A BEGINNING
FOR A SONNET

He who made everything made every part,
And then from everything He chose the fairest,

To let us here look at His very greatest,
And now has done so with His sacred art.

10

SONNET

They make a sword or helmet from a chalice,
And sell the blood of Christ here by the load,
And cross and thorn become a shield, a blade,
And even Christ is being stripped of patience.

He should not come again into this province;
Up to the very stars his blood would spread,
Now that in Rome his skin is being sold,
And they have closed the way to every goodness.

If ever I wished that riches were cut off
What's happening here has changed all that in me;
The Cloak can do as Gorgon did in Atlas.

Yet if high Heaven favors poverty,
But other goals cut off our other life,
What is there in our state that can restore us?

11

MADRIGAL

How much less pain I'd have from dying quickly,
Than, one by one, a thousand deaths to suffer

10—line 11: The Pope can turn one to stone.

From her who wills my death because I love her.
Oh what infinite grief
My heart feels when it chances to perceive
That she I love so greatly feels no love.
How shall I keep my life?
She even says, to increase my agony,
She does not love herself, and I think truly.
How can I hope that she will pity me
If she does not love herself? O sorry fate,
Can it be true that I shall die of it?

12

MADRIGAL

How will I ever dare
Without you, my belov'd, to keep alive,
If I can't ask you to help me as I leave?
Those sighs and those sobbings and those tears
That went with my wretched heart, Lady,
To you, have demonstrated painfully
That I am hurt and that my death is near.
But if it is true that in my absence
My faithful slavery may be forgot,
I leave my heart with you, mine it is not.

13

SONNET FRAGMENT

I see myself as yours, from far invoke
My own approach to Heaven, my derivation,
And reach the bait, you, through the imitation,
Like fish drawn by the line, upon the hook.

And since a heart cut into two shows hardly
A sign of life, both of its parts it gave you;
I'm left not much, you know how much I am.
Since one soul of two things takes the more worthy,
I, if I wish to be, must always love you;
I am wood only, you are wood in flame.

14

FRAGMENT

From something lovely and unusual
My harm arises, from a well of mercy,
And enters in my heart, so made already . . .

15

ROUGH DRAFT OF A SONNET (1521)

O heart, cruel, unpitying and sour,
Entirely bitter although sweetly clothed,
Since it is born only in time, your faith
Lasts less than, in the sweet spring, any flower.

Time passes on, distributing each hour,
A very harmful poison in our life;
We are like straw and it is like the scythe,

     .   .   .   .
For faith is short and beauty does not last,
But seems to eat itself, as much as that,
Just as my harm is what your sin desires.

     .   .   .   .
Always would do among us through all years.

16

FRAGMENT OF UNIDENTIFIABLE
FORM (1522)

The soul tries out a thousand cures, in vain;
Since I was taken from my early road,
Vainly it worries how it can return.
The sea and mountains, and the fire and sword,
All these together, I live in their midst.
The mountain he'll not leave me, who has seized
My intellect, and taken away my reason.

17

UNFINISHED MADRIGAL (1522)

All of the strength that nature
Has used in girl and woman
Was only practice, leading up to this one,
Who now freezes and burns my heart together.
Wherefore no man was ever
Sad with a grief like mine;
Anguish and sighs and pain,
Stronger in source, are greater in result.
Then too in my delight
No one was ever happier than I . . .

18

OCTAVE STANZAS

You have a face more beautiful than a turnip,
Sweeter than mustard; it appears the snail

Has walked on it, it shines so; like a parsnip
The whiteness of your teeth is, and like treacle
The color of your eyes; surely the Pope
To such as this must be susceptible,
Whiter and blonder than a leek your hair;
So I shall die if I don't get your favor.

I think your beauty much more beautiful
Than ever in a church a painted man,
And your mouth is just like a pocketful
Of beans, it seems to me, and so is mine.
Your eyebrows seem dyed in a crucible,
And more than a Syrian bow they twine.
Your cheeks are red and white when you sift flour,
Like fresh cheese and poppies mixed together.

And when I look upon you and each breast,
I think they're like two melons in a satchel,
And then I am like straw, and start to flash,
Although I'm bent and broken by the shovel.
Think, if my lovely cup I still possessed,
I'd follow you past others like a beagle,
And if I thought that getting it was possible,
Here and today I'd do something incredible.

19

SONG

Whatever's born must come to death,
As time flies on, and in the sun
Nothing that's alive is left.
Sweetness fades away, and pain,

Every word and every brain,
And our ancient family line,
The wind's smoke, the sun's shadow.
We have been men like you,
Just as you are, sad and merry,
We are now, though, as you see,
Earth in the sun, of life bereft.

Everything must come to death.

Once on a time our eyes were whole,
Every socket had its light.
Now they are empty, black and frightful,
This it is that time has brought.

20

SONG

What of me now? What would you do again
To a heart when it's wounded, timber burnt?
Love, tell me a little bit,
So that I'll know in just what state I stand.

The years of my course have reached their goal
Like an arrow that has gotten to its target,
And I must quiet down my burning flame.
And I will pardon you all my past evil,
Your arms are blunt and broken in my heart,
Love finds in me for its trials no more room.
And if your buffetings were some new game
Against my eyes, against my heart, wet, timid,
Would it want what it wanted?

Love, it disdains and beats you, you're aware,
Only by being less strong today than ever.

Perhaps you're hoping with some novel beauty
To turn me back into that tangled danger
Where the wisest make much the least defense?
In years grown long, shorter the injury,
And therefore I shall be like ice in fire,
That is split and destroyed but does not catch.
Death at this age will be my sole defense
From savage arm and from the biting darts,
Cause of so many hurts,
That will not hold exempt any condition,
Either because of place or time or fortune.

My soul, which is exchanging talk with Death,
As she with him about herself consults,
Enmeshed in new suspicions every hour,
Whom day by day her body hopes to have left,
Thus on the road she had imagined, starts,
Confused and mingled in her hope and fear.
Ah Love, how rapidly do you appear,
Armed and powerful, reckless and audacious,
And out of me you thrust
The thought of death, even when it is timely,
To bring forth leaves and flowers from a dry tree.

What can I more? What should I? Did you not
Take up what time I had, within your kingdom?
Not one hour of my years fell to my share.
What cheating, what power or what wit
Could bring me back to you, master unwelcome?
Death in your heart, grace in your mouth you bear.

The soul would find no favor,
Ridiculous, ungrateful, if, reborn,
To what gave death before she should return.

The earth awaits all that is born, and soon
From hour to hour all mortal beauties fade;
Those who're in love, I see, cannot be loosed,
Cruel revenge accompanies great sin,
And he who is treated with the least regard
Is the one hurrying to his harm the most.
How would you have me placed,
So that the last good day, which I require,
Should be the one of shame and of disaster?

21

SONNET

I've been a thousand times, in years long past,
Wounded and killed, not to say beaten and tired,
By my own fault, by you; shall my white head
Now once again take up your foolish promise?

How many times you've bound, how many loosed
My sorry limbs, and speared me in the side,
So that I hardly yet can be restored,
Even when many tears water my breast!

Love, my complaint's of you, I speak to you,
Loosed from your wiles; why is it that you must
Take up your cruel bow and shoot at nothing?

When wood is ash, a borer or a saw
Is a great shame, or to dog a man who's lost
All skillfulness and broken off all motion.

22

SONNET FRAGMENT

I let my eyes become my poison's gate
When they let the sharp arrows pass them freely,
And for soft glances made my memory,
Which never will decrease, a nest and crypt.

Bellows my breast, an anvil of my heart,
For the making of sighs with which you burn me . . .

23

CAUDAL SONNET *

Whenever a master keeps a slave in prison
Locked in strong fetters, and entirely hopeless,
He grows so much accustomed to his anguish
That he would hardly ask again for freedom.

Tiger and serpent too are checked by custom,
And the fierce lion, born in the thick forest;
And, toiling at his works, the raw artist
By custom and by sweat doubles exertion.

But fire partakes of no such metaphor.
The sap out of green firewood it may snuff,
But the chilly old man it warms, then nurtures,

And brings him back again so near his youth,
Makes him so young and glad, inflames, restores,
His body and soul are girdled by love's breath.

Though some pretend or mouth
That it is shameful when a man is old
To love what's holy, that is a great fraud.

A soul not off its guard
Will never sin in loving what's in nature,
If it will keep to balance, bound and measure.

24

SONNET FRAGMENT

When it happens that wood does not maintain
Its own dampness, far from its earthly seat,
It can't but be that, more or less, great heat
Will dry it out and kindle it and burn.

My heart, taken by one who'll not return,
Once fed on fire and nurtured on lament,
Now it's away from its own place and seat,
What harm, through death, will not inflict its pain?

25

UNFINISHED SONNET

O lovers, run from love, run from the fire,
The flames are cruel and the wound is deadly.
And after the first thrust there is no virtue
In change of place, in reason or in power.

Run, now that the precedent's not meager
That the arm can be savage, sharp the arrow;

You can read in my face your injury,
And how the game will be ruthless and bitter.

At the first glance, do not lag back, but run;
I thought I could have peace at any time,
But now I feel and you see how I burn.

26

UNFINISHED MADRIGAL

Because unceasingly I feel the lure
Of eyes I hope for and recall, whereby
I am in luck, aside from being alive,
I am constrained by reason and by power,
By nature, love, and old conformity
To gaze upon you all the time I have.
And since by this I live,
If I changed state, I'd die in any other,
And no grace would discover
Except if they were there.
O Lord, how fair they are!
Who lives not on them is not born as yet;
If such come afterward
(Between ourselves a word)
He must as soon as born die on the spot.
None is alive who's not
In love with the beautiful eyes . . .

27

FRAGMENT

All anger, all wretchedness, all power,
Who arms himself with love outdoes all fortune.

28
MADRIGAL

A burning beam from my beloved's eyes
Comes forth and flies; so brilliant is its light,
Into my heart through mine, though shut, it breaks.
Wherefore Love crippled walks,
Having to manage such unbalanced weight;
Giving me light, my shadows he withdraws.

29
MADRIGAL

         . . . not only, but my eyes as well
Find death and life in full
In these of yours, that are unique in beauty.
The less the injury can press and hurt me
The more it wounds and burns;
On the other hand, love harms
The more as the more I am given grace.
And while I think and taste
Evil, good is increasing by the minute;
O strange and novel torment!
Yet I am not afraid;
Since to toil and be wretched
Here, where no goodness ever is, is sweet,
I seek a pain with greater punishment.

30
SONNET FRAGMENT (1525)

I live, dying for me, for sin alive,
My life's indeed not of me, but of sin;

My good by Heaven, my ill by me I'm given
From my loosed will, of which I am deprived.

My mortal part a good, freedom a slave
For me is made; O terrible condition!
I am born to what unhappiness, what living . . .

31
UNFINISHED SESTINA

Even if, besides my own, all other arms
Seem to defend all my most precious things,
Another sword and lance, another shield
Outside of my own powers are as nothing,
Such is the sad behavior that has taken
From me the grace Heaven rains in every place.

Like an old serpent through a narrow place
So may I pass, discarding my old arms,
My soul's behavior be renewed, and taken
During my lifetime from all human things,
Let it be covered with a surer shield,
For the world against death is less than nothing.

Love, I feel myself now being turned to nothing,
And sinful nature is in every place.
O strip me of myself, and with your shield
With your sweet, piteous and trusty arms,
Defend me from myself, all other things
Are as they had not been, and quickly taken.

While my soul from my body is not yet taken,
Lord, who can turn the universe to nothing,

Maker and governor, king of all things,
It's little to you in me to take a place,
As . . . these are mortal arms
That . . . and always be your shield.

O break and crush . . . that buckler and shield,
From which alone I get mercy and place,
For every virile man the genuine arms,
Not having which all men turn into nothing.

32
SONNET *

What sets my love alive is not my heart,
There's no heart in the love I love you by,
It cannot stay where there's mortality
With all its falsehood, nor in vicious thought.

Love, when the soul quit God, made you be light
And brilliancy, and me a steady eye,
So my great longing cannot fail to see
Him in what's mortal in you, to our hurt.

As heat from fire, likewise my admiration
Cannot be parted from eternal beauty,
Praising Him most like it who is its cause.

Since in your eyes you carry all of Heaven,
I, to return there where I loved you early,
Hurry back, burning, underneath your brows.

33

STANZAS IN TERZA-RIMA

The eyelid does not strike the face with color
When it contracts, it's no strain for the eye
To swing from one corner to the other.

The eye, below, turns itself easily,
And a small part of its great sphere reveals,
Exposing less of its calm sight to view.

Covered by it, much less it lifts and falls,
And thus the eyebrows also can be short
And, when it uses them, make fewer wrinkles.

The white white, more than funeral jet,
If that can be, lion-like yellow too,
That makes a passage from this vein to that.

But only touch its edge, above, below,
You won't surround the yellow, white and black . . .

34

UNFINISHED SONNET

Just about here my love, such was his mercy,
Took my heart, a bit further on, my life;
With beautiful eyes he promised me relief,
And, with the same, here wished to dispossess me.

Beyond there did he bind me, here he loosed me,
Here I mourned for myself; with infinite grief

I saw him from this very stone fly off
Who took me from myself, and did not wish me.

35
FRAGMENT OF THE END
OF A SONNET

In you is my life, in me my death,
You sift and divide and grant my time,
My life is long or short as you've desired.

And I am happy in your graciousness;
Blessed the soul that, where there is no time,
Through you has come to contemplating God.

36
UNFINISHED SONNET

He who at once steals time and death will bear
To my heart through my eyes so great a sweetness,
This is the one indeed that gives me solace,
And grows in my distress and lasts forever.

Love, as a lively and watchful power,
Awakes my spirits, is most worth my notice.
He gives me answer: "He is like a corpse
Who leads his life and keeps from me secure."

Love is an idea about beauty,
Imagined or seen within the heart,
A friend of virtue and nobility.

37

UNFINISHED SONNET

From the hard blow and from the biting arrow
My heart would be repaired, if cut clean through,
But this is what my lord alone can do,
Adding to life with added injury.

And though the first blow that he gave was deadly,
A messenger from love came with him too,
To say: "Love, rather burn, for those who die
Have no wings else on earth for a heavenly journey.

"I am the one who in your earliest years
Made your powerless eyes turn to that beauty
That leads up from the earth to Heaven alive."

38

UNFINISHED SONNET

When merry Love would lift me up to Heaven,
Upon this woman's eyes, on the sun rather,
He chases from my heart with rapid laughter
What hurts and aches, and lets her face come in.

And if I long remained in this condition,
My soul, toward me alone a willing grumbler,
Having there, where she always lives, with her . . .

39
SONNET (1529)

O wellborn soul, who show, as in a glass,
In your chaste body, beautiful and dear,
What Heaven and nature can accomplish here,
Yielding to none of their fair creatures else,

O lovely soul, in which, we hope and trust,
Within, as in the outward face appear,
There are love, pity, kindness, things so rare
No beauty ever had, with faithfulness,

Love seizes me, and beauty keeps me bound,
And with their gentle looks kindness and pity
Appear to give my heart firm hope it's so.

What rule and custom of the world demand,
What early or what later cruelty,
That such a beautiful face death not let go?

40
SONNET (1529)

Love, do my eyes, O tell me as a favor,
See the actual beauty I desire,
Or is it in me, so that as I stare
At every point I see her face in sculpture?

You have to know, since you are coupled with her
To snatch all peace from me and raise my ire,
Yet I would never ask less burning fire,
And would not ever wish the least sigh lesser.

The beauty that you see comes from her truly,
But, in a better place, grows by its climb;
Through mortal eyes into the soul it flies.

There it becomes beautiful, chaste and holy,
As the immortal wills a thing like Him;
It's this, not that, that leaps into your eyes.

41

SONNET (1529)

I am complained of and reproached by reason
When I, in love, hope to get happiness.
With true word and with potent illustration
She brings my shame to mind in me, and says:

"What will you garner from the living sun
Except for death, and not the phoenix's?"
But it helps little; if you will fall down,
No other's strong or ready hand suffices.

I understand the truth, and know my hurt,
On the other side another heart's my guest,
That kills me more the more that I submit.

My master is in the middle of two deaths,
One I don't understand and one don't want,
And soul and body die in this suspense.

41—line 6: The phoenix, in mythology, is reborn from his own ashes.

42

UNFINISHED SONNET (1529)

While toward the beauty that I saw at first
I bring my soul, which sees it through my eyes,
The inward image grows, and this withdraws,
Almost abject, and wholly in disgrace.

Love, using all his wits, and with his rasp,
So I won't break the thread, turns back and goes . . .

43

STANZAS IN TERZA-RIMA

By this time certainly the springs and rivers
After my so much sighing, must have dried,
If I did not refresh them with my tears.

And our eternal lights, one hot, one cold,
Sometimes relieve each other in this way,
So that the world will not be more destroyed.

The heart that is enamored, similarly
When it is kindled by too great a heat,
Moist eyes will damp it, and it does not die.

The death and the pain I seek and want
Won't let me die, but bring me a happy future,
For the one who delights us cannot hurt.

And so my little boat will not cross over
To see you on that shore, as I should wish,
That for a season leaves the body here.

Great pain would have me live, too, and subsist,
Like one going faster than the rest, who sees
That he reaches day's end after the rest.

Cruel pity and mercy pitiless
Left me alive and cut you loose from me,
Breaking but not ending our promises.

Not only not taking my memory . . .

44

SONNET

If my rough hammer in hard stones can form
A human semblance, one and then another,
Set moving by the agent who is holder,
Watcher and guide, its course is not its own.

But that divine One, staying in Heaven at home,
Gives others beauty, more to itself, self-mover;
If hammers can't be made without a hammer,
From that one living all the others come.

And since a blow will have the greatest force
As at the forge it's lifted up the highest,
This above mine to Heaven has run and flown.

Wherefore with me, unfinished, all is lost.
Unless the divine workshop will assist
In making it; on earth it was alone.

45

SONNET

When the one who had made me sigh so often
Took himself from himself, my eyes, and earth,
Nature, that wanted him to be our gift,
Was left ashamed, and all who saw it saddened.

Today no boasting, though, of having taken
And quenched the sun's sun like the rest, by Death;
For Love won, taking him to give him life
On earth and, with the other saints, in Heaven.

Thus false and evil Death thought it could quell
The rumor of his virtues, scattered far,
And his soul, which might be less beautiful.

But the reversed effect glows upon paper
With more life than in life was usual;
Dead, he has Heaven; not at all, before.

46

FRAGMENT

As a flame grows the more, the more the wind
Attacks it, every virtue Heaven exalts
Will shine the more, the more it is withstood.

47

FRAGMENT

Your beauty is not something mortal, Love.
There is no face among us that can equal

The image in the heart you hold and kindle;
With other fire, with other wings you move.

48

FRAGMENT

What is there, after many years of her,
O Love, if time must murder every beauty?
Renown of her; yet this as well will flee,
Vanish and go, more than I would desire.
More and less . . .

49

SONG

Oh alas, oh alas, I am betrayed
By flying days and the mirror, which has told
The truth to all who give it steady gaze;
And thus one who, at the end, too long delays,
As I have done, since all my time is fled,
Will find, like me, one day that he is old.
I can't repent, and I cannot be counseled,
Do not prepare, though I am close to death.
Enemy of myself,
I shed my sighs and tears, but uselessly,
Lost time's not matched by any injury.

Oh alas, oh alas, I keep repeating
The time that I have passed, and in it all
Do not discover one day that was mine.
Hopes that were false and wishes that were vain,

Loving and burning, heaving sighs and weeping
(For no mortal feeling to me is novel)
Have held me; this therefore I know and feel.
With truth now plainly far,
I am perishing with danger,
For the short time I had has disappeared,
Yet if it grew, I still would not be tired.

I go weary, alas, not knowing where,
Or rather fear I'll see, time that is gone
Shows it to me, to close my eyes won't help.
And now that time changes and shifts its pelt,
Death and my soul make constant trial together,
The second and the first, of my condition.
And if I am not mistaken
(May God will that I be)
The eternal penalty
For wrongs free, understood, accomplished, true,
I see, O Lord, but what I hope don't know.

50
SONNET FRAGMENT (1531)

If suicide for any on earth were licensed,
Since we by death think we'll return to Heaven,
It would be right for him who lives a bondsman,
Wretched, unhappy, with such true observance.

But since man cannot rise up like the phoenix,
Once more returning to the light of the sun,
I move my foot slowly, lazy my hand . . .

51

FRAGMENT (1531)

During the day any who ride by night
Will sometimes have a need for sleep and leisure.
And this I hope, after I have been hurt,
Life and form I'll have freshened by my master,
For evil does not last where good does not,
But often one is changed into the other.

52

OCTAVE STANZAS (1531–32)

1

I'm certain that if you were made of rock,
By loving you so faithfully I could
Make you come with me, faster than a walk,
And I could make you speak if you were dead,
Were you in Heaven I would pull you back,
When I would lament and sigh and plead.
Seeing you're flesh, here with us and alive,
What's one who loves and serves you to believe?

2

With you there's nothing I can do but follow,
An undertaking that I don't repent,
For you're not fashioned like a tailor's dummy,
That moves within if it is moved without,
And I have hopes someday you'll make me happy,
Assuming that you do not lose your judgment.
Good treatment takes away a serpent's bite,
Like teeth first set on edge by bitter fruit.

3
Nothing can stand against humility,
Set against love, cruelty has no power.
Hardness is always overcome by pity,
In the same way that sorrow is by pleasure.
When the world has a fresh and noble beauty,
The like of yours, its heart will not be other,
For when we see the straightness of a sheath,
It cannot have inside a twisted knife.

4
Also it cannot be you don't consider
My great service at least a little welcome,
Just think, you don't discover everywhere
Loyalty in your friends, but only seldom.

. . . . .

5
And when I cannot see you a whole day,
There is no place at all where I can rest;
To see you then will grip me in the way
That eating always does after a fast.

. . . . .

Like one dying to get his belly emptied,
There's more relief the more distress preceded.

6
Not one of my days can run its course
That in my mind I do not feel or see her,
There's never heat so great in oven or furnace
That would not from my sighs become still fiercer.
And when a while it happens I have her close,
I sparkle then like iron in burning fire,

And want to say so much, if she will listen,
That I say less than when I do not hasten.

7
And if she gives me a smile, even so slight,
Or lets me have a greeting by the way,
It lifts me up like powder that is shot
From any cannon or artillery;
Asks me a question, all at once I'm faint,
And lose both my voice and my reply,
And all at once my great desire surrenders,
And my hope bows submission to my powers.

8
In me I feel great love, I don't know what,
And almost to the stars it might attain,
But sometimes when I want to draw it out,
There's not so big an opening in my skin,
But it would seem much smaller coming from it,
And far less beautiful all that I own.
It's grace alone to speak of love or power,
And he says less of them who flies the higher.

9
I keep thinking about my life at first,
Before I loved you, and of how it went.
There was not one who paid me any notice,
Each day I wasted time till it was night.
Did I perhaps think I would write in verse,
Or keep away from all that other lot?
But now, for good or ill, they know my name,
And they all know that, in the world, I am!

10

You came in through the eyes, through which I shower,
Like a bunch of green grapes into a flask,
Spreading beyond the neck, where it is wider;
Your image thus outwardly makes me moist
And grows inside the eyes, then I grow broader,
As skin will do when fatness makes it vast.
Entering me by such a narrow path,
I can't believe you'll ever dare go forth.

11

And just as when a ball is filled with wind,
And the same breath that opens up the bladder
From outside, keeps it rigid from within,
I feel your beautiful face's image enter
My soul through my eyes in the same fashion,
Open them up and stay locked in thereafter.
And as on the first bounce a ball by a fist,
I, by your eyes struck, up toward Heaven lift.

12

No beautiful woman finds it adequate
To rejoice in the praise of just one lover,
Because her beauty then might die with it.
So if I love, revere you and adore,
My power counts for little in your merit,
A cripple does not match the slowest flier.
Not for one man the sun spreads out its bounties,
But every healthy eye on earth that sees.

13

How you can burn my heart I cannot think,
Entering it through eyes always so wet

They'd quench the fire, much more than just your look.
But all my remedies turn vain and short;
If water lights the fire, all else I lack
To save me from the harm I wished and want,
Except the fire itself. O strange affair,
If the fire's harm is often cured by fire!

53
OCTAVE STANZA (1531–32)

For you, although at great expense, I've bought
A bit of something or other smelling sweetly;
Often by odor I can find my route.
Wherever I am, wherever you may be,
I'm clear and sure of it without a doubt.
I will forgive you if you hide from me,
And, as you go, keeping it always by you,
Even if I were wholly blind I'd find you.

54
SONNET FRAGMENT (1532)

I live on my own death; if I see right,
My life with an unhappy lot is happy;
If ignorant how to live on death and worry,
Enter this fire, where I'm destroyed and burnt.

55
SONNET FRAGMENT (1532)

Since I live most on what most heats and burns,
The more the fire blazes from wood or wind,

The more the one who kills me gives me aid,
And helps me all the more, the more he harms.

56

SONNET

If the immortal wish, the lift and goad
Of others' thoughts, let mine show openly,
It could perhaps even now induce to pity
The house of love's inexorable lord.

But since the soul, by the decree of God,
Has long life, while the body dies so quickly,
Its value and its praise our sense can barely
Describe, being things that it can barely read.

Therefore, alas, how will the chaste wish
That burns my inward heart ever be heard
By those who always see themselves in others?

For me the precious passing day is crushed
With my lord, who gives heed to such a falsehood:
In fact, the unbelievers are the liars.

57

SONNET TO TOMMASO CAVALIERI (1532)

If a chaste love, if an excelling kindness,
If sharing by two lovers of one fortune,
Hard lot for one the other one's concern,
Two hearts led by one spirit and one wish,

And if two bodies have one soul, grown deathless,
That, with like wings, lifts both of them to Heaven,
If love's one stroke and golden dart can burn
And separate the vitals of two breasts,

Neither loving himself, but each one each,
With one delight and taste, such sympathy
That both would wish to have a single end,

If thousand thousands would not be one inch
To love so knotted, such fidelity—
And mere affront can shatter and unbind?

58
SONNET TO TOMMASO CAVALIERI (1532)

You know that I know, my Lord, you know
I have come to enjoy you closer by;
You know I know you know that it is I,
So why put off our greetings longer now?

If the hope you have given me is true,
And true the good desire that's granted me,
Let the wall set between us fall away,
For there is double power in secret woe.

If I in you love only, dear my Lord,
What you love most in you, do not be angry;
The one's enamored of the other spirit.

What in your beautiful face I have wished and learned
Human intelligence can grasp but badly,
He is required to die who wants to see it.

59

SONNET TO TOMMASO CAVALIERI (1532)

If when I first caught sight of it I'd thought
That in this fostering phoenix's warm sun
I'd be renewed by fire, in which I burn,
As is in her extreme old age her wont,

Then, as the swiftest lynx, leopard or hart
Will follow its own good, its suffering shun,
Toward her actions, her laughter, I'd have run,
Toward her chaste words, where now I am quick but late.

But why should I be sorry since I've seen
In the eyes of this single happy angel
That I shall be at peace, rested and safe?

To see or hear her sooner would have been
Perhaps less good, for now, in flight, her equal,
She gives me wings for copying her strength.

60

SONNET

Only with fire the smith can bend the iron
As he's conceived his dear and beautiful work;
And gold, except with fire, to its high mark
No artisan can carry and refine.

And single phoenix cannot live again
Unless it first burns. So, if I die burnt,
Brighter I hope among those to come back
Whom death enhances, time does not demean.

The fire of which I speak, my great good fortune,
Still, to renew me, being within me settled,
Who am almost numbered with the dead already,

If by its nature it goes up to Heaven,
To its own element, and I'm converted
To fire, how can it be it will not take me?

61

SONNET

So friendly to cold rock is the inner fire
That if, drawn out therefrom, it circumscribes,
Burns it and breaks, in some way it survives,
Itself a bond for others, fixed forever.

And if it can outlast winter and summer
In the hard kiln, its earlier worth will rise,
As if a soul returned from Hell, chastised,
To Heaven among the others high and pure.

Me too the fire drawn from me may dissolve,
Whose play has been concealed internally,
And I may have more life, burnt and then cold.

Thus, turned to smoke and dust, I still may live
If I can stand the fire eternally,
For I am beaten not by iron but gold.

61—lines 1–6: Michelangelo's metaphor for himself is stone, which
has fire in it and can be burnt by fire, but which then
survives as mortar.

62

STANZA

This fire shatters stone, and iron it splits,
Though child of their identical hard core.
Then what will Hell's do, since it burns much more,
To a dry straw dovecote that it hates?

63

SONNET FRAGMENT

While I adore you, yet at the same time
The memory of my unhappiness
Returns to me in thought, and weeps, and says
The ones who burn well love well, where I am.

And so I make a shield for me of them . . .

64

SONNET (1532–33)

Perhaps so I will come to pity men,
So I will laugh no longer at men's error,
In my own strength, having no other leader,
My soul that was so worthy once has fallen.

I think no soldier under other ensign
Would trust to get safe off, much less to conquer,
Or in the tumult of the enemy clamor
Not perish, if your power did not sustain.

O flesh, O blood, O wood, O agony,
By you be justice made out of my sin
That I was born in, and my father too.

You are the only good; may your high pity
Give help to my foretold sinful condition,
With death so near and God so far away.

65

OCTAVE STANZAS

1

It is a novel and superior pleasure
To see the daring goats climbing a rock,
Making one peak and then the next their pasture,
And down below their owner, with harsh music,
Pouring his soul out in a rough-hewn measure,
Playing as he stands, or at a gentle walk,
And all the while his iron-hearted lady
With the pigs under an oak stands haughtily.

2

As so it also is to see their home,
On a high spot, made out of straw and mud;
One loads the board; outdoors, one feeds the flame,
Below whatever elm they find is good,
One fattens and pokes the pig and plays a game,
One trains the donkey for its maiden load,
And, sitting outside the door, the aged man,
Saying few words, stays happy in the sun.

3

All that is theirs within without you see,
Peace without gold and quite without ambition,
And when they plow the hills, departing daily,
You can count up their riches one by one.
They have no locks and fear no injury,
But let their house stay open to its fortune.
Then after work they seek out slumber, gay,
Content with acorns fall asleep on hay.

4

Envy can have no place when things are so,
And Pride by its own self would be devoured.
For they feel greed only for some green meadow,
Or grass that is most beautifully flowered.
The height of their treasure is a plow,
The plowshare is the gem by which they're honored.
Their strongbox is in a pair of baskets,
Shovels and spades are all their golden goblets.

5

Miserliness so blind, so low the wits
That have mistreated so the goods of nature,
Seeking out gold and lands and kingdoms rich,
Though potent Pride has charge of your adventure,
And Sloth and Lust, apparently, so teach;
Envy provides and sets harm on another.
You don't see, in insatiable flame,
Little is necessary, short the time.

6

Let those who in the past, in days of yore,
On water and acorns thirst and hunger slaked,

Be your example, guidance, light and mirror,
And hold you back from foods and from delight.
To what I say a little turn your ear;
The one who rules the world, and is so great,
Forever wants, yet cannot find the peace
A peasant and his oxen can possess.

7

Wealth passes sunk in thought, she is adorned
With gold and jewels, but her face is fearful.
Cast down by every rain and every wind,
She watches for each prophecy and marvel,
While merry Poverty, fleeing, has gained
Every treasure, of how and when unmindful,
Safe in the woods, in rough and gray attire,
Free of disputes, incumbrances and care.

8

Giving and having, strange and startling custom,
The better and the worse, the heights of art,
For the peasant these things are all the same,
Water and grass and milk are all his part.
And his rude song, the creases on his palm,
Are tens and scores and budget and account
Of usury that's growing through the world,
And he can yield to fortune unconcerned.

9

He prays to God with honor, love and fear,
For his flock, for his pastures, for his toil,
With faith and with hope and with desire,
For the cow that's with calf, for the fine bull.
Doubt and Perhaps and How and Why can never

Make him do wrong, with them he does not dwell;
He who with simple faith adores and prays
To God and Heaven binds one, the other sways.

10

In pictures Doubt is shown armed and a cripple,
And moves like a locust, with a jump.
Forever, by his nature, he's atremble,
As it might be reed in a windy swamp.
And Why is thin, and all around his girdle
Has many keys, but they will not match up,
And so he has to strain bolts in the gate;
His guide is darkness, for he goes by night.

11

How and Perhaps are very near akin,
They both are giants, and they are so lofty,
Both seem to want to travel to the sun,
And were made blind by looking at its glory.
With their proud breasts they mask it from a town,
And utterly put in the shade its beauty,
Take between rocks a twisted winding road
And test out with their hands which ones are hard.

12

Truth moves along naked and poor and lonely,
Whom humble people hold in great renown,
Her heart a diamond and gold her body,
Shining and pure her eye, which is but one.
In troubles she increases and grows haughty,
In one place dies, though in a thousand born.
Outwardly she is green as emerald
And with her faithful stands, constant and settled.

13

With eyes held downward to the earth, and chaste,
Of various brocades and gold his garment,
Goes Falsehood, who, fighting none but the just,
In outward show loves all, a hypocrite.
Covered and shut from sun, being made of ice,
He seems to long for shade, always at court,
And he makes his defense and company
Of Fraud and of Discord and of Lie.

14

Then there is Adulation, full of trouble,
With handsome person, and with youthful vigor,
Covered with more colors in more apparel
Than Heaven in the spring gives to a flower.
With sweet deceptions getting what she will,
Talking only of what will please another,
Within one wish she has both tears and smiles,
Adores with eyes, and with her hands she steals.

15

In court not only mother of fearful acts,
But she's their nurse as well, and with her milk
Increases them, defends them, and augments . . .

66

OCTAVE STANZAS

1

There is a giant too, whose height is such
From his eyes down to us he cannot see,
And where his foot has trodden he has crushed

And covered up a town repeatedly,
In yearning for the sun, high towers smashed,
To get to Heaven which he cannot see,
For his body, so large and powerful,
Has just one eye, and that is in one heel.

2

Events already past he sees on earth,
And holds his head up straight where stars are near.
From here below we see a two-day length
Of his great legs, skin covered up with hair,
He knows no winter or summer, up from thence,
Seasons for him are all the same and fair.
And, as his forehead's on a par with Heaven,
On earth he makes a plain of every mountain.

3

And as for us a particle of sand is,
So mountains are for him, beneath his steps,
Between the thick hairs of his legs he carries
All kinds of monstrous and enormous shapes;
There would be whales there in the place of flies,
He's only bothered, only mourns and weeps
Whenever in that eye the wind may blow
Smoke or some dust that's moving or a straw.

4

With him, a huge lazy and slow old woman
Upon her milk nurses the ghastly creature,
And always will encourage and sustain
His blind, arrogant and presumptuous ardor.
When not with him, she lives in a closed cavern,
Within the high walls or in some great tower.

She lives in the shadows when he's idle,
And directs only privation for the people.

5

Sallow and pale, and in her heavy breast
The only sign she carries is her master's.
She grows from others' ill, their good her loss,
And is not filled from feeding at all hours.
There's no check or conclusion of her course,
She does not love herself in hating others.
Her heart is of stone, her arms of iron,
And her belly encloses mountain and ocean.

6

Over the earth go seven of their children,
From one to the other pole they search,
Only to just men bring strife and deception,
And there are a thousand limbs on each.
For them the eternal pit is shut and open,
Such beauty in the enormous swarm they catch,
And step by step their limbs will pin us down,
As ivy does a wall from stone to stone.

67

FRAGMENT OF THE END
OF A SONNET

Nature saw to it, it would not befit
Such cruelty if pity should be less;
One moderates the other contrary.
In the same way your face can moderate,
With a little sweetness, all my great distress,
Lightening it, and letting me be happy.

68
SESTINA

O cruel star, or rather, cruel judgment
That leaves my will and power crushed and bound,
There's no bright star working for me in Heaven,
Since that first day in which my sails were loosed,
When first, roving and wandering, I went
As empty boats will swing in all the winds.

Now alas, being here in the burning winds,
I have to launch my boat, and without judgment
Plow the high waves where never once I went.
Thus here below is taken, pressed and bound
What earlier from the tree above was loosed
When I denied myself the prize of Heaven.

Here I am not guided and ruled by Heaven,
But by the haughty and opposing winds
That over me I don't know who has loosed,
Setting them free to take away my judgment.
Thus by another, not my nets, I am bound.
Is it my fault? Unknowing to it I went.

Accursed be the day in which I went,
And the sign that was ruling up in Heaven,
Did I not know no hearts by days are bound,
And no souls forced by them or adverse winds
Against the bounty of our own freed judgment,
Since . . . and by trials we have been loosed.

68—line 11: The apple, sin.

Therefore if ever the heart's pain has loosed
A burning sigh, or if I praying went
Among hot winds to Him exempt from judgment,
. . . merciful for my hot winds,
I am seen, heard, felt and not opposed by Heaven,
Yet that cannot be loosed that is self-bound.

He cannot act who by himself is bound,
And of himself no one is freely loosed.
And as a tree grows upward straight to Heaven,
I pray you, Lord, if ever thus I went,
I may bring back, like one who feels no winds,
Underneath yours, which is so great, my judgment.

The one who has loosed and bound my judgment,
Whither I went among the harassing winds,
Revenge me if you gave me him, O Heaven.

69

SONNET : (*Against the people of Pistoia*)

I've got it, yes, to you my gratitude,
And I have read it twenty times again.
Let teeth be to your nature as much gain
As victuals to a body after food.

I've also, since I left you, understood
That one among your ancestors was Cain,
From whom you have not in the least withdrawn;
You think you've lost when others get some good.

O enemies of Heaven, envious, haughty,
For you neighborly kindness is a trial,
Only to your own damage you are friendly.

Oh Pistoia, learn well
The poet's words, that's all; if you speak kindly
Of Florence, you imagine I'm a fool.

That it's a precious jewel
Is certain, which you cannot understand,
For this small talents cannot comprehend.

70
SONNET TO TOMMASO CAVALIERI (1533)

Since through the eyes the heart's seen in the face,
I have no other way so evident
To show my flame; let this then be sufficient,
O my dear Lord, to ask you now for grace.

Perhaps your spirit, gazing at this chaste
Fire that consumes me, will, more than I credit,
Have trust, and be with me speedy and lenient,
As grace abounds for him who well entreats.

O happy that day, if this is true!
Then at one instant in their ancient road
The hours will be stopped, time, sun, the days,

That I may have, though it is not my due,
My so much desired, my so sweet lord,
In my unworthy ready arms for always.

69—line 13: Dante attacks the people of Pistoia in *Inferno* 24 and 25.

71

STANZA

While I'm deprived and hunted from the fire,
Perforce I'll die where people safely live;
My only foods are those that burn and seethe,
And I can live on what would kill another.

72

STANZAS

I burn, I consume myself, I cry;
O sweet lot! and on this my heart is nourished.
Does anyone live only on his death,
On pain, and on his sufferings, as I?

Ah cruel bowman, you can tell exactly
When to bring quiet to our anxious, brief
Unhappiness, using your hand's strength;
For he who lives on death will never die.

73

FRAGMENT

It is too much when someone looks around
Who kills those standing near him with a look,
Only to show he's on a pleasant round.

It is too much, when day to night he's turned,
His fine fair eyes making the sun grow dark,
To open them often, and whose song and frolic
Strikes others dumb, to be no less adorned.

74

SONNET

I do not know if it's the wished-for light
Of its first maker that the soul can sense,
Or whether, out of popular remembrance,
Some other beauty shines into the heart,

Or someone's formed from dreams, or from report,
Plain to my eyes, and in my heart's presence,
From whom I do not know what smoldering remnants
May be are what now makes my weeping start.

What I sense and I search, and who's my guide
Is not with me, I truly don't see whither
To find it out; it seems I'm shown by others.

This happens to me since I saw you, Lord,
Moved by a yes and no, a sweet and bitter;
I'm sure it must have been those eyes of yours.

75

SONNET

If the fire pouring out of them were equal
To the beauty you have within your eyes,
No part of earth so thoroughly could freeze
It would not then burn like an arrow kindled.

But Heaven, which is kind to all our trouble,
Cuts and deflects our faculty that sees
From all the beauty of which you dispose,
To make our bitter mortal life more tranquil.

So the fire is not equal to the beauty,
For a man catches fire and loves alone
The beauty of Heaven of which he is aware.

Lord, at my age this is what happens to me;
If you don't think I die for you, or burn,
My fire is small because I have small power.

76
SONNET

From an eternal to a short-lived peace,
To grievous laughter from a sweet lament
I've fallen down, for where the truth is silent
Its survivor, cut off from it, is sense.

I don't know if my heart or if your face
Is to blame for the evil, less unpleasant
The more it grows, or else the burning light
Of your eyes which are robbed from paradise.

There is, though, nothing mortal in your beauty,
Divine for us, and made above in Heaven,
So I, losing and burning, have this comfort,

That I cannot be thus with you nearby.
If Heaven allots the weapons of my dying,
Who, if I die, can say you were at fault?

———
76—line 4: Sense—animal sensation.

77

SONNET: (*On receiving a message
from Tommaso Cavalieri*)

O happy soul, who keep, with burning stress,
Life in my old and almost dying heart,
And in much other pleasure and delight
Greet only me, among those more illustrious,

As once you did my eyes, now you refresh,
Through the voice of another man, my thought,
Whence hope, it seems, will hold in check the hurt
That my soul feels as strongly as its wish.

And thus in you he finds, who speaks for me,
Your grace toward me among so many matters,
And he who writes this for the grace is grateful.

For criminal great usury would be
To make you a present of such wretched pictures
To get, in turn, beautiful living people.

78

SONNET

I thought, on the first day I admired
So many beauties, matchless and alone,
I'd pin my eyes, like eagles in the sun,
On the smallest of many I desired.

But then I learned how I had sinned and erred:
To have no wings, yet after an angel run,

Is to strew seed upon a rock in vain,
And words upon the wind, mind upon God.

Hence, if the infinite beauty won't abide
My heart close by, and makes my eyes go blind,
Nor seems to assure or trust me when I'm further,

What shall I do? What guardian or guide
Can ever assist me with you, or withstand?
Nearby you set me on fire, and parting, murder.

79
MADRIGAL (1526–34)

Every object I see begs me and counsels
And forces me to follow and adore you.
Whatever is not you is not my good.
Love, which belittles all the other marvels,
Will have me for my sake seek and desire you,
As the sole sun; my spirit it can hold
Away from all high hope, and from all power,
Willing I live on fire
Not just for you, but any who resembles
Your eyes or brows in any slightest part.
Any who from you part,
O eyes my life, thereafter have no light,
Because it is not Heaven where you are not.

80
SONNET

There is no other image in my fancy,
Of naked shadow or of earthly flesh,

However high my thought, such that my wish
Can arm itself with it against your beauty.

For, leaving you, I find I sink so deeply,
That every power I have love steals and strips;
In hoping to make my pain diminish,
It doubles, and comes prepared to kill me.

So it's pointless for me to strain and fly,
And redouble my enemy beauty's run;
What's slower can't escape from what is fast.

Love with his hands can cause my eyes to dry,
Assuring a reward for all my pain,
And it cannot be trash at such a cost.

81

SONNET

I see within your beautiful face, my Lord,
What in this life we hardly can attest;
Your soul already, still clothed in its flesh,
Repeatedly has risen with it to God.

The evil, foolish and invidious mob
May point, and charge to others its own taste,
And yet no less my faith, my honest wish,
My love and my keen longing leave me glad.

All beauty that we see here must be likened
To the merciful Fountain whence we all derive,
More than anything else, by men with insight.

We have no other fruit, no other token
Of Heaven on earth; one true to you in love
May rise above to God, and make death sweet.

82

SONNET TO TOMMASO CAVALIERI

In the same way that pen and ink embrace
The high and the low style and the middle,
And rich pictures or crude are in the marble,
Whichever our wits are able to express,

Thus, my dear Lord, perhaps within your breast
No less than acts of pride there are the humble.
Yet it is only those that I resemble
That I extract, and show it in my face.

He who has planted tears and sighs and pain,
(The heavenly dew on earth, pure in itself,
For different seeds in different ways will alter)

Sorrow and grief from them will reap and glean;
Who gazes on high beauty in great grief
Draws from it sharp and sure distress and torture.

83

STANZAS IN TERZA-RIMA (1533–34)

An answer to a letter. The comic poet Francesco Berni wrote a terza-rima letter to the painter Sebastiano del Piombo, a friend of Michel-angelo's, speaking of Michelangelo in the highest terms and scathingly of everyone else. The answer is as if written by Sebastiano.

My Lord, as soon as I had heard from you,
I went to look for all the Cardinals,
And said to three on your behalf, "Adieu."

To the great Medicus of all our ills
I showed the same, at which he laughed so greatly,
His nose made two halves of his spectacles.

The one you serve, so estimable and saintly,
Both here and there, just in the way you write,
Liked it so much that he too laughed as greatly.

As for that one, I have not seen him yet,
Who keeps secrets for Medicus the less,
He would feel just the same, were he a prelate.

Many others are here, forswearing Christ
Because you are not here, without a pain;
Not believing is held less tedious.

But I shall take away all of their strain
By this from you; if they're not satisfied
The executioner can let them drown.

The Meat, that in salt is cured and Dried,
And also would do nicely in a broiler,
Seems to have you more than himself in mind.

Our Buonarroti, who is your adorer,
I think, on seeing yours, if I mark well,
Floats up to Heaven a thousand times an hour,

83—line 4: The great Medicus—the Pope, a member of the Medici
                  family.
        line 11: Medicus the less—Cardinal Medici.
        line 19: Meat that is Dried—Mons. Carnesecchi; carne, meat;
                  secchi, dry.

And says that the life that's in his marble
Won't suffice to immortalize your name
As you will make him, with your sacred idyll.

To it, summer and winter do no harm,
Exempt from time and death, which, though it's cruel,
Has no control of meritorious fame.

And as your friend, to me being also loyal,
He said: "To paintings," seeing the handsome verses,
"They pin up a vow or light a candle.

"So I must be considered one of those
Some painter who is blundering and weak
Has dredged out of his paint jars and his brushes.

"For love of me let Berni then be thanked,
The truth of me he understands alone
Of many; they who admire me much mistake.

"But the full light his teaching surely can
Provide me; it will be miraculous
To make a painted man a genuine man."

Thus he spoke to me; I then, if you please,
Commend him to you all that I know how,
Since he will be bearer to you of this.

Yet, as I write it, verse by verse I grow
Terribly red, thinking to whom I send,
Mine being amateur, rough and askew.

And yet nevertheless I would commend
Myself to you as well; there's no news else.
And I am yours at every time and tide.

To you, who are among the rarities,
I offer all myself, and don't consider,
Unless my cowl falls off, I'll be remiss.

Thus I tell you and swear, you can be sure
For you I'd do what I wouldn't for myself;
And don't avoid me since I am a friar.

Command me, and then do it by yourself.

84

STANZAS IN TERZA-RIMA:
(*On the death of his father*)

Though earlier my heart has pressed me so,
For my safety I thought I could express
My great sorrow through my weeping woe.

But fortune, at the fountain of that moistness,
Now makes her roots and veins swollen and fat
Through death, no slighter punishment or sadness,

As you depart; so I must separate
Between the son dying first and you, thereafter,
Of whom I'm speaking, tongue, pen, and lament.

One was brother to me, you were our father;
Love strains toward him, to you my obligation,
I don't know which hurt strains or irks me further.

My brother's painted in my recollection,
And it carves you alive inside my heart,
For face and heart more stain and more affliction.

And yet, as for the debt, it gives me quiet
My brother paid it green, and you mature;
Death in old age makes others feel less hurt.

The matter must become, even to a mourner,
Less harsh and rough when it's more necessary,
For from the senses then truth is securer.

But who is the man who would not cry
For his dear father dead, not seeing again
Him whom he saw infinite times, or many?

For our intensest sorrow and our pain
Are great or small as felt, in any person;
Lord, what they do in me you understand.

And even though the soul consents to reason,
It does it so stiffly, that I'm filled
Far more with more depression later on.

Were not the thought to which I firmly hold
That those in Heaven who have died well feel laughter
About the fear of dying in the world,

My pain would grow; but all the sorrowful clamor
Is tempered by the firm belief that those
Who have lived well in death are settled better.

Upon our intellect so deeply weighs
Our weak flesh, that death seems the more hard
The more that man falsely persuaded says.

For the ninetieth time the sun's bright brand
Had first been dipped and softened in the ocean
Before you had achieved the peace of God.

Since Heaven has now removed you from our burden,
Have some regret for me, who am dead while living,
Since through your means it wished me to be born.

You're dead of dying, and are made divine,
Nor do you fear a change in life or wish;
I hardly write it without envying.

Fortune and time will not attempt to pass
Within your threshold, while with us they make
For doubtful delight and sure distress.

There is no cloud can make your light grow dark,
On you the different hours work no power,
Not bounded by necessity or luck.

The night does not deaden down your splendor,
Nor day, however bright, make it increase,
Even when with us the sun makes heat grow stronger.

By having died my dying you will teach,
Dear father, and I see you in my thought
Where the world hardly ever lets us reach.

Some think that death's the worst, but it is not
For one whose final day grace will transform
To his first eternal, near the holy seat,

Where by God's grace I imagine and assume
And hope to see you are, if reason draws
My own cold heart out from the earthly slime.

And if the best of love in Heaven increases
Between father and son, as virtues all grow . . .

85
SONNET

I want to want, Lord, what I do not want,
An icy veil hides between heart and fire
And damps the fire, making my page a liar,
Since my pen and my conduct do not fit.

I love you with my tongue, then I lament
Love does not reach the heart, and can't tell where
To open the door to grace so it can enter
And thrust all ruthless pride out of my heart.

Tear the veil thou, O break that wall, my Lord,
Which with its hardness keeps in check the sun
Of your own light; on earth it is put out.

Send that same ray of light to your fair bride
Which we are then to have, so I may burn,
And my heart feel you only with no doubt.

86

SONNET TO TOMMASO CAVALIERI

I feel how a cold face that fire has lit
Burns me from far, and turns itself to ice;
Two lovely arms submit me to a force
That does not move, but moves all other weight;

Unique, and grasped by me alone, a spirit
That has no death, but others' death can compass,
I see and meet, that binds my heart, being loose;
From one who helps I feel the only spite.

Lord, from a beautiful face how can it be
Effects so far opposed are borne on mine?
It's hard to give to men what you have not.

As for the happy life he's snatched from me,
He may, if you're not kind, act as the sun,
Which heats the world although it is not hot.

87

SONNET

I with your beautiful eyes see gentle light,
While mine are so blind I never can;
With your feet, on my back can bear a burden,
While mine are crippled, and have no such habit;

Having no feathers, on your wings my flight,
By your keen wits forever drawn toward Heaven,
As you decide it I am flushed and wan,
Cold in the sun, at the cold solstice hot.

My wishes are within your will alone,
Within your heart are my ideas shaped,
When you have taken breath, then I can speak.

It seems that I am like the lonely moon,
Which our eyes fail to see in Heaven, except
The fraction of it that the sun may strike.

88

SONNET

I am dearer to myself than was my habit,
More than myself, since you've been in my heart,
As a bare rock will get much less regard
Than a stone with its carving added to it.

Or, like a written or painted leaf or sheet,
More noted as the more it's torn or scarred,
Such I make myself, since I've been the target
Struck by your face; and I have no regret.

I go as one who bears arms or enchantment
So that all dangers fall away from me,
Made safe in every place with such a seal.

Against fire, against water I am potent,
All blind men in your sign I make to see,
And with my spit all poisoning I heal.

89

MADRIGAL

So that, with heat too great
Which stops and then renews

The closing and the opening of your eyes,
My life in you may still last for the present,
You have become a magnet,
For me, for my soul, O Lord most sweet.
This makes love hesitate,
Shake, fear, before he injures,
Maybe because he is blind,
For to pass to my heart,
I being with you in yours,
He would first have to break your outer rind.
That your life may not end
With mine, he does not kill me. From this anguish
Of deathly suffering but without death,
If I were my own I would be free.
Ah give me back myself so I may die!

90

MADRIGAL

Though time is prodding at me and insists,
Each time with greater hurt,
That to earth must revert
My body, tired and bruised and travel-burdened,
Yet he will make no end
Who brings my soul such grief, me such delight,
Or think to give me peace
Who opens and locks my heart,
Though the hour is at hand
Most doubtful if my after life be quiet,
No, the familiar fault
Keeps strengthening in me as I grow older.
O my fate, more severe than any other!

Too late you rid me now of all my cares;
A heart on fire, on fire for many years,
Will alter, though the mind extinguishes:
No longer a heart at all, but char and ashes.

91
MADRIGAL

If Sense will let its flame, too scorching, scatter
Away from yours to some less beautiful face,
Lord, it has far less force,
As, in its branches, a fierce mountain river.
Then Heart, whose life goes further
In hotter fire, can hardly then agree
With the less burning sighs and rarer tears.
Soul, which can see the error,
Is glad to have it die
And turn to Heaven, whither it aspires.
Then Reason justly shares
The wounds among them, and with tougher bodies
All four of them agree to love you always.

92
SONNET: (*The silkworm*)

With grace to all, to itself only scorn,
A wretched beast is born in grief and pain,
Clothes other's hands, but its own hide unskins,
And only in dying may be called well born.

So too I'd want to have my fate adorn
My Lord, while living, with my dead remains;

As on the rock the serpent sheds its skin,
Only in death can my condition turn.

Oh if I only had the hairy coat
Which, with its plaited fur, makes such a dress,
That clasps so beautiful a breast with pleasure,

I'd have it daytimes; or each little boot
That makes itself his column and his base,
At least I'd carry it in dirty weather.

93
    SONNET

O give back to my eyes, river and fountain,
From that strong vein that is not yours, the water
That swells and lifts you more and with more vigor
Than is according to your natural custom.

And you, dense air, that let the light of Heaven,
Full of my sighs, on my sad eyes be gentler,
Give it back to my weary heart, and clear
Your dark features for my piercing vision.

Let earth then give my steps back to my feet,
So grass may sprout again that was removed,
And deaf echo, my cries back to my voice,

My glances to my eyes from your blessed light,
So that another beauty I may love
Another time, since I am not your choice.

94

STANZAS IN TERZA-RIMA

May I like dry wood in a burning fire
Burn, if I do not love you heartily,
And lose my soul, if it feels for another!

If spirit of love from any other beauty
Except your eyes can make me glow or flame,
Take them from me, who would, without them, die.

If I don't love and adore you, all my warm
Thoughts, with my hope, may then become as dull
As in your love now they are fixed and firm.

95

SONNET

Since I have straw for flesh and my heart's sulphur,
Since I have bones consisting of dry wood,
Since my soul lacks a rein and lacks a guide,
Since I jump at desire, at beauty further,

Since all my brains are weak and blind, and totter,
And since quicklime and traps fill all the world,
It will be no surprise when I am burned
By a flash of the first fire I encounter.

Since I've the beautiful art, that those who bear it
From Heaven use to conquer Nature with,
Even if she can parry everywhere,

If I, not blind or deaf, was born for it,
A true match for my heart's fire-setting thief,
He is to blame who fated me to fire.

96

SONNET TO TOMMASO CAVALIERI

Wherefore should I let loose still more my keen
Longing in mournful words or in lament,
If Heaven, which clothes us all with such a fate,
Strips no one of it ever, late or soon?

Wherefore should my tired heart still urge me on
To die, if others also die? So let
My eyes feel in their final hours less hurt,
All other good counts less than all my pain.

Therefore if I cannot evade the blow
I steal and snatch from him, if it is fated,
Who at least comes between delights and harms?

If capture and defeat must be my joy,
It is no wonder that, alone and naked,
I remain prisoner of a knight-at-arms.

97

SONNET: (*Alluding to Febo del Poggio,*
"Phoebus of the Hill")

I truly should, so happy was my lot,
While Phoebus was inflaming all the hill,

Have risen from the earth while I was able,
With his feathers, and made my dying sweet.

He's gone; I pledged myself less rapid flight
Of happy days, but it was no avail,
For justly to the thankless evil soul
Pity will close its hands and Heaven its gate.

His feathers were my wings, his hill my steps,
Phoebus' lamp for my feet, and dying then
For me no less my safety than my marvel.

Dying without, no soul to Heaven leaps,
Heart is not freshened by remembering them,
For late, after the hurt, who will give counsel?

98
UNFINISHED SONNET

To me Heaven was surely merciless,
Fusing your live beam on two eyes alone,
When, with its rapid and eternal motion,
The journey it gave to you, the light to us.

O happy bird, surpassing us in this,
That Phoebus' beautiful face to you is known,
And, more than the great sight, the extra boon
To fly to the hill from which I fall and crash.

99
SONNET

Since Phoebus does not twist and stretch his bright
Arms all around this damp and chilly earth,

The name that the common people wished
To give that sun, not understood, was night.

And she's so weak that anyone can light
A little torch, and take away that much
Of the life of the night, and she's so foolish
That steel and powder leave her smashed and split.

If there is something that she really is,
She is surely the earth's and the sun's daughter,
For one creates her and one forms the shadows.

Be she what may, to praise her is an error;
She is a widow, and so dark and anxious
A single firefly by itself can fight her.

100
SONNET

O night, O gentle time, however black,
Always at last plunges each work in rest;
He who exalts sees and discerns you best,
Who honors you is sound of intellect.

Each weary thought you cancel, or cut short,
Absorbed into damp shadow and all peace,
And often in dreams carry me from the lowest
To where I hope to go, the highest point.

O shadow of our death, by which the soul
Can erase the heart's enemy, distress,
The last of our afflictions, a good healer,

Our bodies that were weak you can make whole,
You dry our tears, put down all weariness,
And wrest from who lives well all vexing anger.

101
SONNET

Any place covered, any sheltered room,
Whatever any solid circumscribes,
Preserves the night as long as day's alive,
Against the sun playing its glittering game.

And if she's overmatched by fire or flame,
By the sun she'll be ravished and deprived
Of her divine look, baser things besides
Can break her more or less, even any worm.

The rough plowman labors with his blade
Whatever is open for the sun, to blaze
On a thousand different seeds and different plants.

Man can be planted only in the shade.
Therefore the nights are holier than the days
As man is worth more than all other fruits.

102
SONNET

He who created, not from any matter,
Time, which did not exist prior to man,

Made of one, two, gave the high sun to one,
And to the other gave the moon, much nearer.

Wherefrom our fate and chance and fortune were
In one short moment born for everyone;
They allotted to me the darker span,
Being in birth and breeding similar.

And like the man who copies from himself,
Night will grow darker getting underway,
So, doing much wrong, I am troubled and distraught.

Yet this concession gives me some relief:
The sun can make of my dark night bright day,
Having at birth been given you for mate.

103
SONNET

What my eyes saw was nothing that is mortal
When in your beautiful ones I found my peace
Complete, but One within, where sin disgusts,
Who grasps with love His duplicate, my soul.

And if the creature were not made God's equal,
It would not wish more than the eyes' gladness,
The outward beauty; but, since it is false,
Its form moves up into the universal.

I say what dies cannot appease desire
In one who lives, nor ought we to expect
Eternity in time, where men change skin.

Unreined desire, not love, our senses are,
Killing the soul; and our love can perfect
Our friends while here, but more, by death, in Heaven.

104

SONNET TO TOMMASO CAVALIERI

In order to return from whence it came,
The immortal form down to your prison house
Of earth came like an angel, with such grace
It honors earth by healing every brain.

This makes me love, this only lights my flame,
And not simply your tranquil outward face,
For love that houses virtue does not place
Its firm hope in a thing that will decline.

High and strange things no way but this occur
Where Nature stirs herself, and liberally
Heaven itself will for their birth prepare.

God, in His grace, shows himself nowhere more
To me, than through some veil, mortal and lovely,
Which I will only love for being His mirror.

105

MADRIGAL

Beautiful things are the longing of my eyes,
Just as it is my soul's to be secure,
But they've no other power

That lifts to Heaven, but staring at all those.
A shining glory falls
From furthest stars above,
Toward them our wish it pulls,
And here we call it love.
Kind heart can never have,
To enamor and fire it, and to counsel,
More than a face with eyes that they resemble.

106

OCTAVE STANZA

Those who do what they should not hope in vain
(It is a commonplace) for pity or grace.
I was not happy in you, as I'd thought certain,
Stripping me of myself with too much trust,
And do not hope that I'll come back again,
New phoenix to the sun, no time permits;
Yet enjoy my great hurt for this alone:
I'm more mine, yours, than if I were my own.

107

MADRIGAL

Not all men always give so dear a price
For what the senses love
But someone will perceive
How, though it seems so sweet, it is bitter and base.
Good taste's a thing so scarce
He yields to the shifting crowd,
Seemingly, but his inner joy's his own.

Thus do I learn by loss
What none can see outside
Who grieves the soul, and does not hear it moan.
The world is blind; its rank and its renown
Help most who seek in them the slightest part;
They are like whips that teach us while they smart.

108

STANZA IN TERZA-RIMA

To you, who to the world have made the offer
Of soul and body and of spirit too,
I say, your place is here, in this dark coffer.

109

INCOMPLETE MADRIGAL

. . . Lady, how you can
Still live among us, eating, sleeping, speaking,
Like any mortal thing,
Seeing that in your beauty you're divine.
Not to follow you then,
With doubt once settled by your grace and mercy,
What punishment for such a sin were fit?
For in his thoughts a man
With eyes that do not see,
By his own powers arrives at loving late.
Sketch upon me, without,
As I do on bright page or on a rock,
Which having nothing in it takes what I like.

110

MADRIGAL

More than my last resort, my final refuge,
What could be safer, what has not less strength
Than praying and weeping? And they do not serve.
For Love and Cruelty have laid a siege,
One armed with pity and one armed with death,
And one kills me and one keeps me alive.
My soul they thus deprive
Of my dying, her only possible help;
She has often made a step
To go there, where she hopes to be for always,
Where beauty stands alone, without proud ladies.
But to my heart there rises
The true image then, by which I live,
To see that death shall never conquer love.

111

MADRIGAL

It cannot ever be the blessed eyes
Derive from mine, as I from them, delight;
For soft smiles they requite
The sacred face with sad and bitter cries.
Oh hopes of lovers all are fallacies!
How can, being so unlike and so unequal,
This sovereign brightness and this infinite beauty,
To everything about me,
Take fire from me, as I from them, an equal?
Love will grow angry, and depart a cripple,
From one of two faces adverse and unlike.

No force can make it grow upon the other,
Entering as a spark
A gentle heart, and issuing forth as water.

112

MADRIGAL

You with your eyes surpass
Every hardness as much as every glitter.
If it is true that one may die of rapture,
Then that would be the hour
That calls upon great beauty for great grace.
If my soul from long use
Were not on fire, I'd be already dead
After your original glance's promise,
At which my gluttonous
Enemies, rather eyes, never delayed.
But I could not be sad
At this *cannot*, it's not connected with you.
Beauty and grace, equally measureless,
Where most you would assist,
You steal no lives the least,
And cannot not make blind all who observe you.

113

MADRIGAL PERHAPS UNFINISHED

Here pearls and feasts, there kiss, caress, embrace,
But who could ever notice,
Beside her godlike actions, human labor
Wherein the gold and silver

Receive from her and double back their light?
Each jewel grows more bright
From her eyes than it does from its own power . . .

114
MADRIGAL

I can't, Love, and I don't want to suppress
You who have grown so fierce,
Telling you this as certain:
The more you sting and harden,
The more you spur and guide my soul to power.
Therefore, if you should ever
Remit my dying, and my anxious sighs,
I'd feel my heart inside,
As in a man who's died,
Missing, missing my many agonies.
O bright and holy eyes,
Sweet and dear to me is my little grace;
He has well profited who learns by loss.

115
MADRIGAL

If the desire for good
Is borne from earth to God
By anything of beauty,
It's only by my lady,
For anyone with eyes like my eyes made.
All other objects fade,
She is my one concern;

But these are no great marvels,
Since I love, want, and call her all the time.
It's nothing that I did;
The soul itself will lean
By nature on what resembles
In its own eyes the eyes through which it came.
It senses as its aim,
Which makes it honor her, the primal love:
He who adores the lord must love the slave.

116

MADRIGAL

Even though love has many times already
Kindled my heart, which age has now extinguished,
This last time I am punished
Will, unless I should die of it, be deadly.
And therefore, while love heats me,
My soul's desire is that my last day
May be my first in a more tranquil bower.
No other road or safety
Can keep my life away
From dying, except death, cruel and sure.
Against death is no power
Other than death; besides that, all relief
Is double death, for one whom death gives life.

117

MADRIGAL

From the first tears until the final sighs,
Which now are close to me,

Who ever met so hard a destiny
As I do from my star, shining and fierce?
Call her not vile or false;
Outwardly it were better
If scorn from her would make me cease to love her,
But she, the more I gaze,
To my wounds promises
Sweet pity more, although her heart is bitter.
O much awaited ardor!
Against you only fools could win a fight.
I, if I had my sight,
Were grateful for the first and the last hour
I saw her; let the error
Bear me, and be within me permanent,
If all we lose from it is strength and wit.

118
MADRIGAL

Surely the time has come
To let my torment go,
For old age and desire do not agree.
But the soul cannot see
Or hear of death and time
(O Love, how well you know)
And in death's face recalls her still to me;
If bow and string should be
Somehow broken and shivered
In a thousand thousand slivers,
It begs you pass none of its tortures by,
For he who is never cured will never die.

119

MADRIGAL

As you cannot be otherwise than fair,
It cannot be you are not merciful.
So too, being mine in full,
Still less you cannot not murder and crush me.
While in this way my mercy
Continues as your beauty's equal match,
Along with your fair face
And it, in the same hour,
My burning heart will end.
But since the soul, released,
Again goes to its star,
The Lord thereby to win
Who gives all dying men
Eternal bodies, for their rest or agony,
I'll pray that mine, though ugly,
You'll want with you, as it was here, in Heaven,
If beautiful face and piteous heart are even.

120

MADRIGAL

Fire, in which all is harmed,
Burns me, has not consumed,
But not through my greater or its less power.
I, like the salamander,
Only where others die find my support,
And do not know who, calm, prods my distress.
By you yourself your face,

By me myself my heart
Was never made, by us
My love will not be ever torn apart.
That master who has placed
My life within your eyes is higher still.
I love, you do not feel;
Forgive me, as I do this misery
That wills I die outside who murders me.

121

MADRIGAL

The more I seem to feel my ills are great,
If my face lets it show,
It makes your beauty grow
Greater, it seems, so that the pain turns sweet.
My torturer does right
If he makes you beautiful, meanwhile,
Through my unhappy woe;
If my ills give delight,
O my star, wild and gentle,
If I were dead what would you ever do?
If it is really true
Your beauty comes out of my sharp distress,
Which, if I died, would cease,
When I am dead your loveliness dies too.
Let it be therefore so
That I live on in pain for your less hurt,
And if you are lovelier, to my greater ill,
The more calm for the soul,
For a great pain great pleasure can support.

122

MADRIGAL

So eager is this my lady, and so swift,
That she, at the same time that she would kill,
Promises me with her eyes all joy, and still
Can keep inside the wound the cruel knife.
Thus both my death and life,
Opposed, I feel within my soul concurrent
During one little moment.
But still the fatal torment
Mercy can threaten, lengthening the pains,
For evil harms much more than joy sustains.

123

MADRIGAL

So much out of herself
Has kind fair lady pledged,
That I in my slow age,
Watching her, might become as once I was.
But, envious fatal Death
Being at all hours lodged
Between my mournful and her kindly gaze,
I only keep ablaze
The little while his features are forgot.
But when the evil thought
Comes back again to its familiar place,
The lovely fire is quenched by his grim ice.

124

MADRIGAL

If the soul truly, from its body free,
May come back in another's
Only a few short hours,
So for a second time to live and die,
Will she then, whom I see
As a lady of great beauty,
In returning, as now, show such despite?
If she will hear my plea,
I would expect her mercy
To be abounding, of all hardness stripped.
I think if she has shut
Her beautiful eyes, she'll have, in the renewing,
Pity upon my death, when she knows dying.

125

MADRIGAL

Not only death, but even its fear will save me
And keep away the lady,
Evil and fair, who steadily tortures me;
And if the fire scorches me
Much more than usual, in which I've strayed,
I have no other aid
But her face in my heart's center firm,
Because where death is, love will never come.

126

MADRIGAL

Not always to throw off
And escape fear of dying,
But rather leave it in its place at rest,
Would let strong cruel love,
With hardness never tiring,
Make on the gentle heart a pitiless test.
But since the soul at last
Hopes elsewhere to rejoice, through death and pity,
One who cannot not die clings to the fright
To which all others bow.
No other course against
The haughty woman's beauty,
Novel and high, will suit,
From both her scorn and kindness to withdraw.
Not being believed, I'll vow
That, against her who on my sorrow smiles,
He only helps and keeps me safe who kills.

127

MADRIGAL

By greater light, and by a brighter star,
At night the heavens theirs from far set burning,
And only you keep turning
More beautiful as less beautiful things are near.
Which, this or that, can more
Move, spur the heart to soften,
So, while I burn, at least they will not freeze
Who give you, without having,

Your sweet and lovely person,
Your beautiful blonde hair, your face and eyes?
Thus to your hurt from these
You shrink, from me as well,
If beauty on beauty grows
Where none are beautiful.
But if what Heaven stole
From us, Lady, and gave you, you should replace,
Ours would be more, less beautiful your face.

128

MADRIGAL

You have a godlike face,
In which there can be danger
If the soul is so near
Death as to feel it always, as do I.
I take arms and advice
For my defense from it before I die,
And yet your courtesy
Will not, though near my end,
Give me myself again,
Nor from such mercy any hurt unloose;
One day does not unbind the year's long use.

129

MADRIGAL

Beneath two beautiful brows
The strength of love renews,
In the season that sneers at wing and bow.
Greedy for every miracle that has

Likeness with this, my eyes
Act as the gate to more than one sharp arrow.
Meantime a point of view,
Bitter and strong, assaults me with the sweetness;
Yet love won't lose through greater hurts or fears,
An hour can't stop the habit of long years.

130

MADRIGAL

All the time that my past is in my presence,
Which often is repeated,
Then, O false world, well do I grow acquainted
With humankind's punishment and offense.
Heart that at last consents
To your allurements and your foolish pleasures
Purchases for the soul a sorry hurt,
As well they know who sense
How often you promise others
A peace and blessedness that you have not
And cannot ever get.
For him who stays here more, mercy is slighter;
Who lives the less returns to Heaven lighter.

131

MADRIGAL

Led on through many years to my last hours,
I understand too late your pleasures, Earth.
Repose that is dead before its birth
And peace you do not have, you promise others.
Old age's shame and terrors,

Which the Heavens now require,
In me do but refresh
The old delightful errors.
Too long a lifetime there
Murders the soul and hardly helps the flesh.
In Heaven the luck is best—
I say it and I know, the proof is I—
Only for him who, born, could soonest die.

132
MADRIGAL

"Blessed are you who up in Heaven profit
From the tears that the world will not redeem;
Does love still do you harm,
Or are you now by dying free of it?"
"Our everlasting quiet,
Outside all time, is free
Of agonized laments and lovers' envy."
"Then I, as you can see,
Live for no benefit,
To serve and love where sorrows are so many.
With Heaven to lovers friendly,
And the world good for nothing,
What was I born to, loving?
To live for long? And this fills me with terrors;
Little's too much, for who well serves and labors."

133
MADRIGAL

While life is running out in me through time,
Love does me still more harm,

And won't remit an hour,
As I after so many years had thought.
My soul with a trembling scream,
Like a man dead by error,
Complains of me and of the eternal cheat.
Between fear and deceit
I feel such doubt then of my love and death
That I seek in one breath
The better of them, and then take the worse,
Good counsel thus undone by evil use.

134
MADRIGAL

The soul has poured and spouted
Its inner waters out
Only so they will not
Put out the fire to which it is converted.
Your fire has always started
Tears in me, so, though tired
And old, I could not get other assistance.
My destiny is hard, my fortune thwarted,
Yet they are not so hard
But that their sting, where more you burn, decreases.
And so your burning glances,
Outwardly weeping, I shut up within me,
And what most die of only enjoy and live by.

135
MADRIGAL

Since, Love, for joy you'd have us weep and suffer,
Dearer to me is each more cruel dart,

That, between death and hurt,
Leaves scarcely any space, and time still shorter,
So that, killing a lover,
You lose the weeping, and decrease the torture.
I am grateful to you, therefore,
Only for dying, and not for my grief;
He heals all ills who takes away my life.

136

MADRIGAL

Humbly I offer the harsh yoke my neck,
Before the evil luck my face is happy,
And to my enemy lady
My heart is full of fire and faithfulness.
From no pain do I shrink,
But instead always fear it may grow less;
For if her quiet face
Food and life from a great pain supply,
What cruel harm can ever make me die?

137

MADRIGAL

No other soul in a more lovely garment,
Or a less kind one, Lady,
Than yours, carries its sweet breath and its motion.
Eternal punishment
Is better fitted to your gift of beauty
And graceless will than, to my suffering, Heaven.
I'll not say or keep hidden
Whether or not my sin like yours I'd wish,

And so, if not alive, be with you dead,
Or, with you kind, that my eternal peace
Should be where all my pain has its reward.
If I would think Hell good,
Being with you, then what can Heaven hold?
Reward there is twofold:
Only I could enjoy, of the sacred choir,
Both Heaven's God and Earth's that I adore.

138

MADRIGAL

If the soul comes at last
Back to its sweet and longed-for flesh again,
As runs belief, when Heaven damns or saves,
Then Hell would hold less pain
If by your beauty graced,
So long as others see you there and gaze.
But if to Heaven it rise,
As I with it would wish,
And with such warm affection and such care,
I shall enjoy God less
If nothing else can please
Like your sweet holy semblance, just as here.
I hope to love you more
If the damned are more helped by pain decreasing
And there's no harm in Heaven from scanter blessing.

139

MADRIGAL

As you, Lady, keep brief and little faith
With my high hopes, if my eyes see it true,

Lest worse be, I'll enjoy
The outward promise of your beautiful eyes.
In spite of pity's death,
It does not mean great beauty does not please;
If I sense you oppose,
By your actions within, your eyes' mercy,
I seek no certainty,
But pray, where happiness is incomplete,
To him whom truth may harm let doubt be sweet.

140

MADRIGAL

Perhaps, I imagine, so
As not to leave dead embers,
When the years are not green in my cold breast,
Love suddenly drew his bow,
Because he well remembers
In gentle heart he cannot miss his thrust.
Old age is refreshed
By a fair face; worse, at the final dart,
The second fall than when I first was hurt.

141

MADRIGAL

The more that all my days remaining speed
In little life and short,
The more the fire is shut
In a small space, to my more pain and ache.
For Heaven will give no aid

Against old habits, when the time's so quick.
And since you are not slaked
By a flame thus surrounded,
In which not even rock maintains its form,
Much less a heart, I thank
You, Love, if the less solid
Remains in the closed fire so short a time.
My luck is in the harm;
I do not care for living with your burden
Of weapons, if the dead at least you pardon.

142

MADRIGAL

Ahead of myself I pass
With high and virtuous concept,
And promise time for it
I shall not have, O foolish vain conjecture!
Because, when death is close,
I lose the present, robbed too of the future.
Burning for pretty features,
I am hoping to be healed, and, dead, to live
In the years to which life does not arrive.

143

MADRIGAL

If she enjoys and you, Love, only live
Upon our griefs, and I like you support
My life with aching heart,
With tears, for the most part, and with ice,
Why then, we'd be deprived

Of our lives by a goodly lady's grace,
The worst would be the best.
Contrary foods' results are contrary;
Taking our life from us, her joy from her,
So you too guarantee
Death the more as the more help you offer.
To my soul, in its fear,
Long life with a hard lot is far more worth
Than kindness when it is so near to death.

144

MADRIGAL

Your glances you discard,
But I am kept excluded;
It isn't theft, not giving what's your own,
But if you sate the crowd,
And beasts, and I'm denuded,
It's murder, hurrying my dying on.
Love, why do you condone
That your most precious favor
A beauty takes from him
Who wants and knows its savor,
And gives to foolish men?
Ah, make her over again,
So kind within and ugly outwardly,
That she'll displease, and fall in love with, me.

145

MADRIGAL

"Tell me now, if this woman's soul, O Love,
Were gracious as her face is beautiful,

Would any be a fool
To give her himself, self from himself remove?
And I, how could I serve
Or love her any more if she were friendly,
Since as an enemy
I love her more than it would then behoove?"

"I tell you, it is best for you to brave—
O powerful gods—your being pushed aside.
But, after you have died,
And she loves you as now you burn for her,
You can take vengeance, and with every right.
Alas for him who has so long to wait
For me so late to come to him with cheer.
But still, if you see clear,
A proud and generous and noble heart
Forgives and loves all those who do him hurt."

146

MADRIGAL

Lady, with surer safety,
Less graciousness would keep me living yet,
And down each rivulet
My eyes would not be moistening my breast.
My little strength, by double courtesy,
Is so outmatched it is shadowed and suppressed.
No wise man ever wished,
Unless himself spurred on
And raised it, greater joy than he could handle.
Vain folly is excess,
For any modest person

In humble fortune will remain more tranquil.
I do not like what is permissible:
Giving someone yourself, by him not planned,
In the excess of pleasure death's contained.

147

MADRIGAL TO VITTORIA COLONNA

I cannot not fall short in wit and art
Of her who takes my life,
Her help being so excessive
That far more from less grace we realize.
Then does my soul depart,
As when a too great brightness hurts the eyes,
And, far above me, rise
To my impossible; it has not drawn
Me with it to my high and tranquil mistress,
To let me match her least gift; I must learn
What I can do will lead me to her worthless.
She, with abounding graces,
Strews them and sets us with some flame alight;
The too much burns less warmly than the slight.

148

SONNET

Great mercy no less than great distress,
Lady, is death for a convicted man,
Empty of hope, frozen in every vein,
If he is suddenly set free by grace.

Likewise if you, with more than wonted kindness
Toward my unhappiness, so full of pain,
With too much pity make me be serene,
More than my tears it seems to leave me lifeless.

This is the way with news, gentle or harsh;
In their reversals death is swiftly present,
So that the heart too much contracts or swells.

Your beauty thus, which Love and Heaven nourish,
To have me live must check this great content.
My feeble powers surpassing bounty kills.

149

SONNET

The best of artists never has a concept
A single marble block does not contain
Inside its husk, but to it may attain
Only if hand follows the intellect.

The good I pledge myself, bad I reject,
Hide, O my Lady, beautiful, proud, divine,
Just thus in you, but now my life must end,
Since my skill works against the wished effect.

It is not love then, fortune, or your beauty,
Or your hardness and scorn, in all my ill
That are to blame, neither my luck nor fate,

If at the same time both death and pity
Are present in your heart, and my low skill,
Burning, can grasp nothing but death from it.

150

MADRIGAL

Just as we put, O Lady, by subtraction,
Into the rough, hard stone
A living figure, grown
Largest wherever rock has grown most small,
Just so, sometimes, good actions
For the still trembling soul
Are hidden by its own body's surplus,
And the husk that is raw and hard and coarse,
Which you alone can pull
From off my outer surface;
In me there is for me no will or force.

151

MADRIGAL

Not only, empty of finished
Work, does the mold expect to be refilled
With silver fire has melted,
Or gold, that only breaking can remove,
But with the fire of love
In me, I too replenish
The empty desire of infinite beauty
With the one whom I cherish,
Who, to my fragile life, is soul and body.
The high and longed-for lady
Descends within me such a little span,
To withdraw her I must be crushed and slain.

152

MADRIGAL

Above myself so high,
Lady, you make me leap,
Not only I cannot speak
But cannot think it, being no longer I.
Then why do I not fly,
If you will lend your wings,
Rising more often to your lovely face,
Thereby with you remaining,
If Heaven will allow
My body to ascend to paradise?
Only that, by your grace,
I am cut off from my soul, and it alone
With you evades its death and makes my fortune.

153

MADRIGAL

Between my fortune, Lady, and your kindness,
Conclusions differ so
That I have come to know
The middle between bitterness and sweetness.
While you, being good and gracious
Within, show outwardly
To my hot wish that you are beautiful,
Fortune, false, rancorous,
Our pleasure's enemy,
Hurts our enjoyment with unmeasured trouble.
If, afterwards reversing all that evil,
It bends toward my desires,

Your kindness all retires.
From tears to laughter, such opposed extremes,
To diminish great grief there are no means.

154
MADRIGAL

Lady, up to your high and shining crown
By the long narrow route
None can attain, without
Your adding your humility and grace.
The climbing stiffens and my strength runs down,
And by the halfway point I am out of breath.
It seems the ranking place
Your beauty holds can make my heart content,
Which yearns greedily for all special height;
And yet, to revel in your loveliness
I long for your descent
Where I can reach; thus reassured in thought
That your foreseeing slight
Toward me who hate your high state, love the lower,
May grant yourself forgiveness for my error.

155
MADRIGAL

Your merciful and sweet
Help, when we are together,
My vital spirits scatter,
Lady, through my far members from my heart.
And my soul, which is kept
From its own natural action,
You separate from me, the joy's too quick.

But when you cruelly quit,
Then, for my life's protection,
Scattered spirits rejoin the heart too thick.
If I see you come back,
Again from my heart I feel them vanish;
So it is equal anguish,
I see both help and injury are mortal,
For one who loves too much, the worst's the middle.

156

MADRIGAL

Love, it appears you thrust
Death by force from my mind,
And with such kindness bind
My soul that, lacking, it were more content.
The fruit is fallen now, dry is the husk,
I seem to feel as bitter what was sweet.
It only can torment,
In this my last brief hour,
To have such infinite joy with time so short.
Your pity, strong and late,
Thanks to this, makes me fear,
To the body a death, to joy a hurt.
Wherefore I thank you for it,
In this my age, for if I die of this,
You do it less by death than by your grace.

157

SONNET TO VITTORIA COLONNA

So that I might at least be less unworthy,
Lady, of your huge high beneficence,

To balance it, my poor wits at first
Took to plying my own wholeheartedly.

But then, seeing in me no potency
To clear the way to grasp that goal exists,
My evil fault for its forgiveness asks,
And the sin makes me wiser constantly.

And well I see how anyone would stray
Who thought my flimsy, transient work could equal
The grace pouring from you, which is divine.

For wit and art and memory give way;
In a thousand attempts none who is mortal
Can pay for Heaven's gift out of his own.

158

SONNET TO VITTORIA COLONNA

When anyone is bound by a great bliss,
Revived, say, by another from the dead,
What is there that can then repay such aid,
So that the debtor is let free and loose?

And, if there truly were, it would exhaust
The overflow of infinite gratitude
Toward him who was well served, and so impede
The offering to it of counter-service.

Therefore, to have your kindness stay high over
My state, Lady, in me I have desired
Only ingratitude, not courtesy.

For where each equally contents the other
My much beloved would not be my lord,
For there's no lordship in equality.

159

MADRIGAL TO VITTORIA COLONNA

What kind of acid lime
Makes your tired carcass shrivel and decrease,
Sick soul, forever? When will time release
You from it, back to where you were in Heaven,
Happy and bright beforetime?
Although I change my skin
For short years toward the end,
I cannot change old ways to which I'm used,
That with more age push and compel me more.
To you, Love, I must own
My envy of the dead.
I am frightened and confused,
Such, for myself, my soul's convulsive fear.
Lord, in the final hour,
Stretch out thy pitying arms to me, take me
Out of me, make me one that pleases Thee.

160

MADRIGAL TO VITTORIA COLONNA

Now on my right foot, now upon my left one,
Toward my salvation shifting in my searches,
Between vices and virtues
My heart wearies and burdens me, distraught
Like one who sees no Heaven

And upon every road is lost and late.
I offer a clean sheet
To take your sacred inks:
Let love inform me, truth be inscribed by pity;
Free to itself, the spirit
Not bend toward our mistakes
My short time left; let me not live so blindly.
Tell me, high sacred Lady,
Whether in Heaven less honor is bestowed
On humble sin than on the sovereign good.

161

MADRIGAL TO VITTORIA COLONNA

While still I shun and hate myself the more,
The more, Lady, with proper hope I call
On you; in me the soul
Is less afraid, as I to you draw near.
In your face I aspire
To what I am pledged from Heaven,
And in your beautiful eyes, full of all safety.
And often I see clear,
At all the others gazing,
Eyes without heart possess no potency.
Lights that I never see,
Nor shall see, and my wish is more than that,
For rarely seen is neighbor to forgot.

162

MADRIGAL

As a trustworthy guide in my vocation,
When I was born I had a gift of beauty,

In both the arts my lantern and my mirror.
Who otherwise believes has a false notion;
Only this to the heights the eye will carry
Where I prepare to be painter and sculptor.

And even if judgments that are rash and futile
Tie sense to beauty, which will only bear
To Heaven the most wise intelligence,
No eye can reach the holy from the mortal,
Infirm and always firmly set just where
It's vain to think of mounting without grace.

163

MADRIGAL

Though what our eyes find easy brings constraint
With use, meanwhile in part
We lose our heads with fright,
And, being most deceived when self-assured,
In the heart as beauty paint
What a little beauty would have overpowered.
Lady, I give my word
It was not ease or use that captured me,
So rarely is it that my eyes see yours,
Surrounded where desire can scarcely climb.
One instant kindled me;
I have not seen you more than that one time.

164

SONNET

My eyes, nearby or far away, can truly
See your fair face wherever it may appear,

But feet are not allowed to carry there
My arms and either of my hands, O Lady.

The soul, the mind when it is sound and steady,
Rises up through the eyes wider and freer
To your high beauty: yet so great a fire
Gives no such privilege to the mortal, heavy

Body of man, wingless as well, which thus
Can scarcely follow if an angel fly,
And boasts and praises only are for sight.

Ah, if you can in Heaven as with us,
Then make my body all one single eye,
No part of me not having your delight.

165
MADRIGAL: TO LOVE

Now Death, O Love, out of the very place
Where once in me you lorded it, stripped bare,
As much as with your bow and pricking dart,
Drives you away and slights you, its grim ice
Quenches and leaves few days to your sweet fire.
You count for less than it in each man's heart;
Even though I was caught
By wings you wear, you run away with fear;
All blooming youth is shy at the last hour.

166
MADRIGAL

Since half of me, descended from the Heavens,
Thereto with longing flies and turns again,

While I remain in one
Woman of beauty, and am ice on fire,
She keeps me in two portions,
So opposite each robs the other one
Of the good I should only have entire.
But if she should alter
Her ways at any time, while Heaven lets
Its half go, during the time she'd have me,
My weary scattered thoughts
Would then completely be upon my lady;
If while she's gentle to me
Heaven bars the soul, I'll hope at least a while,
To be a half no more, but hers in full.

167

MADRIGAL

While my desire is hot
This woman makes me a plaything,
Gracious she seems, her heart is wild and fierce.
I said, Love, did I not,
That it would come to nothing,
We lose our own, hoping from someone else.
If she would have me perish,
It is my fault, my hurt, to have trusted her
Who stints a little one who expected more.

168

MADRIGAL

A blazing flame, by a great beauty strewn
Through a thousand burning hearts,

May be compared to weights,
Slight and small upon many, fatal to one.
When narrowly shut in,
Hard rock is turned to lime,
And water then dissolves it instantly,
As he who observes the truth well knows by test.
Divine, she sets a flame
For a thousand men in me,
Which leaves my heart burnt to the innermost.
But tears that never cease
May yet dissolve what was so strong and tough;
Better not be than burn and not have death.

169

MADRIGAL

If beautiful things are in the memory,
There must be death as well, which can withdraw
His face therefrom, as it has him from you,
And turn laughter to tears and fire to frost.
Then they're the enemy,
Such that the empty heart no more they boast.
But still, if he should cast
Toward the familiar spot his beautiful eyes,
They'll be as dry sticks to a flaming blaze.

170

MADRIGAL

This woman here is bound,
In her ungoverned rage,

That I'm to burn, and change
To what won't even weigh an ounce, and perish,
My blood lets, pound by pound,
Unnerves my body, for my spirit worthless;
It gives her joy to furbish
Before her trusted mirror,
Where she observes herself as fine as Heaven,
Then turn to me to cherish,
Who, age apart, can render
Her face by mine more beautiful therein,
Heaping me with disdain.
In such a fire I find old age is best,
The hurt is less where evil does not last.

171
MADRIGAL

If happy heart makes beautiful face, and sad
Makes ugly, and a beautiful cruel lady
Does it, who can she be
That won't take fire from me as I from her?
Because my eyes were made
By my bright star to see
The difference between the fair and fair,
She is no less severe
Often against herself
When I say: from my heart my face turns pale.
For if one paints himself,
Painting her, what can he
Do for her, while she sets him this ordeal?
For both it would be well
To draw her heart happy, her face clear;
Me she would make not ugly, herself fair.

172

MADRIGAL

Seeing you this much, Lady, outwardly,
Though the eye cannot reach the truth inside,
I hope my weary, tired
Thoughts may find rest a little longer still;
And greater knowledge, maybe,
Of you within, would worsen what is ill.
If a heart can be cruel
Whose beautiful eyes promise
Genuine pity to our every plaint,
This hour would be well;
Chaste love hopes nothing else
Other than what you outwardly present.
If your eyes are against
Your soul, Lady, and I opposed to it,
I rejoice in a beautiful lady's cheat.

173

MADRIGAL

Not yet, O Love, healed from your shafts of gold,
Not even of my smallest older wound,
Yet my prophetic mind
You shift to even worse from earlier bad.
If less you stir the old,
I should escape, unless you fight the dead.
Against me, lame and naked,
Setting wings to your bow,
Your eyes as your banner,

That murder more than your most painful dart,
How shall I be relieved?
Not shield or helmet now,
Only what shows me honor
In loss, and blame to you if you will burn me.
A weak old man, and tardy
And slow to run, I find escape in that:
Who wins by fleeing will not stay to fight.

174

MADRIGAL

To your dear beauty there was no requirement
Of any sort of cord to bind me prisoner,
Since, if I well remember,
One glance alone had made me prey and captive.
And, passing through such torment,
At once, perforce, the weak heart is submissive.
But who will ever believe,
A few days captive to your beautiful eyes,
That in dry burnt-out wood the green revives?

175

EPITAPH (1543)

Here lies, by death before her time bereft,
This sacred beauty, still, for us, alive.
Had she but known with her right hand to strive,
She had been saved, but did not—she was Left.

176

SONNET (1543): (*To the lover of Mancina,
asking for her portrait*)

In Heaven this fresh great beauty I'd consider
Unique, not only in the base vile world,
Whose name after her Left arm has been labeled
By the blind crowd that never did adore her;

Who was born for you only, I could not form her
With paper that I brushed or stone I chiseled,
But to her beautiful living face I should
Perhaps bring all your hopes where they may anchor.

And so if she can overcome our mind
As the sun does with every other star,
To you thereby she should be no less sweet.

For her fresh beauty has been made by God;
Thus I'd content you, at your high desire,
And that not I, He only, could create.

177–226

FORTY-EIGHT EPITAPHS, A SONNET,
AND A MADRIGAL, ON THE
DEATH OF CECCHINO BRACCI (1544)

177

The beautiful eyes are closed here in the tomb,
Before their time, and only this can cheer:
That pity, dead for them when living here,
Since they are dead, in many lives for them.

178

If there are those who pity me at all,
Here shut away, and from the world detached,
Oh save your tears to bathe your face and breast
For them who still are under Fortune's rule.

179

"Why, Death, to faces that the years had spoiled
Did you not come, so that too soon I died?"
"Because in Heaven may not rise or bide
What has known age or what the world has soiled."

180

Death did not wish not to destroy without
Years as its weapons, and superfluous time,
The beauty lying here, but let it climb
To Heaven now, not having lost a trait.

181

The beauty lying here did so transcend
In all the world every most lovely creature,
That Death, being at enmity with Nature,
Killed and destroyed it, so to make a friend.

182

Here I am, of the Bracci, and too weak
To fight against my death and so not die.

182—line 1: The word Bracci means Arms.

Better if I had been the Feet to fly
Than to be Arms and yield to the attack.

183

Here I am buried, though it was of late
That I was born, to whom Death was so rapid
And rough that my soul, which still is naked,
Is hardly conscious she has changed her state.

184

He who shut me within cannot through death
Return the beauty showered on me alive
To all the others whom He had deprived,
If He at last must form me again on earth.

185

The soul within could never see, like us,
The outward face now in this chamber shut.
Death itself could not have drawn her out,
If there were not in Heaven as fair a house.

186

Though Nature here is overcome by death
In this fair face, it will be fairer even

When the body rises up divine to Heaven
Out of this tomb, and thus revenge the earth.

187

Here the fair eyes are shut, which, being open,
Made the most holy and shining seem less bright.
Now dead, they give so many back their light,
Whether it's good or harm we are not certain.

188

Here I'm thought dead; for the world's cheer I lived,
A thousand true loves' souls were in my breast.
And therefore I'm not dead, though life is lost,
Merely through having one of them removed.

189

That the soul stays alive outside the body
Mine, which seems to have broken with me here,
Shows, when I cause in living men such fear
As none could bring about by dying wholly.

190

MADRIGAL

If, as it does, the soul outlives the body,
Released from what against its will it schools

Only while God so rules,
Not till then is it blest, only forthwith
After it is made holy
By dying, as it had been born for death.
And therefore all the grief
We each have for our dead
In laughter without sin should be suppressed,
If they, removed from dread,
From frail flesh enter their true rest
When the hour comes at last.
This ought to be as much the friend's desiring
As God more than the world is worth acquiring.

191
SONNET

I scarcely once had seen, while they were open,
The beautiful eyes that were your life's delight,
When on their last departure day they shut,
And opened to contemplate God in Heaven.

I know and weep; not that I was mistaken
If my heart came to prize their beauty late,
But that death came so soon that it is cut
No whit from you, but all from my hot longing.

Therefore, Luigi, to make in living stone
Cecchino's matchless form (it's he I mean)
Eternal, seeing he is dust among us now,

If lover turns into beloved one,
And lacking that my art must be in vain,
I needs must, to portray him, draw from you.

192

My fate too early here would have me sleep;
I am not dead, although I change my home.
Since one in love takes on the other's form,
I stay alive in you, who see and weep.

193

"If two hours' span your hundred years denies,
Five years must needs defraud eternity."
"No, in a day he lives a century
Who in that time learns everything, and dies."

194

I see my luck in dying was the best,
A heavenly dowry without growing old;
Since I could not have better in the world,
Everything else than death would have been less.

195

My flesh now earth, my bones of their fair eyes
Here dispossessed, and of their charming face,
Will prove to him whose joy I was and grace
How, here below, the soul in prison lies.

196

If pleas made for a second life for me
Should be as flesh and blood to these my bones,

Then he were pitiless who in pity moans
To bind again the soul in Heaven now free.

197

He who laments me dead here hopes in vain,
Bathing my bones and sepulcher, that he
May restore me like fruit to a dry tree,
For dead men do not rise in spring again.

198

You alone know, O stone that shut me in,
If once I lived; if any recollect me
He thinks he's dreaming; death consumes so quickly
That what once was seems never to have been.

199

Much more I fear, quit of the years and days
That bound me here, a coming back to life,
If such can be, than I did going off,
Because I then was born where dying dies.

200

Bracci I was, portrayed, and then deprived
Of my soul, finding now that death is sweet,
Because that work has such a happy fate
And painted goes where I could not alive.

201

I was born Bracci; after the first wail
My eyes saw sunlight only a short space.
I am here forever, nor would wish it less,
In him who loved me greatly living still.

202

I was no more than live, now I am dead,
Both live and dear to him from whom death stole me.
If he loves more than when he had me wholly,
Who grows by lessening must find death good.

203

If death has buried here the finest flower
Of the world and of beauty, not yet open,
Before its time had come, then I am certain
Who dies of age will not be mourned for more.

204

From Heaven divine and full my beauty came,
From my father my mortal beauty only.
Since with me dies what God bestowed upon me,
What can from death the merely mortal claim?

205

To death forever, I was given first
To you one hour only; with such gladness

I wore my beauty, leaving with such sadness
Never to have been born had been the best.

206

Here sets the sun that still you burn from, weeping.
The cherishing light it gave was a short pleasure.
Far longer lasts less bounty and less treasure;
Death comes to the unhappy late and creeping.

207

Here it behooves a while I stop and rest,
My earthly cover's beauty to restore.
For Heaven has no grace or beauty more
That could be nature's exemplar and test.

208

Open, my eyes were breath and peace to one.
Now they are closed, who is his peace and breath?
Not beauty, which has disappeared from earth;
Since all his good lies here, it is death alone.

209

Since I alive on earth was life for him
To whom here now this dust is all my beauty,

It's more than death, it's cruel jealousy,
That someone does not die for me before him.

210

Braccio, whom I enclose here, had no peer
In wounding others with his beautiful face.
And so Death snatched him off, if I can guess,
Because it fell to him to kill the lesser.

211

Here Braccio's buried; God through him had aimed
That nature by his face might be amended,
But, since a good is lost when not attended,
Showed to the world, then speedily reclaimed.

212

Herein the dead Cecchino Bracci lies;
What life you had was from his dazzlement.
Who saw him not, lost not and lives content;
Who saw him loses life, unless he dies.

213

To dust the dust has been returned by death,
The soul to Heaven; in trust is given to him

Who loves me still, though dead my beauty and fame,
To eternalize in stone my earthly sheath.

214

The sacred beauty of Braccio here I guard,
And, as the soul is form and life to the body,
So it for me is to the work's great beauty,
For such a sheath implies the finest sword.

215

If, like the phoenix, Braccio's beautiful face
Ever returns, to be admired still more,
It's best who did not know this good before
Should find it, after it is lost a space.

216

Besides the Bracci sun, the sun of nature,
Put out forever, I imprison here.
Death murdered him without a sword or spear;
A flower of spring a little wind can capture.

217

I once was Bracci, here my life is death.
And if alone of all the world my lot
Is Heaven, then let its gates forever shut,
For Heaven is detached today from earth.

218

Cecchino has laid down a frame so goodly
In death, the sun had never seen its peer.
Rome weeps for it, and Heaven takes pride and cheer;
The soul rejoices, parted from the body.

219

Here Braccio lies; no one could ask more meet
Tomb for his body, his soul has holy room.
Dead, more than live, he has a worthy home
In earth and Heaven, and finds death fair and sweet.

220

Death stretched an Arm, the bitter fruit he seized,
Or no, the flower; at fifteen years he's gone.
He is enjoyed and owned by this one stone,
And grieved for by all the world besides.

221

Brief, as mortal Cecchin, my stay on earth,
Heaven I have forever, made divine.
Of death I boast, and of its change so fine
That gave to many dead, me living, birth.

222

Cecchino Bracci's eyes here Death has closed,
Untying body and soul; he is departed

Before his time, his life being now converted
To what after long life is often refused.

223

Bracci I was; here, of my soul deprived,
Being from beauty turned to dust and bone,
Pray do not open my concealing stone:
I'll remain fair to him who loved me alive.

224

That the soul lives I who am dead am sure,
Also that I was dead while I had life.
Bracci I was, and if my time was brief,
Who lives the less may hope for pardon more.

225

His beautiful form to sacred Bracci is given
Again, it is not here; pity, before
The great day, took it from earth; if then he were
Still buried, none but he were worthy Heaven.

226

Since Heaven lends the soul and earth the body
For a long time, yet Bracci here is dead,
By what goods can he ever be repaid,
Being the creditor of such years and beauty?

227

MADRIGAL

My eyes, you must be certain
The hour grows nearer with the passing time
When mournful tears will find their passage barred.
Pity must keep you open
So long as my divine
Lady will deign to live within the world.
If grace leaves Heaven unbarred,
As for the saints is done,
And this, my living sun,
Departs from us, again ascending there,
What will you have to see hereafter here?

228

SONNET

To let the world retain all of your beauty,
But in a woman less severe and kinder,
I pray that it may be redeemed by nature
As it declines in you continually,

And serve to form again, out of your godly
And gentle face, a noble heavenly figure,
And let it then be Love's concern forever
To make her a new heart, filled with kind pity.

And then my sighs he is also to recover,
And bring together all my scattered tears,
Making for him who loves her then a gift.

He who is born upon that hour will move her
Perhaps to pity with my very cares,
The grace I am bereft of not be lost.

229
M A D R I G A L

No time is left, Love, for my heart to flame,
Or human beauty to enjoy or fear.
The final hour is here,
When he who has least time most mourns its loss.
The great blows that your arm
May give me, Death will lower,
Heightening his much more than was his use.
The words and the thoughts
Which, to my harm, shot out in fire from you,
Have now turned into water,
And with them, all together,
May God will that my sins be poured out too.

230
M A D R I G A L

They march against their will no differently,
Who are brought by a just court
To where soul quits the heart,
From the way in which toward my death I go.
Death is as close to me,
Except that my remainder runs more slow.
Yet love does not allow,
For all that, one hour's life,

Between two dangers, where I sleep and start.
In one, humble and low,
My hopes hearten and lift,
While, old and tired, the other keeps me hot.
Not knowing what's less hurt
Or best, I fear Love more, who kills the faster,
Using your gaze, for having started later.

231
SONNET

If slight slow fire, wide open since my prime,
Can rapidly destroy a fresh new heart,
Then what will happen to one often burnt
When final hours shut in a greedy flame?

If passing of more time provides less room
For my life, for my powers and my might,
To a thing that must die in nature what
Will fire do then, keen from the amorous game?

Me it will make just what one would expect,
Ash in a wind as mild as it's severe,
Robbing my body from the worms' disdain.

If, green in a small flame, I burned and wept,
In one so large shall I now hope for more?
For my soul in my body to remain?

232
MADRIGAL

Whatever does not come from you is not
My eyes' mirror, to which my heart yields, weary;

If it sees other beauty,
It's death, Lady, if it is not like you,
As in a glass without
Some back, a thing's absorption is not true.
A prototype, and awe
Would come to him who is hopeless
Of your mercy in his unhappy state,
If the fair eyes and brow
With your true gentleness
Should turn and make me, aged, yet content.
Being born unfortunate,
If my hard fate such luck and grace should master,
You will have overcome Heaven and nature.

233
MADRIGAL TO VITTORIA COLONNA

A man, a god rather, inside a woman,
Through her mouth has his speech,
And this has made me such
I'll never again be mine after I listen.
Ever since she has stolen
Me from myself, I'm sure,
Outside myself I'll give myself my pity.
Her beautiful features summon
Upward from false desire,
So that I see death in all other beauty.
You who bring souls, O Lady,
Through fire and water to felicity,
See to it I do not return to me.

234

If our divine part has imagined well
Someone's gestures and face, then double strength
Therefrom, with only a crude and rapid sketch,
Makes the stones live; it's not the power of skill.

With rougher papers it is parallel;
Before a ready hand can take the brush,
The finest, most alert of learned wits
Checks and reviews, and has composed his tale.

Likewise with me, a sketch when I was born,
Of no account, to be reborn from you,
High worthy Lady, a thing high and perfect;

If you in mercy trim my surplus down
And build my little, what is my fierce fire due
As penance, when you punish and correct?

235
UNFINISHED SONNET

There is much joy for just and perfect taste
In work of the first art, when it assembles
From gestures, faces, and the liveliest members,
A human body in stone or clay or wax.

If time thereafter, hurtful, harsh and base,
Breaks it, or twists, or thoroughly dismembers,
The beauty earlier there he still remembers,
And keeps the vain joy for a better place.

I o gia facto ūgozo īqueſto ſteto
Chome fa lacqua agacti ī lonbardia
ouer daltro paeſe cheſiſia
cha forza luētre apicha ſotto lmēto

I abarba · alcielo · ellamēmoria ſeto
īſullo ſcrignio eſpetto fo darpia
eſpēnel ſopraluiſo tuttauia
melfa gocciando ū richo pauimēto

E lōbi entrati miſō nella peccia
e fo delcul p̄ chōtrapeſo groppa
epaſſi ſeza ghochi muouo īuano

Dimāzi miſalluga lachortaccia
ep̄ pregarſi adietro ſiragroppa
e tēdomi comarcho ſoriano

p̄o fallace eſtrano
ſurgie iliudicio ch̄ lamēte porta
ch̄ mal ſipra p̄ cerboctana torta

lamia pictura morta

diſedi orma giouanni elmio onore
nō ſedo ī loᵍ bō ne io pictore

Medici Tomb, about 1521

Phaeton, 1533

Sheet of Sketches, about 1525

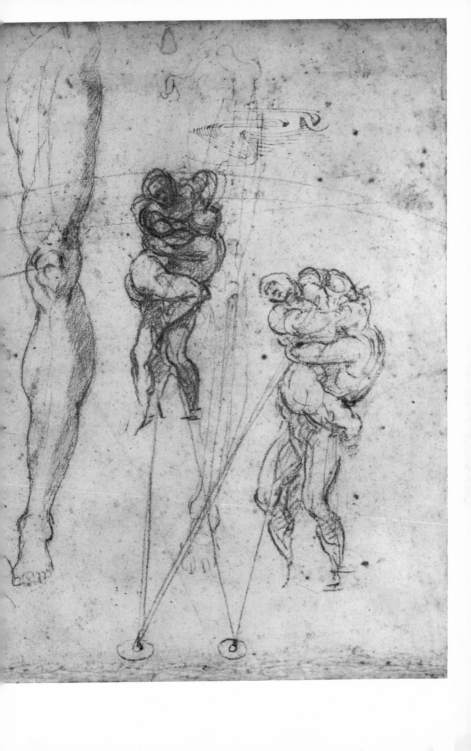

Resurrection, about 1532
REPRODUCED BY GRACIOUS PERMISSION OF
HER MAJESTY QUEEN ELIZABETH II

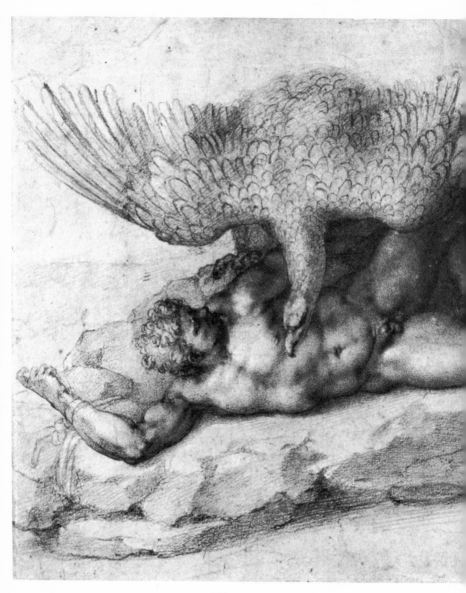

Tityos, 1532

Children's Bacchanal, 1533
REPRODUCED BY GRACIOUS PERMISSION OF
HER MAJESTY QUEEN ELIZABETH II

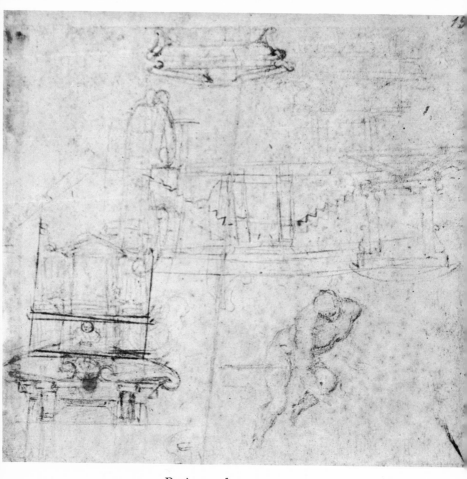

Projects, about 1540-45

Annunciation, about 1545-50

Crucifixion, 1550's

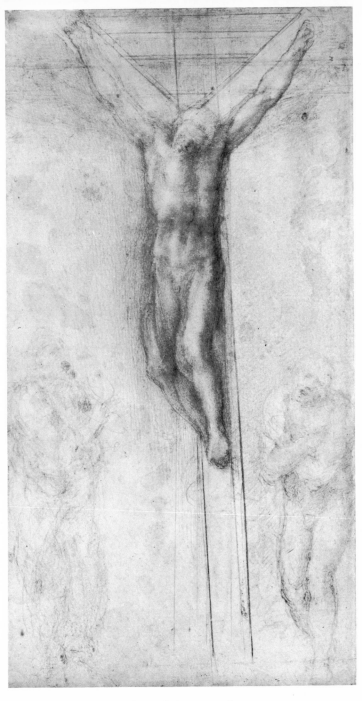

Crucifixion, 1550's

Madonna, about 1560

236
UNFINISHED SONNET

If a soul is ordained to live forever
Where it has quiet rest, it's not unworthy,
Having enriched us with the only money
That's coined by Heaven or here paid out by nature.

237
SONNET

How can it be, Lady, what long acquaintance
Lets everyone observe, that the live figure
In the hard mountain stone can last far longer
Than its maker, whom age returns to dust?

The causes yield and bow to the results;
Hence it is art that overpowers nature.
I know, I've tested it in beautiful sculpture,
Time and death to the work will not keep trust.

Thus I can give a long life to us both,
By either means, with carving or with paint,
Portraying both the faces of us two,

So that a thousand years after our death
They'll see how you were beautiful, I faint,
And that I was no fool in loving you.

238
MADRIGAL

Here art would have lived on
In just a living stone,

As long as there are years, one woman's features.
Then how should Heaven treat her,
This being mine and she its handiwork,
Not to my eyes alone
A goddess and no creature?
Yet after a little stay her flight is quick,
And crippled in its right hand is her luck,
If a stone can remain, and death dislodge her.
Who then will revenge her?
Nature alone, if here alone can stay
Work of her child, and time steals hers away.

239
MADRIGAL

Searching through many tests and through much time,
The wise man will attain the true idea,
Only when death is near,
For a live image in the rough, hard rock,
Since it is late we come,
And little keep the great and the unique.
If nature does the like,
From age to age, from one face to the next
Passing, and finds in yours, divine, the acme
Of beauty, she is old, and soon must perish.
So fear, being intermixed
Thoroughly in with beauty,
On curious food my great desire will nourish.
What more impairs or profits
I cannot think or say, seeing your face:
. The ending of the world, or the great bliss.

240

MADRIGAL

As, in hard stone, a man at times will make
Everyone else's image his own likeness,
I make it pale with weakness
Frequently, just as I am made by her,
And always seem to take
Myself for model, planning to do her.
The stone where I portray her
Resembles her, I might
Well say, because it is so hard and sharp;
Destroyed and mocked by her,
I'd know, at any rate,
Nothing but my own burdened limbs to sculpt.
And yet if art can keep
Beauty through time only if she endure,
It will delight me, so I'll make her fair.

241

SONNET

Every time that my idol is presented
To the eyes of my strong and feeble heart,
In between the two objects death is brought
And drives it off the more, the more I'm frightened.

Such havoc leaves my soul far more contented
In joy, than hope of any other sort;
Unconquered Love, with his most brilliant court,
Then arms for his defense, which thus is stated:

Death, as he says, can happen only once,
There's no rebirth; what next for one who dies
With my love, if he had it not yet dead?

Then, burning love, by which the soul's let loose,
Since it's a magnet to its matching blaze,
Like gold purged in a fire returns to God.

242

MADRIGAL

If pain makes beauty grow, as some have thought,
Weeping a stolen beautiful human face
I can get life and grace
From my distress, and being sick is well;
Bitter sweetness is what
My foolish thought desires, against the soul.
Fortune, however ill,
Against one flying lowly
Cannot, wheeling, boast of a great collapse.
With what a kind good will
Poverty, bare and lonely,
Scourges me gently with uncommon whips.
The soul, a pilgrim, reaps
Far less, whether in pastime or in war,
From knowing a little gain than losing more.

243

MADRIGAL

If the face that I mean, which is in her,
Had not withheld her eyes debarred against me,

Then, Love, how would you test me,
With further trials of a hotter blaze,
Since, seeing her no more,
You burn me in no small sort with her fair eyes?
"The man who does not lose
Has least part in the sport,
If every longing vanishes in pleasure;
When a thing satisfies,
Hope has no place to sprout
In the sweetness that cancels every torture."
Of her I tell you, rather,
If her great wealth surrenders to my yearning,
Your kindness will not calm my height of longing.

244
MADRIGAL (1546)

I see your only pleasure is my ill,
And ask you nothing else for all my love;
There is no peace for you unless I grieve,
For you the worst you do me is not to kill.
For if I pack and fill
My heart with sorrows, at your haughty wish,
From such life to escape,
What kind of ruthless help
Torments and slays me and won't let me perish,
Since dying would be short
When your long running cruelty is so fierce?
Any unjustly hurt
Hope for mercy no less than for great justice.
Wherefore the soul that's honest
Bears it and serves, and hopes for sometime later,

Not, though, what you can offer;
Not among us is the reward for torture.

245

EPIGRAM (1545–46)

I prize my sleep, and more my being stone,
As long as hurt and shamefulness endure.
I call it lucky not to see or hear;
So do not waken me, keep your voice down!

246

SONNET ON DANTE (1546)

When he'd come down from Heaven, and had seen,
Still in his flesh, both Hells, the just and good,
He went again alive to look on God,
So as to let us have the whole true gleam;

This was a shining star, and with its beam
The nest where I was born unfairly glowed.
No prize for him were the whole wicked world;
That art Thou only who created him.

Dante I mean, while his ungrateful city
Had hardly any knowledge of his action;
Only the just do they deprive of safety.

If I could have been he! Born to such fortune,
To have his bitter exile and his virtue
I would forego the world's most splendid portion.

246—line 2: The good Hell is Purgatory, the just one Hell itself.

247

MADRIGAL ON FLORENCE

"For many, Lady, no, for a thousand lovers,
You were created, in an angel's shape;
Now Heaven seems asleep
When one can own what's given to many others.
Return to us, your mourners,
The sun of your eyes; it seems you would recoil
From those born into poverty of its bounty."

"Ah, let not be disturbed your sacred ardors:
He who seems to rob you of me and spoil
Cannot enjoy great sin, fearing so greatly.
For a lover's condition is less happy
Where great excess brings great desire to a stop
Than when his wretchedness is filled with hope."

248

SONNET ON DANTE

As much as should be said of him we cannot,
He was too brightly shining for the blind;
The town that hurt him can be more condemned
Than all the greatest rise to his least merit.

This is he who went down where sin is quit,
For our advantage; then to God he climbed.
Though Heaven's gates against him did not stand,
His country's to his just desire were shut.

I call her thankless, and of her own fortune
To her own hurt the nurse, which is a symbol
How the most perfect come to the most harm.

Among a thousand other proofs just this one;
If his unworthy exile had no equal,
A like or greater man was never born.

249

SONNET TO LUIGI DEL RICCIO

Often, in the pleasure of tremendous kindness,
Some attack on my life and dignity
Is masked and hidden, and it is so heavy
That it can make my health become less precious.

To give the shoulders wings, then draw the noose
At the same time, in gradual secrecy,
Will leave love's kindled burning charity
Most smothered where it longs to burn the most.

Maintain therefore, Luigi mine, the luster
Of that first grace to which my life is due,
And which no wind or tempest is to alter.

All gratitude disdain can learn to master,
And, if I've learned to know why friends are true,
A thousand joys can't match a single torture.

250

MADRIGAL TO LUIGI DEL RICCIO

A gift is too injurious,
As kind as it may be,
Whenever it leaves another caught and fettered;
So my freedom, at this,
Your height of courtesy,

Laments and weeps more than at being cheated.
And, as the sun leaves shattered
The power of the eye, which ought to grow,
Spurred on by it to see and have more light,
Desire would wish uncrippled
My courtesy as well, derived from you.
Often the small gives up before the great
And does not pardon it.
For love wants only friends (this makes them rare)
Equal and like in fortune and in power.

251
MADRIGAL

If in my early years I had taken heed
Of the then outward fire now burning in me,
Lest worse be, I had not only
Quenched it, but from my soul torn my weak heart.
I blame it, now it's dead,
But only our first error is at fault;
Unhappy soul, if at the very start
A man could not resist,
Late he is killed and burns
By the first fire that's lighted.
For he who cannot not be burnt and captured
During his youth, when there is light and mirror,
Is destroyed, old and tired, by much less fire.

252
MADRIGAL

For me, so old and weary
I return and re-enter,

As to a weight its center
Which finds no rest except for that, O Lady,
Heaven has keys made ready.
Love twists and turns them round,
Opens this woman's bosom to the just,
Forbids my evil, deadly
Desires, and I am drawn,
Worthless and tired, up to the few who are blest.
From her there comes a grace
Strange and sweet, and whose potency is sure;
He lives for himself who dies for her.

253
MADRIGAL

Lady, while you are swerving
Your beautiful eyes near me,
In them, myself I see,
Just as yourself, in mine, you are observing.
From all the years and slaving,
Whatever I am they render to me fully,
As mine do you to them, more than bright star.
It needs must anger Heaven
That in fair eyes I see myself so ugly,
And you in mine, ugly, see yourself so fair.
Within, sharp and severe
Decree will let you pass
Through them to my heart, but bar
Me out of yours no less.
This since your mighty prowess
Heightens its hardness toward each lower level,
For love would have youth and condition equal.

254

MADRIGAL

If one part of a woman's beautiful,
And ugly every other,
Because I take great pleasure
In that one only, must I love them all?
The part that makes appeal,
While my joy feels depression,
To reason, still would have me
Pardon and love the innocent mistake.
But Love will only tell
Of the disgusting vision,
And keeps repeating, angry,
None such his realm will bid for or expect.
But Heaven would have me seek
That kindness toward the unpleasing not be empty;
Habit heals for the eyes what is unshapely.

255

UNFINISHED SONNET

Why is it not more frequent, why so late,
That fire within me, with its steadfast faith,
That takes my heart, lifting me from the earth,
Where of itself its power does not permit?

Perhaps each interval is granted it
Between your first and next loving despatch,
Because all rare things have more force and strength
The less the nearness and the more the want.

The night's the interval, the day the light,
One freezes and the other inflames my heart
With love, with faith, and with a heavenly fire . . .

256

MADRIGAL

However true it is, the beauty of God
Your beautiful and human face here shows,
Lady, those distant joys
Are brief for me, and yours I do not quit;
Every other hard road
The journeying soul finds is too steep or strait.
Wherefore my time I allot,
Giving my heart the nights, my eyes the days,
And yearning for Heaven no interval.
Thus from my birth my fate
Has stopped me in your rays,
And no rise permits to my burning will.
If nothing else can pull
My mind to Heaven, by grace or charity,
The heart is late to love what eyes can't see.

257

SONNET

My hope now and again can climb indeed
With my inflamed desire, and not be false;
For if our feelings all leave Heaven displeased,
To what end was the world then made by God?

And for my love of you, what better ground
Than glorifying that eternal peace
Where the divine in you, my joy, arose,
As it makes all kind hearts be chaste and good?

Hope only of that love is spurious
That dies with beauty, lessening each instant,
Ruled by a beautiful face's variation.

It's sweet indeed where the heart's virtuous,
And at an altered skin or final moment
Won't fail, but gives us here a taste of Heaven.

258
SONNET TO TOMMASO CAVALIERI

Violent passion for tremendous beauty
Is not perforce a bitter mortal error,
If it can leave the heart melted thereafter,
So that a holy dart can pierce it quickly.

Not hindering high flight to such vain fury,
Love wakens, rouses, puts the wings in feather,
As a first step, so that the soul will soar
And rise to its maker, finding this too scanty.

The love for what I speak of reaches higher;
Woman's too much unlike, no heart by rights
Ought to grow hot for her, if wise and male.

One draws to Heaven and to earth the other,
One in the soul, one living in the sense
Drawing its bow on what is base and vile.

259

SONNET

If luck and grace to long postponed desires
Are more than pity often given them early,
Mine hurts and pains me, since my years are many,
For aged pleasure a short time endures.

A flame in what by rule are freezing years,
Like mine for a woman, makes the Heavens angry,
If they're concerned for us, and so I tally
My ripe age by my sad and lonely tears.

Yet perhaps, though I'm at the end of day,
With sun already set below the horizon,
And amid the thick shadow, cold and somber,

Since love inflames us only when halfway,
And that's true, for I'm old but burn within,
There's a woman who'll make my end my center.

260

MADRIGAL

Can't you do what you want,
O Love, if you're a god?
Do for me what I would
For you if I were Love, unless you can't.
Great desire is unfit
To hope for a high beauty,
Still less to have it, when my death is close.
So let me take your seat;

Can I treat pressure gently?
Torture is doubled by a moment's grace.
I would also tell you this:
If death is hard for the unhappy, what
Of him who dies reaching his high delight?

261

MADRIGAL

One woman's fresh new beauty
Unchains, whips, spurs me on:
When tierce not only is gone,
But nones and vespers, and the evening's close.
Playing with death the one,
The other cannot here give me full peace.
I who was at my ease,
With my white head and with my many years,
Held in my hand my other lifetime's ticket,
Such as the penitent heart could well assure.
More loses who less fears,
Making his trust be in his own power
Against accustomed ardor.
Though only the ear's left, with memory,
Except with grace age is no remedy.

262

MADRIGAL

As I so long have carried in my breast,
Lady, the stamped impression of your face,
Now that my death is close

Let love so stamp my soul, with copyright,
Seeing that it is blest
To drop the earthly prison's heavy weight.
Whether in storm or quiet,
With that mark be it safe,
As is the cross against all its opponents;
And whence in Heaven nature snatched you off
Let it return, model to high bright spirits
To learn its reappearance,
And leave on earth a spirit wrapped in clay,
So after you your beautiful face will stay.

263

MADRIGAL ON THE DEATH
OF VITTORIA COLONNA (1547)

So not to need from many to reclaim
That gathered beauty—other there was none—
It has been made a loan
To a high pure lady, under a bright cloak.
For, having to redeem
From all the world, Heaven scarce could be paid back.
Now, in a short speck,
No, in a second, God
From the unwatchful earth
Again has seized it, from our eyes removed.
But memory cannot fade,
Despite the body's death,
Of all she has written, sacred, sweet, belov'd.
Cruel pity, you prove,
If the ugly had such loans from Heaven as she
And now called them through death, we all would die.

264

SONNET ON THE DEATH
OF VITTORIA COLONNA (1547)

What wonder if, since I was burnt and crushed
Next to the fire, which outwardly is spent,
Inwardly it can still consume and hurt,
And bit by bit reduces me to ash?

So shining, as I burned, I saw the place
Which was the source of my oppressing torment,
That just the sight of it made me content,
Games and delights for me death and abuse.

But Heaven has taken away from me the splendor
Of the great fire that burned and nourished me;
I am left to be a coal, covered and burning,

And if Love will not offer me more timber
To raise a fire, in me there will not be
A single spark, all into ashes turning.

265

TERZA-RIMA STANZAS

I live shut up here, like the doughy middle
Inside the bread crust, poor and all alone,
Like a genie shut up inside a bottle.

And in my somber tomb, a narrow run,
The spider and her thousand works and toilers
Have become their own bobbin as they've spun.

There is the dung of giants at my doors;
Those who eat grapes or take some medicine
Go nowhere else to empty, in great numbers.

Then I have made acquaintance too with urine
And the tube it comes out of, through the slit
That summons me before it's day each morning.

Any who have a cat, corpse, stool or pot,
For keeping house with, or to save a journey,
Won't ever come to change my sheets without.

My soul has this advantage of the body,
That if a purging made the smell diminish,
Bread and cheese would not keep her company.

Only my cough and cold prevent my death;
If she does not go out the lower gate
My mouth can scarcely just emit my breath.

I am broken up, ruptured and cracked and split
From my labors so far; death is the inn
Where I by paying rent can live and eat.

I get my happiness from my dejection,
And these disturbances give me my rest;
To him who asks it, God may grant ill fortune!

Good for the one who saw me at the feast
Of the three Magi! or saw here, still better,
Among these splendid palaces, my house.

Love in my heart has not kept up a flicker,
And (since a great drives out a little care)
My soul is plucked and shaved of every feather.

I keep a hornet in a water jar,
Inside a leather sack some strings and bones,
And in a canister three balls of tar.

My pale blue eyes are powdered into grounds,
My teeth are like keys on an instrument,
So, when they move, my voice is still or sounds.

My face has the shape that causes fright;
In wind when there's no rain my clothes would scare
Crows from the seed, without another dart.

A spider web is nestled in one ear,
All night a cricket in the other buzzes;
With spitting breath I do not sleep, but snore.

Love, and the flowered grottoes, and the muse,
My scrawls for tambourines or dunces' caps,
Go to innkeepers, toilets, bawdy houses.

What use to want to make so many puppets,
If they have made me in the end like him
Who crossed the water, and then drowned in slops?

My honored art, wherein I was for a time
In such esteem, has brought me down to this:
Poor and old, under another's thumb,

I am undone if I do not die fast.

266
MADRIGAL

My age is now detached
From desire, blind and deaf;

I make my peace with death,
Since I am tired and near the end of speech.
Love that fears and respects
What the eyes cannot see
Keeps me from your fair face, O Lady, far,
As out out of something perilous in its charms.
Love that does not give way
To truth, with hope and fire
Gladdens my heart again, tells me, it seems,
What I love is not human . . .

267

MADRIGAL

Now with hot fire, again with cruel ice,
Now armed with shame, again with age or torture,
I mirror out the future
Within the past, my hope mournful and sad.
My good, being short, no less
Than my evil I feel a wounding goad.
Of my bad fortune just as of my good,
Tired of me, I beg pardon constantly.
And swift short hours, as I can plainly see,
Must in our life be the best luck and grace,
Seeing that death's the doctor for distress.

268

FRAGMENT

You always give me what you have left over,
And ask of me things that do not exist.

269

UNFINISHED SONNET

On you, Love, with you, many years I've fed
My soul, and also partly if not all
My body, and with most miraculous skill
Desire, with my hope, has made me good.

Hence now I lift my thought on wings, and, tired,
Spur myself to a point more safe and noble,
Your paper promises of no avail,
And your honor I moan of and upbraid.

270

SONNET

Restore me to the time when curb and rein
Were mild and loose on me, in my blind flame;
Return whence it's with virtue in the tomb,
The face that was angelic and serene,

And my steps, close together, with such strain,
Which are so slow in one who's passed his time;
Restore the fire and water to my bosom
If you will gorge yourself on me again.

And if, O Love, you only live indeed
On mortal creatures' sweet and bitter tears,
Now you'll gain little from one old and spent.

My soul has almost reached the other side,
And more compassionate darts shield me from yours;
Fire makes a poor test on a wood once burnt.

271

UNFINISHED SONNET

Though always One alone, the only Mover
Of everything, however high or wide,
Won't always let us see a single side,
But more and less, just as his mercies shower,

One way to me and others everywhere,
More and less shining, or more brightly clean,
According to the weakness of the mind,
Shattered when set against a sacred measure.

To the most able heart most He will lean,
If one may say that; thus His face and power
To it alone become a guide and light,

. . . . .

And find what matches His own inmost part.

272

SONNET

Oh make me so I'll see you everywhere!
If ever I feel by mortal beauty burnt,
Set beside yours I'll think it fire that's spent,
And as I was I'll be, in yours on fire.

No one but you I call on and implore,
Dear Lord, against my blind and useless torment,
You only can renew, within, without,
My will, my mind, my slow and little power.

You gave this sacred soul to time, O Love,
Imprisoned it within this frail and tired
Body besides, and with a savage fate.

What other can I do not thus to live?
I without you lack all that's good, my Lord,
It is God's power alone to change a lot.

273

UNFINISHED SONNET

Down from a great cliff, from the highest mountain,
Where I was cloaked and hidden by great rock,
I came to be exposed in this low spot,
In such a tiny stone, and still unwilling.

Born with the sun, and, as decreed by Heaven . . .

274

SONNET

In an instant there runs from eyes to heart
Whatever object they believe has beauty;
And being so ample and so broad, the roadway
On thousands, much less hundreds, will not shut,

Of every age and sex; and I feel fright,
Burdened with troubles, more with jealousy,
And of such differing faces cannot say
Which before death would give me whole delight.

If mortal beauty stops a passionate flame
Completely, it did not come down together
From Heaven with the soul; it's human will.

But if, Love, it moves on, it jeers your name,
Seeking another God, fearful no longer
You'll come to grapple with a prey so vile.

275

SONNET TO VASARI,
on the publication of his
Lives of the Artists (1550)

If you had with your pen or with your color
Given nature an equal in your art,
And indeed cut her glory down in part,
Handing us back her beauty lovelier,

You now, however, with a worthier labor,
Have settled down with learned hand to write,
And steal her glory's one remaining part
That you still lacked, by giving life to others.

Rivals she had in any century
In making beautiful works, at least would bow;
At their appointed ends they must arrive.

But you make their extinguished memory
Return blazing, and themselves, and you,
In spite of her eternally alive.

276

EPIGRAM

Those who don't care for leaves
Should not come here in May.

277

UNFINISHED SONNET

To what am I spurred by a beautiful face's power,
Since on earth I rejoice in nothing else?
To rise alive among the chosen spirits
With such grace there's no good in any other.

If maker and his work agree together,
What blow is it I should expect from justice,
Because I love, no, burn, with holy thoughts,
And every noble person praise and honor?

278

UNFINISHED SONNET

My soul, uncertain and disquieted,
Finds in itself no cause but some great sin
Unknown to it, but still not therefore hidden
From the huge grace that is a wretch's aid.

I speak to you, for all my attempts, O Lord,
Except your blood, will not redeem a man.
Have mercy upon me, since I was born
Under your law; it's not a thing untried.

279

UNFINISHED SONNET

As once in the cold ice my burning flame,
Now burning flame for me is all cold ice;
That indissoluble knot, O Love, is loose,
Death is for me what once was sport and game.

And that first love that gave it place and time
In my last misery is hard distress
To my tired soul . . .

280

FRAGMENT (1552)

With so much slavery, with so much boredom,
And with false notions and the greatest danger
To the soul, here to be carving holy things.

281

FINAL SECTION OF A SONNET (1552)

The fresh green years cannot, O my dear Lord,
Feel how much at the final step we change
Our tastes and our love, our thoughts, our will.

The soul gains more the more it's lost the world,
And death and art do not go well together.
What should I of myself then hope for still?

282

FINAL SECTION OF A SONNET (1552)

If, in your name, I have conceived some image,
It is not without death joined onto it,
So that my art and understanding flee.

But if, as some believe, I too acknowledge,
We shall return to life, then in that lot
I'll serve you, if perchance my art will follow.

283

SONNET (1554)

My course of life already has attained,
Through stormy seas, and in a flimsy vessel,
The common port, at which we land to tell
All conduct's cause and warrant, good or bad,

So that the passionate fantasy, which made
Of art a monarch for me and an idol,
Was laden down with sin, now I know well,
Like what all men against their will desired.

What will become, now, of my amorous thoughts,
Once gay and vain, as toward two deaths I move,
One known for sure, the other ominous?

There's no painting or sculpture now that quiets
The soul that's pointed toward that holy Love
That on the cross opened Its arms to take us.

284

UNFINISHED SONNET

My thoughts, innumerable and much to blame,
In my last years of living ought to be
Condensed to only one, to let me see
How its eternal days will be made calm.

But, Lord, how can I if you do not come
With wonted inexpressible courtesy?

285

UNFINISHED SONNET

From day to day, and since my early years,
Lord, you have been my helper and my counsel.
And that is why still now my soul is trustful
Of double aid now in my doubled cares.

286

SONNET (1555) •

The world with its fables has removed
The time I had for contemplating God;
His mercies I not only put aside,
But with, more than without them, turn depraved.

Foolish and blind, where others can perceive,
My own mistake tardily understood,
Hope growing less, desire is magnified
That you will loosen me from my self-love.

Cut down by half the road, O my dear Lord,
That climbs to Heaven! You will have to aid me
If I am going to climb even that half.

Cause me to hate the value of the world
And what I admired and honored in its beauty,
So before death to taste eternal life.

287

      SONNET (1555) '

There's not a thing on earth so low and base
As without you I am and feel myself,
So that my own feeble and weary strength
Beseeches pardon for my exalted wish.

Oh proffer, my Lord, that chain that clasps
Together to itself each heavenly gift,
Toward which I press and strain; I speak of faith.
I by my fault have not complete full grace.

The gift of gifts for me, as it is rarer
Will be the greater, greater if without it
Earth has not in itself content and peace.

And since with your blood you were no miser,
What will your mercy be in such a present,
Since Heaven won't open for us with other keys?

288

     SONNET

With a vexatious heavy load put down,
O my dear Lord, and from the world set free,

I like a fragile craft turn to You, weary,
From fearful tempest into gentle calm.

The thorns and nails, the left and the right palm,
Your face, benign, humble, and filled with pity,
Pledge that for great repentance there is mercy,
To the sad soul give hope You will redeem.

Let not your holy eyes with justice watch
My past, and let not your immaculate ear
Make your unsparing arm stretch out to it,

Only your blood my trespass wash or touch
And more abound as my old age grows more,
With ready aid and pardon absolute.

289

UNFINISHED SONNET

I think, I know, some sin, to me a secret,
Is driving my spirit to great grief.
My senses and their own fire have bereft
All hope from my desire, peace from my heart.

But who with you, O Love, feels fear of what
Might make his grace decline before he left?

290

UNFINISHED SONNET

My prayers to you would be a joy indeed,
If, for my praying, you would give me strength;

There is no portion of my feeble earth
Where good fruit on its own account can breed.

Of pure, good acts you are the only seed,
Where you take part in them they come to birth;
No one can follow you by native strength,
If you do not point out your holy road.

291
SONNET

Loaded down with my years, and filled with sin,
Bad habits having roots in me, and power,
My first and second deaths, I see, are near,
And all the while I feed my heart on poison.

The strength that I would need I do not own
To make my luck, love, life and customs alter,
Unless by your divine and shining succor,
From every false direction guide and rein.

It's not enough, my Lord, that you dispose me
To go again there where the soul can be
Created, not from nothing as before;

Before you strip and draw it from the body
Reduce by half, I beg, your high steep way,
And make my coming back more bright and sure.

292
SONNET

I'm pained and grieved, but meanwhile I am glad
For every thought that puts my memory

On my past time, and bids me justify
The lost days that can never be redeemed.

I'm only glad before death to have learned
How short a time all human joys deal fairly;
I'm grieved, for seldom can we count on mercy
And grace for many sins, close to life's end.

Even though we are mindful of your promise,
Perhaps it still is daring, Lord, too much
To hope love will forgive each needless wait.

But yet it seems that in your blood we sense
That, as your torture for us had no match,
So are your precious gifts without a limit.

293
SONNET

Certain of death, but not when it will be,
Life's short, and I have little of it left,
Joy to the senses, but no resting place
For the soul only begging me to die;

The blind world and its bad example, though,
Leave all right practice swallowed and suppressed.
The light is spent, and with it all assurance,
The false is king, the truth cannot break through.

When will it be, O Lord, what we await,
Your true believers? All the great delay
Cuts off our hope, making the soul be mortal.

What good to promise men so great a light
If death comes first, pinning us just the way
We are attacked, with no escape at all?

294
     SONNET (1555)

Though often it happens great desire will promise
To my so many years still many more,
It won't keep Death from always drawing near,
And where he gives less pain he hurries less.

Why wait on living longer to rejoice,
If God in misery only we adore?
For our good luck, only by lasting longer,
Does us more harm the more that it delights.

If sometimes by your grace that burning zeal,
O my dear Lord, comes to attack my heart,
Which gives my soul comfort and reassurance,

Since my own strength's no use to me at all,
To turn to Heaven at once would then be right,
For with more time good will has less endurance.

295
    UNFINISHED SONNET (1555)

Though a long span of wretched foolish habit
Needs longer, to be cleaned, its opposite,
My death, already near, will not allow it,
Nor check my evil wish from what it wanted.

296

SONNET

It no more grieved and vexed the chosen spirits
Than made them glad, that you, not they, had suffered
Death, and had thus reopened with your blood
To earthly man the Heavens' shuttered gates.

Glad that you had redeemed him from the first
Sin of his wretched lot, whom you had made,
Grieved when they knew your torment, sore and hard,
Becoming on the cross servant of servants.

Of who and whence you were Heaven gave such sign
That it darkened its eyes, split earth apart,
Made mountains tremble and the waters churn,

Snatched the great fathers from the shadowy zone,
The ugly angels drove to greater hurt,
And only man rejoiced, baptized, reborn.

297

SONNET OF THANKS (1555)

By the mule, by the candles, by the sugar,
Not to mention a giant flask of malmsey,
So far outmatched is all my property
That the scales to Saint Michael I'll restore.

My sails collapse so in the too fair weather
That my frail boat, without a wind at sea,

296—line 12: Redeemed the Old Testament prophets and patriarchs
from limbo to Heaven.

Loses its pathway, and appears to be
A bit of wood in the rough cruel water.

Considering the great gift and the kindness,
The food, the drink, the traveling so often,
Meeting and satisfying all my wants,

O dear my Lord, clearly in terms of fairness
To give you all I am would still be nothing;
It is no present when we pay our debts.

298
SONNET TO BISHOP BECCADELLI
(1556)

Through grace, the Cross, and all we have endured,
We'll meet in Heaven, Monsignor, I'm convinced,
And yet before the ultimate last gasp,
To enjoy the earth I'd also say is good.

The rough road, mountains and sea, may hold
One away from the other; feeling and impulse
Care nothing, though, for blocking snow and ice,
Nor do the wings of thought for chain and bond.

So I thereby am constantly with you,
And weep, and speak of my Urbino dead,
Who now might be there with me, were he living,

As I had had in mind. His dying, too,
Hurries and draws me down a different road,
Where he awaits, that I may share his lodging.

299

UNFINISHED SONNET (1560)

By many things my eyes are filled with sadness,
My heart by all the things that are on earth;
What would I do with life, without the gift
That you made of yourself, noble and precious?

For my bad habits, from the bad examples
In the thick shadows where I find myself,
I hope not only pardon but relief;
To whom you show yourself, this you must promise.

300

UNFINISHED SONNET (1560)

In no way else you take out of myself
My love, my dangerous and vain emotion,
Than by strange happenings or adverse fortune,
Whereby you loose your chosen from the earth.

Dear Lord alone, who dresses and strips off
Each soul, your blood its healing, its purgation
From infinite sin and from the human motion . . .

301–327

MINOR FRAGMENTS, CHIEFLY OF
UNIDENTIFIABLE POETIC FORM

301

(1501)

Desire provokes desire, and then knows care.

302

At the sweet murmur of a little stream,
That dims with green shadow a shining spring,
The heart may stay . . .

303

I saw a beautiful woman
That I . . . my fate
I felt myself completely comforted.

304

. . . a sweet lodging in Hell

305

. . . God devotedly

306

. . . that in the . . . Phoebus
. . . of his beautiful lovely stay
. . . in the shadow I escape the day
. . . with his light he gilds the meadows
. . . where, from either one of them, my sorrows
        . . . discolors

307

Man keeps you, Lord,
In thought . . .

308

Fever, sides, pain, sicknesses, teeth, and eyes.

309
        (1507)

She burns me, binds me, holds me, seems like sugar to me.

310

Loving therefore takes my energy,
For victory is like an enemy.

311

To the eyes, and to virtue, and your strength.

312

They have no other pleasure
In living where I am deceased and dead,
Indeed, indeed, of nothing I am made.

313

(1523)

One goes off in the same way with my fate,
The other, gazing, still proffers me help.

314

Not otherwise was Daedalus awakened,
Not otherwise the sun drives out the shadow

315

. . . or my breath tired
. . . or the evil hour
. . . light to my pleasure
. . . in frost and shade.

. . . drives out the shadows
. . . and the other plume
. . . carries within
. . . consoling Heaven

316

. . . can be all boredom and anxiety
. . . the only remedy
. . . among us there is nothing human
. . . the heart, the mind, the soul will then
. . . the evil of all error

. . . disdain and anger
. . . the first and the second death drive out
. . . in my fate.

317

. . . and inhuman
. . . love to the flower comes close
. . . a haughty woman
. . . through eyes to heart will pass.

318

Made scorched and burnt by the sun and greater heats.

319

Thus either in or outside of its rays
I am inside the fire that burns my body . . .
And know . . .
And thus, brimful of grace and full of love,
A secret thought will show me and will say:
I await your seeing her another time;
It makes me see her again with mournful looks.

320

Two dry eyes, they are mine, make the world sad.

321

Make it another evening, this one's rainy,
And one expected elsewhere will talk badly.

322–327
FRAGMENTS OF LOST MADRIGALS

322

I had no strength before

. . . . .
Your face within mine
Can well be seen, by your good will and kindness,
By one who can't see you for too much brightness.

323

No one has mastery
Before he is at the end
Of his art and his life.

324

When sometimes I'm beset by your great mercy,
I fear and chafe no less than at your rigor;
At one extreme or the other
The wound from the blows of love is deadly.

325

What can I, should I, would you, I still try,
O Love, before I die?
                .   .   .   .
Tell her always each day,
Her mercy's overcome by your wild star.

326

I don't know if with other beams it happens
              .   .   .   .   .
My fortune, though, has overcome his custom.

327

And in this wretched state it is your face
That lends me light and shadow, like the sun.

NOTES TO THE POEMS

4 Written on the back of a sheet of paper with a draft of a letter from Bologna to his brother Buonarroto, December 24, 1507.

5 Written in 1509–12, the period when the Sistine Chapel ceiling was being painted. Five sonnets from Giovanni of Pistoia to Michelangelo exist, but there are no other references by Michelangelo to Giovanni. Nothing is known of the personality of Giovanni, who was a Florentine civil servant as late as 1540.

6 Pope Julius reigned from 1503 to 1513. On Michelangelo's work for him see the Introduction.

10 It has been proposed that this was written in 1512 and addressed to Giovanni of Pistoia.

12 An early date is deduced from the fact that the madrigal was set to music by Bartolomeo Tromboncino, and appears in a book of his songs published in Naples in 1518. It was the first poem by Michelangelo to be printed in any form.

14 These three lines appear on the same sheet and

the second rhymes with the third. For this reason they are here presented as one fragment, although Girardi considers them two separate ones, lines 1–2 (his number 16) and line 3 (his number Appendix 21). This is the only disagreement with Girardi in this book.

15 Written on the back of a letter of April 20, 1521, to Michelangelo in Carrara.

16 Written on the back of a letter of April 27, 1522, to Michelangelo in Florence.

29 The manuscript is torn.

30 Written on the back of a letter of October 8, 1525, to Michelangelo in Carrara.

44 Michelangelo continues the thought by writing in prose under the poem: "Lionardo. It was alone in exalting virtues in the world with great virtue; it had no one to handle the bellows. Now in Heaven it will have many companions, because there is no one there except those whom the virtues pleased, so that I hope my hammer will finish up there above. At least it will have someone in Heaven to handle the bellows, while down here it had no companion at the forge where virtues are exalted." Most writers have considered this poem to refer to the death of Vittoria Colonna. But Girardi considers the handwriting to belong to an earlier time, before Michelangelo even knew her, and that it may refer to the death in 1528 of his brother Buonarroto, whose son Lionardo is addressed in the prose footnote.

54–55 Written on the back of a letter of June 8, 1532, to Michelangelo in Florence.

57 This and the next two poems are all written on a

sheet containing a letter of August 5, 1532, to Michelangelo in Rome.

61 Under the poem Michelangelo wrote: "If what is sent is marked 'to Raffaello' the poem will get back." He was sending it to Luigi del Riccio to read and arranging for its return through his assistant, Raffaello da Montelupo.

74 This poem exists in many drafts, of which the earlier ones are to an unknown woman, the later ones probably to Tommaso Cavalieri.

79 This poem was also rewritten several times with great changes, like 74.

89 Michelangelo sent this madrigal to Luigi del Riccio with the note: "Old stuff for the fire, without witnesses." He enclosed it in a brief letter, whose casual references to "my love" and "a third party" have been unconvincingly interpreted with the aim of settling the date.

91 This madrigal was sent (probably long after it was written) to Luigi del Riccio, with a note expressing pleasure that the composer Jakob Arcadelt had set another of the madrigals to music (145) and asking advice about what present to give him.

104 Michelangelo later sent a copy of this sonnet for explication to Benedetto Varchi, at Tommaso Cavalieri's request (see letter 79).

107 This madrigal is accompanied by a letter to Luigi del Riccio with greetings to friends, but, again, the letter was probably written long after the poem.

108 Accompanying a drawing of a skeleton holding a box.

128 Michelangelo sent this and the next madrigal to Luigi del Riccio, it seems in September or October 1542, with a note: "Master Luigi, you who have

the poetic spirit, would you please shorten and smooth one of these madrigals, whichever you think is the less poor, because I must give it to a friend of ours. Yours, Michel . . ." But as in other cases the poems may have been written earlier.

130 A manuscript of this madrigal was sent "To Master Donato, the polisher of badly made things, my greetings." This was Donato Giannotti, a friend who shared Michelangelo's interests in Dante and in Florentine liberty, and who gave a vivid sketch of him in his dialogue "On How Many Days Dante Passed in Hell." Number 133 was also sent to him.

141 A manuscript was sent to Riccio with the postscript: "I thank you for the melons and wine and pay with a squib."

143 This too was sent to Riccio with a note: "This is for the cheese; the next will be for the olives, if it's worth that much."

144 Besides the numerous manuscripts of this poem reported by Girardi, there is another in the Huntington Library, apparently the only page of Michelangelo's poetry not known to him. It was published in *The Art Bulletin*, 1940, incorrectly identified as an unknown sonnet to be added to Michelangelo's work, and again in the same magazine, 1944, as a draft of this madrigal. Two additional lines on the sheet, not part of the poem, have now been identified as a draft of 106 (by Girardi in a letter to the writer).

145 Set to music by Arcadelt and published by him in 1543, to Michelangelo's pleasure (see note to 91). The first half was quoted by Giannotti in his

"Dialogue" (see note to 130) and by Varchi in his
lecture on sonnet 80. Partly as a result, some mod-
ern editors have treated this as two poems. They
have interpreted the second as a political allegory,
encouraged by the difficult syntax of the first two
lines. In addition to Girardi's arguments against
this, another disproof is that in the second part, if
it were a separate poem, the first line would have
no rhyme; instead it rhymes with lines in the first
part, a typical arrangement in the madrigals.

146   On the manuscript sent to Riccio, Michelangelo
added the prose line: "When somebody only
wants half a loaf of bread, to give him a palace is
not to the point."

149   The fame of this sonnet began when it was the
subject of an elaborate lecture of explication by
Varchi in Florence on March 6, 1547. See letters
77 and 79.

154   Annotated by Michelangelo: "To be polished by
day."

155   Underneath Michelangelo wrote: "This is for the
trout; the sonnet I told you of will be for the pep-
per, which is worth less, but I cannot write. My
regards to you."

157   One of the manuscripts contains both the sonnet
and letter 60, which is essentially a paraphrase of it.

159   One of the manuscripts also contains the first line
of a letter: "Lady Marchioness, I don't think, since
I am in Rome . . ." The whole letter (61) ap-
pears elsewhere.

160   Accompanied in the manuscript by letter 61.

165   Sent with the postscript: "For yesterday evening's
duck."

167 Sent with the postscript: "This is really a squib, and my greetings to you." When sending 168, Michelangelo also gave a new last line for 167, with the note: "Put this line below the squib I sent you, because the one that's there is not to the point."

169 An accompanying note to Riccio reads: "Master Luigi, please send me the last madrigal, which you don't understand, so that I can polish it, because the squib carrier, who is Urbino, was so prompt that he didn't let me look it over. As for getting together tomorrow, I must beg you to excuse me, because the weather is bad and I have business at home; we will do later the same that we would do tomorrow, this Lent at Lunghezza with a big keg."

170 Beneath, Michelangelo writes to Riccio: "This one I put not as a squib but as a dream."

171 This was written on a piece of blue paper, and Michelangelo noted: "Of holy matters one speaks in an azure field."

175 Epitaph on the death of Faustina Mancina Attavanti, to whose death other poets also dedicated themselves. This was doubtless written at the request of Gandolfo Porrino; see the next note. The word Mancina means Left.

176 Gandolfo Porrino, a poet and courtier, wrote three sonnets to Michelangelo, the first praising *The Last Judgment*, the other two requesting the portrait of Mancina. Michelangelo here answers the second of the three, using the same rhyme sounds. That procedure was typical of the exchange of sonnets when they were being used as complimentary letters.

177 Francesco Bracci (Cecchino is a nickname for Francesco) died January 8, 1544. He was Luigi del Riccio's nephew, and the epitaphs in their almost absurd logical variations result from Riccio's request to Michelangelo, accompanied by gifts, to provide a sculpture and epitaph for the tomb.

184 Michelangelo added: "Your friend speaks, and says: If Heaven took all beauty from all other men on earth to make me alone beautiful, as it did, and if, by divine law, on the Day of Judgment I must return the same as I was alive, it follows that it cannot return to those from whom it took it the beauty it gave to me, but I must in eternity be more beautiful than the others, and they ugly. And this is the contrary of the idea you told me yesterday, and the one is false and the other is true. Yours, Michelangelo Buonarroti."

188 "If you don't want any more, don't send me anything any more," Michelangelo wrote below to Riccio.

190 The accompanying note to Riccio reads: "Not to talk properly [literally: "in grammar"] sometimes would be shameful to me, since I have so much to do with you. Master Donato's sonnet seems to me as fine as anything done in our times, but since I have bad taste, I cannot esteem less a new cloth, even if it is from the Romagna [that is, rough village work], than used garments of silk and gold that would make a tailor's dummy look good. Write him about it and tell him about it and present him with it and give him my greetings." Donato Giannotti was one of several others who had also written poems on the death of Cecchino.

191   To the second manuscript version of this Michelangelo added the note: "Master Luigi, the last four lines of the above eight of the sonnet I sent you yesterday contradict themselves, so please send it back to me, or insert these in place of those, so it will be less awkward, and you polish it for me."

192   Sending this, Michelangelo wrote: "I didn't want to send this one, because it's very awkward, but the trout and truffles would force Heaven itself. My greetings to you."

193   "One who sees Cecchino dead and speaks to him, and Cecchino answers him."

194   "Now the promise of fifteen squibs is finished; I am not obligated for any more, unless something else comes down from Heaven, where he is."

195   "Take these two verses below, which are a moral thing; and I send this to you for the balance of the fifteen squibs:

Show him, to whom in bed I had such grace,
What he embraced, and in what the soul lives."

196   "For the salted mushrooms, since you will have nothing else."

197   "This stupid one, told a thousand times, for the *finocchi*." (A type of greens.)

199   "This the trout say, not I; so if you don't like the verses, don't marinate them again without pepper."

204   Sending Riccio this one for the second time, revised, Michelangelo wrote: "I send you back the melons with the squib, and the drawing not yet; but I shall do it without fail the best I can draw. Give my greetings to Baccio . . ." The drawing was the design for Cecchino's tomb.

205 "For the tortoise; for the fish Urbino will take care, having gobbled it up."

206 "Polish it your own way."

209 "Stupid things! The well is dry, we must wait for rain, and you are in too much of a hurry."

212 "The tomb speaks to whoever reads these lines. Stupid things, but from your wanting me to make a thousand of them, perforce there will be all sorts."

214 "Above the grave."

216 "For the fig bread. Under the head, which speaks."

217 "Till we meet again this next St. Martin's, if it doesn't rain."

221 "Since poetry has been in a calm tonight, I send you four scrawls for the constipated man's three good ones. And my regards to you. Yours, Michelangelo at Macel de' Corvi." Poems 218–221 were sent on one sheet.

226 "For the fun of it, not for the quantity."

229 "For Lent; your Michelangelo greets you."

233 A copy of this and the sonnet following were sent to Giovan Francesco Fattucci later, with letter 80.

239 Sent to Riccio with the note: "Since you want some squibs I cannot send you any but what I have. It's you that suffer, and your Michelangelo greets you."

240 At the foot Michelangelo wrote: "For sculptors."

243 Opposite line 7 Michelangelo wrote: "Reply."

244 This poem was originally written, but not finished, in the form of a long poem in octave stanzas on the back of a letter of 1524 to Michelangelo, and again in the same way on the back of another of 1534.

245 The Florentine Giovanni Strozzi addressed a com-

plimentary epigram to Michelangelo on his statue of *Night*: "The Night you see sleeping in such a sweet pose was carved by an Angel in this stone, and since she is sleeping she is alive; wake her, if you don't believe it, and she'll speak to you." Number 245 is marked "Buonarroti's Answer" in the manuscripts.

246 In Donato Giannotti's "Dialogue" on Dante, in which Michelangelo is portrayed as an interlocutor, he is asked to "recite that sonnet you wrote a few days ago in praise of him." An early draft of this then follows.

247 The manuscript is captioned by Riccio: "By Master Michelangelo Buonarroti, meaning Florence by the Lady."

248 Under a manuscript Michelangelo wrote: "Master Donato, you ask me for what I do not have."

250 There is also a reply to this by Riccio.

251 On the earlier of two manuscripts Michelangelo wrote: "Song born at night lying in bed, to be polished tomorrow evening," and on the later: "It would be as sweet as Adam's fruit, but I have no apples in my body."

252 Michelangelo's postscript: "Old love has stuck out a branch, or rather a heel."

283 An early draft is of 1552. The sonnet was sent to (but not written for) Giorgio Vasari with letter 95. Vasari replied with another with the same rhyme sounds.

286 At the foot of one of the manuscripts, Michelangelo wrote: "Master Giorgio, I send you two sonnets, and though they are a silly business, I do it so you can see where I turn my thoughts, and

when you are eighty-one years old like me you will believe me. Please give them to Master Giovan Francesco Fattucci, who has asked me for them. Yours, Michelangelo Buonarroti in Rome." He also sent it to Bishop Lodovico Beccadelli, who replied with a sonnet with the same rhyme sounds.

297 The donor of the presents is usually assumed to have been Vasari, but the evidence is dubious.

298 The sonnet is a reply (but not with the same rhyme sounds) to one addressed to Michelangelo by the Bishop from Dalmatia. He regrets not seeing him, but expects to in Heaven.

301 The fragments 301–327 are so brief that they do not constitute complete thoughts. They are placed at the end because their brevity makes it generally impossible to know when they were written.

315 These were completed verses, lost when the paper was cut. The same applies to 316, on another sheet.

322 This and the following five fragments are known to us only as they were quoted by Varchi in his lecture on Michelangelo's poetry in 1547. That is, they were complete poems, now lost. Since they have disappeared, in spite of having been in semi-public circulation, it may well be that many others have been lost completely.

LETTERS

1

In the name of Christ, July 2, 1496

Honorable Lorenzo etc.: Just to inform you that we arrived safely last Saturday and went at once to visit the Cardinal of St. George,[2] and I presented your letter to him. He seemed to be happy to see me and wanted me to go and see certain figures immediately, in which I occupied that whole day, and so I did not give your other letters that day. Then on Sunday the Cardinal came to the new house and asked for me; I went to him, and he asked me what I thought of the things I had seen. I told him what I felt about them, and certainly I felt that there were some very fine things. Then the Cardinal asked me whether I was up to making something fine. I answered that I would not do such great things, but he would see what I would do. We have bought a piece of marble for a life-size figure, and I shall begin to work on Monday. Then last Monday I pre-

---

1 A rich but non-political cousin of the famous Medici.
2 As told in the Introduction, Raffaello Riario, Cardinal of St. George, nephew of a previous Pope, had bought Michelangelo's *Cupid* in the belief that it was an ancient Roman sculpture. Michelangelo had, in fact, had it buried and dug up, not to deceive, but to prove his talents.

sented your other letters to Paolo Rucellai, who handed me
that money, and the ones at the Cavalcanti's likewise.
Then I gave the letter to Baldassare [1] and asked him for
the child, for which I would give him the money back. He
answered me very harshly, and would sooner break it in a
hundred pieces, and he had bought the child and it was his,
and he had letters that he had given satisfaction to the ones
who sent it to him, and he had no notion of being obli-
gated to give it back; and he complained a great deal about
you, saying that you had spoken ill about him; now some
of the Florentines have intervened to get agreement be-
tween us, and haven't done anything. Now I am counting
on doing so by means of the Cardinal, for I am so advised
by Baldassare Balducci. [2] You will hear what comes out of
it. No more in this one; my duty to you; God keep you
from harm.

Michelangelo in Rome

(*outside:*) SANDRO BOTTICELLI [3] IN FLORENCE

2

(TO HIS FATHER IN FLORENCE;
ROME, JULY 1, 1497)

In the name of God, July 1, 1497

Most revered and dear father: Do not be astonished that I
have not come back, because I have not yet been able to

---

[1] The dealer who had paid Michelangelo thirty ducats for the *Cupid*
and sold it for two hundred ducats.
[2] A friend of Michelangelo. He worked in the banking house of Jacopo
Gallo.
[3] The letter was addressed to Botticelli, the painter, presumably be-
cause it was risky to write to a member of a family that had fallen from
power only two years before.

work out my affairs with the Cardinal, and don't want to leave if I haven't been satisfied and reimbursed for my labor first; with these great personages one has to go slow, since they can't be pushed, but in any case I hope to be clear of everything this coming week.

I should inform you that Friar Lionardo [1] returned here to Rome and says he was obliged to flee from Viterbo and had his robe stolen, and wanted to go to you, so I gave him a gold ducat that he asked me for, to go with, and I suppose you must know this since he must have arrived there.

I don't know what else to tell you, since I am in suspense and don't know how things will go yet, but I hope to be with you soon. I am well and hope the same of you. Give my friends my greetings.

Michelangelo, sculptor, in Rome

3

Giuliano: I have learned from one of yours how the Pope took my departure badly, and how His Holiness is going to make a deposit and do what he had agreed, and that I should come back and not be doubtful about anything.

As for my departure, it is true that on Holy Saturday I heard the Pope, speaking at table with a jeweler and the Master of Ceremonies, say that he didn't want to spend a penny more either on large or small stones, which amazed me a good deal. Still, before I left I asked him for part of

---

[1] Michelangelo's brother; a partisan of Savonarola.
[2] The subjects covered in this letter, Michelangelo's flight from Rome and the negotiations for his return, are described in the Introduction.

what I needed for going on with the work. His Holiness answered me that I should come back Monday; and I came back there Monday and Tuesday and Wednesday and Thursday, as he saw. Finally, on Friday morning I was sent out, that is, chased away, and the fellow who sent me out of there said that he knew me but those were his orders. So, since I had heard those words on Saturday, and then seeing the result, I got extremely desperate. But this was not the entire cause of my departure; there was also another thing, which I don't want to write; suffice it that it made me think that if I stayed in Rome my tomb would be built before the Pope's. And this was the cause of my sudden departure.

Now you write me on the Pope's behalf, and thus you will read this to the Pope; and His Holiness should know that I am more disposed than ever to go on with this work, and if he wants the tomb built no matter what, it shouldn't bother him where I build it, so long as at the end of the five years that we agreed on it is put up in St. Peter's, wherever he likes, and is a fine thing as I have promised; for I am certain, if it is made, the whole world will not have its equal.

Now if His Holiness wants to go on, he should place that deposit here in Florence, I'll write him where, and I have many marbles on order in Carrara which I shall have brought here, and I shall also have those brought here that I have there; although it would be quite a disadvantage to me, it wouldn't bother me if I could do that work here, and I would send the things as they were done, piece by piece, in such a way that His Holiness would be pleased, just as if I stayed in Rome, or more so, since he would see things done without having any other bother about them. And as for that money and that work, I shall obligate myself as His

Holiness wishes, and shall give him whatever security he asks here in Florence. Be it what it will, I'll guarantee it no matter what, and all Florence should be enough. I have this to tell you too: that it is not possible that I could do that work in Rome for this price, as I can here on account of the many advantages available which don't exist there, and besides, I shall do it better and more lovingly because I shan't have to think about so many things. In the meantime, my dear Giuliano, I ask you to make me an answer, and quickly. There's nothing else.

May 2, 1506

Yours, Michelangelo, sculptor, in Florence

4

(TO HIS BROTHER BUONARROTO IN
FLORENCE; BOLOGNA, DECEMBER 19, 1506)

Buonarroto: I have received one of yours today, this nineteenth of December, in which you recommend Pietro Aldobrandini to me and ask me to serve him in what he asks. Know then, that he writes that I should have a dagger blade made for him, and that I should do it in such a way that it would be a marvelous thing. However, I don't know how I can serve him quickly and well; one thing is, that it is not my profession; the other, that I have no time to attend to it. But within a month I shall figure out how he can be served the best I know how.

I understand all about your affairs and Giovansimone's.[1] I am glad he is going into your shop and that he wants to do well, because I want to help him like the rest of you. If

---

[1] Giovansimone, a happy-go-lucky younger brother, was a source of considerable annoyance to Michelangelo.

God helps me as he always has, I hope by this Lent to have done what I have to do here, and shall return there to do what I have promised you, no matter what. As for the money that you write me Giovansimone wants to invest in a shop, I feel he should delay four months more and have the lightning and the thunder both at once.[1] I know you understand me, and that's enough. Tell him on my behalf to attend to doing well, and even if he wanted the money you write me about, it would have to be taken out of what's there, since I don't have any here yet to send him, because I am getting a small price for what I am doing, and it is a doubtful thing too, and something might happen that would absolutely undo me. Therefore I call on you to be patient for these few months, until I come back there.

On the matter of Giovansimone coming here, I don't advise it yet, since I'm in a poor room here and I have bought only one bed, in which four persons sleep, and I would have no way to receive him properly. But if he still wants to come, he should wait until I have cast the figure I am making, and I will send Lapo and Lodovico back for him, who are helping me, and send him a horse so that he won't come like an animal. Nothing else; pray God for me and for things to go well.

Michelangelo, sculptor, in Bologna

5

(TO HIS BROTHER BUONARROTO IN FLORENCE; BOLOGNA, FEBRUARY 1, 1507)
Buonarroto: I have gathered, from one of yours, how things went in the matter of that little farm; I was very much re-

---

[1] A proverb, meaning to do everything at one time.

lieved by it and am very glad, so long as the matter is quite sure.

As to the affairs of Baroncello, I am quite well informed, and from what I am told, the matter is much more serious than you make it out; still, I for my part would not ask for it, since it is not just. We are all of us obligated to do a good deal for Baroncello, and so we shall, and most of all in those things that are in our power.

Let me tell you that Friday evening, three hours before sunset, Pope Julius came to my house where I work and stayed for half an hour to look while I went on working; then he gave me his blessing and went away; and he indicated that he was happy with what I am doing. Wherefore I feel we have to thank God in the highest, and so I pray you to do, and pray for me.

I also want to let you know that Friday morning I dismissed Lapo and Lodovico who were working for me here. Lapo I chased out, since he is a ne'er-do-well and a scoundrel and didn't do a job for me. Lodovico is certainly better, and I would have kept him two months more, but Lapo, so as not to be blamed all by himself, corrupted him in such a way that they were both in it together. I write you this, not because I care anything about them, since they are not worth three coppers between them, but so that Lodovico [1] won't be astonished if they come to talk to him; and tell him not to lend an ear to them on any account, and if you want to find out all about their activities, go to Master Agnolo the herald of the Council, since I have written him everything, and he will give you the news, since he is a good fellow.

I understand about Giovansimone; I would like him to

---

[1] Michelangelo's father.

go into your masters' shop and attend to doing well, and urge him to do so because, if this matter turns out all right, I have hopes of setting you up well, if you are smart. On the matter of those other lands next to Mona Zenobia's, if Lodovico likes, tell him to attend to it and let me know. I believe, or rather it is said here, that the Pope will leave here around carnival time.

First of February, 1506 [1]

> *Michelangelo son of Lodovico son of Buonarroto Simoni, sculptor, in Bologna*

6

(TO HIS FATHER IN FLORENCE; BOLOGNA, FEBRUARY 8, 1507)

Eighth of February 1506

Most revered father: Today I received one of yours from which I learn that you have been given news by Lapo and Lodovico. I am happy for you to reprove me, since I deserve to be reproved for a sorry sinner, as much as others and perhaps more so. But let me tell you that I have not sinned at all in this matter for which you reprove me, neither against them nor anybody else, unless in doing more than it was right for me to do; and all men with whom I have ever been involved know very well what I give them, and even if they don't, it's Lapo and Lodovico who know it better than the rest, for one of them had twenty-seven ducats in a month and a half, and the other eighteen broad florins and expenses, so please don't let them knock you off your perch. When they complained of me, you

---

[1] The Florentine New Year's Day was on March 25, so that days between January 1 and March 25 are recorded in the year previous to our system.

should have asked them how long they worked for me and what they got from me, and then you would have asked what they were complaining about. But what made them suffer most of all, and especially that sorry Lapo, was this: they gave everybody to understand that they were the ones doing this work, or that they were in association with me, and they never realized they were not the master, especially Lapo, except when I chased him away; only then did he realize he was working under me, and since he had got involved in so many affairs and had begun to boast of the Pope's favor, it seemed strange to him that I chased him out like a dog. I am sorry he has seven ducats of mine, but if I return there, he'll give them back to me no matter what, though he ought to give me back the rest he has had too, if he has any conscience—enough of that. I won't carry this on further, since I have written Master Agnolo enough about their affairs, and I beg you to go to him, and if you can, take Granacci [1] along with you; take him and have him read the letter I wrote him, and you'll understand what riffraff they are. But please keep secret what I write about Lodovico, because if I can't find anyone else to come here for the casting, I would see about getting him back, since I really didn't chase him away from here; but Lapo, since it was too humiliating to leave alone, corrupted him as well to make it lighter on himself. You will learn everything from the herald, and how you should act in the matter. Don't come to words with Lapo; it's too shameful, since our situation has nothing to do with him.

As for Giovansimone's affairs, I don't feel he should come here, since the Pope is leaving this carnival time and I think will come straight to Florence, and he is not leaving

---

[1] A painter who had studied as a fellow pupil with Michelangelo.

good order here; there is some suspicion here, according to what people say, but it mustn't be pursued or written down, it's just that if anything happens (which I don't expect), I don't want to have the obligation of brothers on my hands. Don't be surprised about this, and don't speak of it to any man on earth, because if I were to need men, I couldn't find any who would come; and besides, I still think things will go well. I shall be there [in Florence] soon and shall do things so that I'll satisfy Giovansimone and the others, please God! Tomorrow I'll write you another letter about certain money I want to send there, and what you are to do with it. I know about Piero; he will answer you for me, since he is a good man, as he has always been.

Yours, Michelangelo in Bologna

I have more to tell you in reply to that "strange treatment" Lapo says I have inflicted on him. I want to write you just one thing, and that is that I bought seven hundred and twenty pounds of wax, and before I bought it, I told Lapo he should enquire who had some and bargain for it, and I would give him the money and he was to get it. Lapo went and came back and told me it couldn't be had for a penny under nine broad ducats and twenty bolognini for a hundred pounds, which is nine ducats and forty coppers, and I should take it quickly, since I had found a lucky bargain. I answered by telling him to go and find out if he could knock off those forty coppers per hundred, and I would take it. He replied that these Bolognese are by nature such that they wouldn't knock a farthing off what they ask. At that point I got suspicious and let it go. Then the same day I called Piero aside and told him secretly to go and find out for how much he could get a hundred-weight of wax. Piero went to the same man as Lapo and bargained him down to eight ducats and a half, and I took it and then sent Piero for the broker's fee and that was given to him too. And that is one of those "strange treatments" I have inflicted on him. In fact, I know he felt it was strange that I saw through that fraud. The eight broad ducats a month and expenses were not enough; he also figured out how to defraud me and may have defrauded me many times I don't know about, since I trusted him; and I never saw a man that had more the color of goodness than he, which makes me believe he has tricked others under the guise of goodness. So do not trust him in anything, and act as if you didn't see him.

7

(T O   H I S   B R O T H E R   B U O N A R R O T O   I N
F L O R E N C E ;   B O L O G N A ,   J U L Y   6 ,   1 5 0 7)

Buonarroto: Let me tell you that we have cast my figure, in which I didn't have very good luck, because either through ignorance or accident Master Bernardino did not melt the material well, which would be too long to write about, it's enough to say that my figure came out up to the waist, and the rest of the material, that is, half the metal, remained in the furnace and wasn't melted, so that in order to get it out I'll have to take the furnace apart, and that is what I am doing, and this week I shall have it done over again and next week recast it from above and finish filling the form, but not without the greatest suffering and work and expense. I would have credited Master Bernardino to melt it without fire, I had such faith in him; nevertheless, it isn't that he is not a good master and didn't do it lovingly. He who does may go amiss. And he has really gone amiss to my hurt and his own, because he has been so abused he can't hold up his head in Bologna.

If you should see Baccio d'Agnolo, read him the letter
and ask him to inform Sangallo in Rome and greet him for
me, and greet Giovanni da Ricasoli and Granacci for me.
I think if the thing goes well, I'll be out of it in fifteen or
twenty days, and return there. If it should not go well, I
might have to do it over; I'll keep you informed.

Let me know how Giovansimone is.

July sixth

Along with this will be one going to Rome to Giuliano da
Sangallo. Send it carefully and as quickly as you can, and
if he should be in Florence, give it to him.

8

(TO HIS BROTHER BUONARROTO IN
FLORENCE; BOLOGNA, NOVEMBER 10, 1507)

Buonarroto: I find it strange that you write me so rarely. I
believe too that you must have more time to write me than
I you, so let me know often how you are making out.

I learned from your last that you wanted me to come
back quickly for a good reason, and that made me spend
several days worrying; so when you write me, write boldly
and explain things properly, so that I can understand them;
enough of that.

Let me tell you I desire far more than you to come back
quickly, because I am in the greatest discomfort here, with
the hardest kind of toil, and I'm busy with nothing but
working day and night, and I have endured and am endur-
ing such labor that if I had another such again I don't
think my life would be long enough, because it has been a
very large piece, and if it had been in someone else's hands
something would have gone wrong with it. But I think the
prayers of a few people have helped me and kept me

healthy, for it was contrary to the opinion of all Bologna that I would ever get it completed after it was cast; and even earlier nobody believed I would ever cast it. Suffice it that I've brought it just about to completion, but won't finish at the end of this month as I expected; but next month it will certainly be finished and I'll come back. So all of you keep cheerful, for I shall do without fail what I promised. Soothe Lodovico and Giovansimone on my behalf, and write me how Giovansimone is getting on, and attend to learning and keeping the shop, so that you'll know how when you have to, which will be soon.
Tenth of November
Michelangelo in Bologna

9

(TO HIS FATHER IN FLORENCE;
ROME, JUNE 1508)

Most revered father: I learn from your last how it has been said there that I am dead. It's a thing that matters little, since I am really alive. So let those who say it say it, and don't talk of me to anybody, as there are evil men. I am attending to work as much as I can. It's now thirteen months since I've had money from the Pope, and I expect to have some in a month and a half no matter what, as I shall have put all I had to excellent use. If he were to give me none, I would have to beg money to return there, since I don't have a penny. So I cannot be robbed. May God let it work out for the best.

I understand about Mona Cassandra.[1] I don't know what

---

1 The widow of Michelangelo's uncle, who had sued to recover her dowry. There is no record of the outcome.

to say about it. If I could find some money, I would en-
quire whether the lawsuit could be transferred here without
loss to me—that is, of time—and I would have to get a
lawyer, and so far I have nothing to pay with. Let me know
when the time comes how the affair is going, and if you
need money go to the Hospital Director at Santa Maria
Nuova, as I told you before. There's no more to tell you. I
am unhappy and not in too good health staying here, and
with a great deal of work, no instructions, and no money.
But I have good hopes God will help me. Give my greet-
ings to Giovanni da Ricasoli and to Master Angelo the
Herald.

Yours, Michelangelo in Rome

10

(TO HIS BROTHER GIOVANSIMONE IN
FLORENCE; ROME, JULY 1508)

Giovansimone: They say that those who do good to the
good make them better, and to the bad, make them worse.
I have been trying for some years now, with good words
and deeds, to get you to the point of living decently and in
peace with your father and the rest of us, and you continu-
ally get worse. I'm not telling you you're bad, but you're
acting in a way I don't like any more than the others do. I
could make you a long speech about your affairs, but they
would be words, like the others I've spoken to you. To
make it short, I can tell you for certain you haven't a thing
in the world, and your spending money and household
necessities are what I give you and have given you for some
time now, for the love of God and thinking you were my
brother like the rest. Now I know for certain you are not
my brother because if you were you would not threaten

my father; no, you are an animal, and I shall treat you like
an animal. Let me tell you that whosoever sees his father
threatened or struck is obligated to interpose his own life,
and that's all. I tell you you have nothing in the world, and
if I hear the slightest thing about your activities, I shall
come posthaste all the way there and show you your mis-
take, and teach you to tear up your things and set fires in
the house and farms you didn't earn; you are not where you
think. If I come there, I'll show you something to make
you cry hot tears, and you'll know on what it is you base
your pride.

I have to tell you this over again besides, that if you want
to attend to doing right and honoring and reverencing
your father, then I'll help you like the others and set you
up in a short while in a good shop. If you don't do that,
I'll be there and arrange matters for you in such a way
you'll know what you are better than you ever did, and
know what you have in the world, and see it everywhere
you go. Nothing else. Where I lack words I shall supply
with deeds.

Michelangelo in Rome

I can't keep from writing you two more lines, and that is,
that I have gone all over Italy wretchedly for ten years past,
borne every humiliation, suffered every toil, scourged my
body in every labor, placed my own life in a thousand dan-
gers only to help my house, and now I have begun to raise
it up a little, you alone wish to be the one to smash and
ruin in an hour what I have done in so many years and
with so much strain; Body of Christ if it isn't true! For I
am ready to crush ten thousand like you if I have to. So be
sensible, and do not tempt one who is suffering for another
reason.

11

Most revered father: I learned from your last how things
are going there and how Giovansimone is behaving. For
ten years I have not had worse news, because I believed I
had their affairs all set, that is, in such a way they could
hope to have a good shop with my help, as I promised
them, and in that hope attend to making something of
themselves and learning, so that later they could manage
it. Now I see they are doing the opposite, and Giovansi-
mone most of all, and if I could have, on the day I got your
letter I would have taken horse and would have set every-
thing to rights by now. But since I cannot do that, I am
writing him a letter about how I feel, and if he doesn't
change his nature from now on, or if he removes anything
from the house worth a pin, or does anything else you don't
like, please let me know, because I shall see to it I get the
Pope's permission and come there and show him his mis-
take. I want you to be sure that all the labors I have always
endured were for you no less than for myself, and what I
have bought I bought so that it would be yours as long as
you lived, for if it hadn't been for you I wouldn't have
bought it. So when you would like to rent the house and
lease out the farm, do so at your own pleasure, and with
that income and what I'll give you you will live like a lord,
and if it wasn't getting on into summer, as it is, I would say
do it now and come to stay here with me. But it isn't
the right time, since you'd have a poor life here in the sum-
mer. I have thought about taking the money he [Gio-
vansimone] has in the shop and giving it to Gismondo,[1]

---

[1] Another of Michelangelo's brothers.

and for him and Buonarroto to work it the best they can
and you rent those houses and the farm at Pozzolatico, and
with that income and the help that I'll give you besides,
settle in some place where you can live nicely and have
someone to take care of things for you, either in Florence
or outside Florence, and leave that rascal up the creek.
Please think about your affairs and that I want to help you
all I can and know how, so that it will be up to you in
everything you want to do. Let me know. On the matter of
Cassandra I have been advised as to shifting the lawsuit
here. I have been told I'll spend three times as much here
as one will there, and that is certainly so, for what can be
done there with one broad piece cannot be done here with
two gold pieces. The other thing is that I have no friend
here to trust, and I couldn't attend to anything of this kind.
I feel that if you want to wait, you should go about your
ordinary life as reason dictates and defend yourself as best
you can and know how; and as for the money that has to
be spent, I shall not fail as long as I have any, so be as little
fearful as you can, for it is not a life-and-death matter.
That's all. Let me know, as I said above.

Yours, Michelangelo in Rome

12

(TO HIS BROTHER BUONARROTO IN
FLORENCE; ROME, OCTOBER 17, 1509)

Buonarroto: I got the bread. It is good but not for trading,
since there is little profit. I gave the porter five carlini, and
he would hardly give it to me. I have the information from
your last about Lorenzo [1] coming by here, and that I

---

[1] Lorenzo Strozzi was a Florentine wool merchant.

should show him a good time. I guess you don't know how I live here. All the same, I excuse you. What I can I shall do. I understand that Gismondo is coming here to speed up his business. Tell him from me he is not to make any plans based on me, not because I do not love him as a brother, but because I cannot help him in anything. I am obliged to love myself more than others, and I cannot provide myself with necessities. I live here in great toil and great weariness of body, and have no friends of any kind and don't want any, and haven't the time to eat what I need; so I must not have any more bother, since I couldn't bear another ounce.

As for the shop, I urge you to be prompt, and I am glad Giovansimone has got on the way to doing well; use your heads to increase honestly what you have or at least keep it, so that later you will know how to handle something bigger, since I have hopes that when I return there you will be acting on your own, if you are men enough. Tell Lodovico I haven't answered him because I haven't had time, and don't be surprised when I don't write.

Michelangelo, sculptor, in Rome

13

(TO HIS FATHER IN FLORENCE;
JANUARY 5, 1510)

My very dear father: I wrote you in my last how I thought you ought to buy. Now you inform me that you have another farm available at Pozzolatico besides Girolamo Cini's. I would buy both of them if the security is good, but be sure you keep your eyes open so there won't be any lawsuits later. Act with all diligence so as to be secured. On

the matter of the house [1] they give me fair words. Not that
it is important, since I know it only means the rent for the
time I live there. No need to be excited otherwise. Buonar-
roto writes me about getting married; I write you my feel-
ing, such as it is, and that is that I have a scheme to free
you all in five or six months and give you everything of
mine you have had up to today, and then you are to do
anything you like, and I, as I can, shall always help all of
you no matter what. But I do urge Buonarroto not to get
married this summer, and if I were nearby I would say why;
since he has been so long already, he won't be older for
waiting six months. Buonarroto writes me also that Ber-
nardino, son of Pier Basso, has a wish to come here to work
for me; if he wants to come, he should come now, before I
take on someone else, since I want to begin to do some-
thing. For salary I'll give him what you wrote me, that is,
three ducats a month and expenses. It is true I live in my
house simply, and I want to stay that way. Tell him this,
and do not delay; and after eight days, if he doesn't like
my ways, he can return there and I'll give him money
enough to get back. Nothing else occurs to me.
Fifth of January
                    Michelangelo, sculptor, in Rome

14

(TO HIS FATHER IN FLORENCE;
ROME, JANUARY 1510)

Revered father: About Bernardino's affairs, I answered you
that I first wanted to settle the matter of the house that

---

1 Michelangelo had been paying rent for a house in Rome since he
started work on the tomb of Julius. By a new agreement he was to
have the house rent-free until the tomb was done.

you know about, and I answer you the same way now. I first sent for him, because it was promised me that in a few days it [1] would be arranged and I would begin to work. Then I saw it would be a long affair, and in the meantime I am looking around to see if I can find another suitable one in order to get out of this, and I don't want to have any work done until I am settled. So give him the news of how the matter stands. For the boy who came that rascal of a muleteer cheated me of a ducat; he took his oath it had been agreed so, that is, for two broad ducats in gold; and all the boys who come here with muleteers are paid for at no more than ten carlini. I was more annoyed than as if I had lost twenty-five ducats, because I see it's a notion of his father's, who wanted to send him very honorably on a mule. Oh I never had such a good thing before, not I! The other thing is that the father had said to me, and the boy too, that he would do everything and look after the mule and sleep on the ground if necessary; and I'm the one that has to look after him.[2] This business was just what I needed besides what I've had since I got back! For I've had my apprentice that I left here sick on my hands from the day I got back up to now. It's true he's better now, but he has been on the point of death, doubted of by the doctors, for about a month, during which I never went to bed; not to mention many other things. Now I have this nasty mess of this boy who says he doesn't want to lose time, he wants to learn; and back there he said two or three hours a day would be enough, but now the whole day isn't enough, he

---

[1] The new contract for the tomb of Julius.
[2] Some time before Michelangelo had written to his father to look around for a boy, used to hard work, who could come to run errands and learn in his spare time, "because here they are all good-for-nothings."

wants to draw all night too. It's the father's advice. If I said anything, he would say I didn't want him to learn. I need to be taken care of, and if he didn't feel he could do it, they shouldn't have put me to this expense. But they are disingenuous and work toward a definite end. But I won't take any more. Please have him taken away from me, because he has bothered me so I can't stand it any longer. The muleteer has had so much money he can just as well take him back; and he is a friend of his father's. Tell the father to send for him. I would not give him another farthing, and I have no money. I shall be patient just so long until he sends for him, and if he doesn't, I'll send him away. Though I chased him out the second day and other times too, and he doesn't believe it.

As for the affairs of the shop, I'll send you a hundred ducats there next Saturday, with this proviso, that if you see they are attending to business, give it to them and make me creditor, as I did with Buonarroto when he left; if they should not be attending to it, put it to my account of Santa Maria Nuova. It's not time to buy yet.

Your Michelangelo in Rome

If you should speak to the boy's father, tell him about it nicely, that he is a good boy, but too soft and not fit for my service, and he should send for him.

15

(TO HIS FATHER IN FLORENCE;
ROME, JANUARY 1510)

Very dear father: I send you a hundred broad ducats in gold, with the understanding that you will give them to Buonarroto and the others and have them make me a creditor of the shop, and if they will make it their business to behave properly, I'll help them bit by bit as much as I can; tell them. So when you have seen this, go to Bonifazio or to Lorenzo Benintendi, you and Buonarroto, and he will pay them over to you; he will pay you a hundred broad ducats in gold in exchange for the same amount that Baldassare Balducci has from me here. I answered you that it wasn't time for buying yet. With my affairs here I shall do the best I can; God will help me. I wrote you about the boy, that his father should send for him to come back, and I wouldn't give him any more money, and this I repeat; even the wagoner is paid to take him back there. There the boy is good, to stay and learn and remain with his father and mother; here he is not worth a penny and makes me labor like a beast, and my other apprentice is still not out of bed. It is true I don't have him in the house, because when I was so exhausted I couldn't stand it any more, I sent him to the room of a brother of his. I have no money. This that I am sending you I have wrenched from my heart, and I don't feel I can properly ask for any, since I am not having work done and by myself I work little. When I have this business of the house settled, I hope to begin to work vigorously.

Michelangelo, sculptor, in Rome

16

(TO HIS FATHER IN FLORENCE;
ROME, SEPTEMBER 5, 1510)

Very dear father: I have had one from you this morning, September 5, which made me suffer greatly, to learn Buonarroto is ill. Please as soon as you have seen this, let me know how he is, because if he were really bad, I would come up there by the post this next week, although it

would damage me very much, because I am still to receive
five hundred ducats through the agreement, which I have
earned, and the Pope was to give me another equal amount
to start on the other part of the work.[1] And he has left here
and left no order for me, so that I find myself without
money and don't know what I am to do. I wouldn't want
to annoy him and lose what is mine if I went away, and to
stay is something I can hardly do. I have written him a
letter and am waiting for an answer; yet if Buonarroto is
in danger, let me know, because then I shall leave every-
thing. Make good arrangements and don't let money be a
reason for failing to help him. Go to the Hospitaler at
Santa Maria Nuova, and show him my letter if he doesn't
trust you, and get him to give you a hundred and fifty
ducats, as much as is needful, and have no scruples. Do not
suffer, for God has not made us to abandon us. Answer at
once and tell me definitely to come or not.

Yours, Michelangelo, sculptor, in Rome

17

(TO HIS FATHER IN FLORENCE;
ROME, SEPTEMBER 15, 1510)

Very dear father: I have given Giovanni Balducci here
three hundred and fifty broad florins in gold, for him to pay
to you there. So when you have seen this go to Bartolomeo
Fazi, and he will pay them out to you; that is, he will give
you three hundred and fifty broad florins in gold. When
you have received them, take them to the Hospitaler and
have him take care of them, as you know he has taken care
of the rest for me. You still have a few loose ducats which

---

1 The work for the Pope is the Sistine Ceiling (1508–12).

I wrote you you should take; if you haven't, take them at your convenience, and if you need more, take what you need; for I give you as much as you have need for, even if you spend it all, and if I need to write anything to the Hospitaler, let me know.

I understand from your last how the matter goes; I suffer very much; I cannot help you in any other way, but don't be frightened because of that, and don't give yourself the least distress, because if we lose property, we don't lose life. I shall provide you with so much that it will be more than what you lose, but I must remind you, don't treat it as precious, since it's all an illusion. So do your work, and thank God that since this trouble had to come, it came at a time when you could help yourselves better than you could have in the past. Attend to living, and let property go sooner than suffer discomforts, for I would rather have you alive and poor, because if you were dead, I wouldn't care for all the gold in the world, and if those chirping crickets there [in Florence] or anyone else reproves you, let them talk, for they are ignorant men and without love.
Fifteenth of September
        Yours, Michelangelo, sculptor, in Rome
When you take the money to the Hospitaler, take Buonarroto with you, and to be on the safe side, don't you or he speak to any man in the world; that is, neither you or Buonarroto say that I send you sums of money, neither this nor others.

18

(TO HIS BROTHER BUONARROTO IN
FLORENCE; ROME, JANUARY 10, 1511)
Buonarroto: I had a letter of yours some days ago, from which I learned your thoughts exactly; and since it would

be long to answer each thing, I shall tell you briefly how I feel. In the affair of the shop I am of a mind to do all I promised, when I return there; and though I wrote that some property should be bought now, I am still of a mind to set up the shop, because when I finish here and collect the balance due me, there will be enough to make up what I promised. As for your finding someone who would provide you with two or three thousand ducats and set you up in a shop, this is a better purse than mine is. I feel you should accept no matter what, but watch out not to be deceived, for you don't come across people who wish better for others than for themselves. You tell me this individual would like to give you a daughter of his to wife; and I tell you all the offers he makes you will vanish, except the wife, when he has hung her on you, and of that you'll have more than you want. I tell you besides that I don't like you getting mixed up with baser men than you are out of avarice; avarice is a great sin, and nothing can come to a good end where there is sin. I feel you should give out fair words and delay the matter until I have finished here, so I can see how I stand. All this will be three more months or thereabouts. Now do as you feel. I couldn't answer you sooner.
Tenth of January

Michelangelo, sculptor, in Rome

19

(TO HIS FATHER IN FLORENCE;
ROME, MAY 1512)

My very dear father: I learned from your last about the farm that you got from Santa Maria Nuova, and that it's a good thing, which gave me the greatest pleasure; and although it may cost a great deal, I believe you have seen to it that it's good value, and if it were overpaid by a hundred ducats, it isn't expensive, with the security it has. I thank God I am out of this business. Now I have only one thing left to do, and that is to have a shop set up for those others, and I think day and night of nothing else. Then I shall feel I have satisfied my obligations, and if I live beyond then, I shall want to live in peace.

Giovanni da Ricasoli has written me a letter that I have no time to answer. Please make my excuses. This next Saturday I shall answer him. That's all.

Yours, Michelangelo, sculptor, in Rome

20

(TO HIS BROTHER BUONARROTO IN FLORENCE; ROME, SEPTEMBER 5, 1512)

Buonarroto: I did not write you some days ago, because nothing has happened; now, learning here how things are going there, I feel I should write you my mind, and this is, that since the Country [Florence] is in a bad way, as they say here, you should see about withdrawing somewhere where you would be safe and abandoning property and everything, since life is worth much more than property; and if you don't have the money to leave there, go to the Hospitaler and have some given to you; and if I were among you, I would take out all the money of mine that the Hospitaler has and come to Siena and take a house and stay there until things settle down. I think the power of attorney I made out for Lodovico has not expired yet, so that he can still draw out my money; so take it if necessary, spend what is needful in such cases of danger and keep the rest for me. As for the matter of the Country, don't get involved in anything, either in words or actions, and act as if it were the plague; be the first to run away. That's all. Let me know of anything as soon as you can, because I am very much disturbed.

Michelangelo, sculptor, in Rome

21

(TO HIS BROTHER BUONARROTO IN FLORENCE; ROME, SEPTEMBER 18, 1512)

Buonarroto: I learned from your last that the Country stood in great danger, which made me suffer terribly. Now it is said again that the Medici family has entered Florence and everything is smooth, so that I believe the danger is over, that is from the Spanish, and I no longer think there is any need to leave; so stay in peace, and don't be friendly or intimate with anyone but God, and don't speak good or ill of anyone, because the end of things is not known; just attend to your own affairs.

As to the forty ducats Lodovico withdrew from Santa Maria Nuova, I wrote you a letter the other day that in case of mortal danger you should spend not just forty, but all of them; but aside from that I did not give you permission to touch it. I can tell you that I haven't a farthing and I'm barefoot and naked, one might say, and I can't get my balance until I have finished the work; and I suffer the greatest toil and discomfort. So if you should be bearing some discomforts too, don't be distressed, and as long as your own money will help you, don't touch mine, except in case of danger as I said. And even if you should have some very great need, I beg you to write me first. I shall be there quickly. It cannot fail that I'll be there at All Saints at the very latest, if it please God.

18th of September

Michelangelo, sculptor, in Rome

22

(TO HIS FATHER IN FLORENCE;
ROME, OCTOBER 1512)

My very dear father: I learn from your last that I ought to avoid keeping money in the house and not carry it on me, and also how it has been said there I have been talking badly about the Medici.

As for the money, what I have I keep in Balduccio's bank, and don't keep more than what I need from day to day in my house or on me. As to the matter of the Medici, I have never said a single thing against them except in the way that every man did generally, as over the affair of Prato,[1] which the stones would have talked of too, if they had known how to talk. Then too, many other things have been said here which, when I heard them, I said: "If it is true they are doing so, they do wrong"; not that I believed them, and may God will they are not true. Besides, a month ago someone who is making a show of being my friend said many bad things to me about their affairs, and I reproved him and said they do wrong to talk so, and not to talk to me any more about it. So I wish Buonarroto could see about learning discreetly where that person has heard I spoke badly of the Medici, to see if I can discover where it comes from, and if it comes from any of those who show themselves as my friends, so I can be on guard against it. I have nothing else to tell you. I am still not doing anything, and waiting for the Pope to tell me what I have to do.

Yours, Michelangelo, sculptor, in Rome

---

[1] When the Medici were trying to re-enter Florence and overthrow the Republic, their allies, the Imperial troops, sacked the town of Prato with a cruelty that shocked all Italy.

23

My very dear father: From your last I learned how things
are going there, though I knew part of it before. It is neces-
sary to have patience, trust in God, and repent one's errors,
for these adversities come from nothing other than those,
and especially from pride and ingratitude, for I never dealt
with people more unfair and prouder than the Florentines.
So, if justice comes, it is only right. Of the sixty ducats you
tell me you have to pay, I find it dishonest and suffered
very much over it; still it is necessary to have patience, as
long as it may please God. I shall write two lines to
Giuliano de' Medici,[1] which will be enclosed here; read
them, and, if you would like to take them to him, take
them to him, and you will see if they help at all. If they
don't help, consider whether what we have might be sold,
and we can go and live elsewhere. In addition, if you
should see that you were treated worse than other people,
make an effort not to pay and sooner let what you have be
taken away, and let me know. But if they do to our other
equals what they do to you, be patient and have hope in
God. You tell me you have provided for thirty ducats;
take thirty more of mine and send me the balance here.
Take them to Bonifazio Fazi and have him get Giovanni
Balducci to pay them to me here, and have Bonifazio give
you a receipt slip for the aforesaid money, and put it in
your letter when you write me. Attend to living; and if you
can't have the honors of the country as the other citizens

---

1 The Medici family, back in power, appear to have fined the Buonar-
roti family, perhaps because they had been sympathetic to Savonarola.
Apparently Michelangelo's letter to Giuliano was effective and the
family was restored to favor.

do, let it suffice you to have bread and live virtuously in
Christ and poorly, as I do here, for I live meanly and don't
bother about life or honor, that is, the world, and I live
with the greatest toil and a thousand worries. It has now
been about fifteen years since I have had a happy hour; I
have done everything to help you, and you have never rec-
ognized it or believed it. God pardon us all. I am ready to
do the same again as long as I live, so long as I can.

Yours, Michelangelo, sculptor, in Rome

24

(TO HIS BROTHER BUONARROTO IN
FLORENCE; ROME, JULY 30, 1513)

Buonarroto: Michele the stonecutter has come here to
work for me and has asked me for some money for his
family there, which I send you. So go at once to Bonifazio,
and he will give you four broad ducats, and give them to
Meo di Chimenti, stonecutter, who works at the Cathedral
Works, and give him the letter that is with this, which is
for him, and have him sign a voucher in his own hand that
he has received it from me for Michele, and send it to me.

The same Michele has told me you showed him that you
spent about sixty ducats at Settignano. I remember you
told me this here, also, at table, that you had spent many
ducats of your own. I pretended not to hear you, and I
wasn't surprised at all, because I know you. I believe you
have them written down and are keeping an account to be
able to ask us for them one day. And I would just like to
know from your ingratitude what money it was you earned
them with, and the other thing I would like to know is
whether you keep an account of those two hundred and
twenty-eight ducats of mine that you took from Santa

Maria Nuova, and many other hundreds I have spent upon the house and for you, and of the toils and discomforts I've had to help you. I would just like to know if you keep an account of them. If you had sense enough to recognize the truth, you would not say: "I have spent so much of mine"; and you also would not have come here to promote your affairs with me, seeing how I have borne myself with you in the past, but instead you would have said: "Michelangelo knows what he has written us, and if he does not do it now, he must have some hindrance we do not know about"; and keep patience, because it is not good to spur the horse that's running as fast as it can and faster than it can. But you have never known me and do not know me. God pardon you! because He has had such mercy on me that I am able to bear what I bear, or have borne, so that you could be helped; but when you don't have me you'll know it.

I should tell you that I cannot come there this September, because I am so pressed I have no time to eat. God will I can bear it; however, when I can, I want to give Lodovico the power of attorney, for I have never forgotten it, and want to put in your hands a thousand broad ducats in gold, as I have promised you, so that, with the rest you have, you can begin to act for yourself. I don't want any of your earnings, but I want to be sure that at the end of ten years, if I am alive, you will return me these thousand ducats in goods or money if I should want them back, which I don't think will happen, but if the need should come, I can have them back again as I said. And this will be a check on you not to let them go to waste; so give it some thought and consideration and write me how you want to do it. The four hundred ducats of mine that you have I want divided into four parts, each to get a hundred, and I hereby give them to you. A hundred to Lodovico, a hundred to you, a hundred to Giovansimone, a hundred to Gismondo, with this proviso, that you can do nothing with them but keep them together in the shop. There's nothing else. Show the letter to Lodovico, and decide what you want to do, and give me an assurance as I have written. Thirtieth of July. Keep in mind to give Michele the money I am sending you.

Michelangelo, sculptor, in Rome

Note on the back, in his father's writing: About the hundred ducats he is giving to his brothers and me, which I never got.

25

(T O   H I S   B R O T H E R   B U O N A R R O T O   I N
F L O R E N C E ;   R O M E ,   A U G U S T   1 ,   1 5 1 5)

Buonarroto: I saw from your last how the money stands, the account book, and the papers. I was very glad, because I have a notion to withdraw it soon, as I wrote you, and I shall notify you when it is time. Inside this will be one that goes to Michele; be sure you give it to him. I am not writing to him because I don't know he's crazy, but because I need a certain quantity of marble and don't know how to manage.[1] I don't want to go to Carrara myself, because I can't, and I can't send anyone else who would take care of what is needed, because even if they aren't crazy, they are untrustworthy and miserable, like that rascal of a Bernardino who cost me a hundred ducats extra while he was living here, aside from going all over Rome whining and

---

[1] The Medici command that Michelangelo should get his marble from their territory instead of from Carrara had involved him in great difficulties. (See Introduction.)

complaining of me, and since I have got here he knows it. He is a great rascal; keep away from him as you would from fire, and don't let him into the house for any reason. Nothing else occurs to me. You will give Michele the letter.

Michelangelo in Rome

26

(TO HIS BROTHER BUONARROTO IN FLORENCE; ROME, SEPTEMBER 8, 1515)

Buonarroto: From your last I understand that the balance of the money is at Santa Maria Nuova. I wrote you to put it back in, believing, in view of what you had written me, that you had given it to Pier Francesco to send by a muleteer; and since I didn't like that, I wrote you to put it back where it was. Now you tell me you didn't take it out; hence the matter is all right, no need to speak of it further. If I need it I'll let you know. You write me in such a way that it seems you believe I am more concerned about the things of this world than is fitting; well, I have more concern for you than myself, as I always have. I don't believe gossip and am not a bit crazy as you think; I believe too that from now on for some time you'll find more to your taste in the letters I have been writing you for the past four years than you do at present, if I'm not mistaken; and if I am mistaken, I am not mistaken about things that are evil, for I know that all times are good for feeling concern about oneself and one's affairs. I remember about eighteen months ago you wanted to take up a certain proposition, or perhaps a bit longer ago or less; I wrote you it wasn't time yet, and you should let a year pass to be on the safe side. In the meantime, a few days after that the King of France died, and you answered me, or rather wrote later, that there was no danger of anything in Italy any more, and that I was paying heed to gossip and friars' talk, and you made fun of me. But you see that King is not really dead,[1] and if you had been ruled my way several years ago it would have been better for all of us; and that's enough of that. Along with yours I had a letter from Carrara, from Zara, and he manifests a desire to serve me; I am not writing him anything, because I wrote to Master Antonio da Massa, chancellor of the Marquis of Carrara, in the last that I sent you. I suppose you have sent it on to him, and don't want to give someone else another commission before I have his answer. That's all there is.

Michelangelo, sculptor, in Rome

27

(TO HIS FATHER IN SETTIGNANO;[2] FLORENCE, 1516)

My very dear father: I was amazed at your actions the other day, when I didn't find you at home; and now at hearing that you are complaining about me and saying I chased you away I am more amazed still, because I know for a certainty that never from the day I was born up to now has it been in my mind to do anything against you, big or little, and always all the toils I have borne I have borne for love of you; and since I have come back from Rome to Florence, let me tell you I have always taken your part, and let me tell you I reaffirm to you what I said, and it was not many days since, when you were ill, I told you and promised never to fail you with all my powers as long as I live,

---

1 Louis XII had died, but the accession of Francis I gave little promise of peace for Italy.
2 A village just outside Florence where the Buonarroti had property.

and so I reaffirm. Now I am amazed that you've forgotten everything so soon. After all, you have had experience of me for thirty years, you and your sons, and know that I have always thought and done good for you when I could. How can you go about saying I have chased you away? Don't you see the reputation you give me if it's said I chased you away? That's all I lack, aside from the troubles I have and all the other things, and I have them all for love of you! You're returning me a nice reward for it! Now, however anyone may wish, why so be it; I desire to regard myself as having always hurt and shamed you, and I ask your pardon just as if I had. Consider pardoning a son of yours who has always lived badly and done you all the harm that can be done in the world; and likewise again I ask you to pardon me like the wretch I am, and don't give me this reputation up here of having chased you away, because that matters more to me than you believe; I am your son after all!

The bearer of this will be Raffaello da Gagliano. I beg you for the love of God and myself to come as far as Florence, because I have to go away and have to tell you something that is quite important, and can't come up there. And since I have learned certain things I don't like about my workman Piero,[1] from his own lips, I am sending him this morning to Pistoia and he will not return where I am, because I don't want him to be the ruin of our house; and all of you who knew I didn't know about his behavior ought to have told me about it long ago, and no such scandal would have arisen.

I am pressed to go away and I'm not leaving if I don't

---

[1] Piero d'Urbino was Michelangelo's servant and helper. Michelangelo must have changed his mind about him, as he continued to be his servant and confidant.

speak to you and leave you here in the house. I beg you to put by all your distress and come.

Yours, Michelangelo in Florence

28

(TO DOMENICO BUONINSEGNI IN ROME;[1]
CARRARA, MAY 2, 1517)

Master Domenico: Since I last wrote you I have not been able to attend to making the model, as I wrote you I would; the reason would be too long to write. I had first sketched out a little one in clay that would do for me here, which I want to send you in any case even though it is as twisted as a honeybun, so that this matter won't seem like fakery.

I have several things to tell you; read on a little with patience, it's important. That is, that I feel capable of doing this work, the façade of San Lorenzo, so that it can be the mirror of all Italy in architecture and sculpture, but the Pope and the Cardinal must decide quickly whether they want me to do it or not. And if they want me to do it, they must reach some decision whether to assign it to me by contract and trust me entirely for everything, or in some other way, I don't know what, do as they think best; and you will understand the reason for this.

I have ordered many blocks of marble, as I wrote you, and also since I wrote you, and given money here and there, and had digging started in many places. And in some places where I have spent money the blocks did not come out right, in my opinion, because they have faults, and especially these large blocks that I need, wanting them as fine as I want them; and in one block which I have already had

―――――――
[1] Michelangelo's agent in Rome; his intermediary in dealing with the Pope.

cut certain faults showed up, toward the place called Peak, that could never have been guessed, so that two columns I wanted to make from it are a dead loss, and I have thrown away half the investment. And so, with these snarls, I can only get so little out of so much marble that it won't add up to more than a few hundred ducats' worth, and I don't know how to keep accounts, and in the end I won't be able to show I have spent anything except for the quantity of marble I deliver. I would willingly do like Master Pier Fantini,[1] but I do not have enough ointment. Then too, because I am old, I don't feel like losing so much time in order to save the Pope two or three hundred ducats over this marble, and I am being pressed for my own work from there; I must come to a decision no matter what.

And this is my decision. If I knew I had to arrange labor and price, I wouldn't worry about throwing in four hundred ducats, because I would not have to render an account, and I would take three or four of the best men there are and assign all the marbles to them; and the quality of the marbles would have to be like that of the ones I quarried already, which are wonderful, though I have just a few. And for this and the money I would give them I would have good security in Lucca, and as for the blocks I have, I would give orders for them to be shipped to Florence and for work to be started, both the Pope's and my own. And if the above-mentioned arrangement with the Pope were not made, it wouldn't work out for me, and even if I wanted, I couldn't ship the marbles for my own work to Florence and then have to ship them to Rome later, but I

---

[1] Pier Fantini was a doctor who supplied ointment to his patients without charge. The story of Michelangelo's difficulties, torn as he was between conflicting assignments, is told in the Introduction.

would have to come to Rome right away to work, since I am pressed, as I mentioned.

The cost of the façade, in the style in which I propose to have it done and get it under way, including everything, so that the Pope would not have to bother about anything afterwards, cannot be less than thirty-five thousand gold ducats, according to the estimates I have made, and for this I would undertake to do it in six years, with this understanding, that in six months from now I would need another thousand ducats on account for the marbles; and if the Pope does not want to do this, either the expenses I have begun to have here for the above-mentioned work will have to go to my account and loss and I will return the thousand ducats to the Pope, or else he should put someone on it who will follow up the project, since for various reasons I want to get away from here no matter what.

About the price mentioned: at any time after the work is begun, if I should realize it could be done for less, I shall go to the Pope and the Cardinal with so much good faith that I would inform them of it far sooner than as if the loss fell on me; but I expect to do it in such a way that it's far more probable the price will not be adequate.

Master Domenico, please answer me definitely about the state of mind of the Pope and Cardinal, and this will be the greatest favor to me, besides all the others you have done me.

29

(TO DOMENICO BUONINSEGNI IN ROME; FLORENCE, MARCH 1518)

Domenico: The marbles have turned out fine and like the ones suitable for the work at St. Peter's, and are easy to cut out and nearer the shore than the others, that is, in a place called the Corvara; and from this place to the shore there is no outlay for building a road except in the bit of marsh that is near the coast. But when marbles for figures are called for, such as I need, the road will have to be widened from Corvara all the way above Seravezza, about two miles, and for about a mile or less it will have to be all new, that is, it will have to be cut into the mountain with picks up to the point where these marbles can be loaded. So if the Pope won't make arrangements except where needed for his own marbles, that is, the marsh, I have no way to arrange the rest, and wouldn't be able to get the marbles for my work. And if he doesn't do it, I wouldn't be able to check at the same time on the marbles for St. Peter's [sic] as I promised the Cardinal; but if the Pope does it all, I would be able to do everything I had promised.

I have written you all this in other letters. Now you are prudent and wise, and I know you wish me well, so I beg you to arrange the matter with the Cardinal in your own way and answer me quickly, so I can set up an agreement, and if nothing else, go back down there where you are on the old basis. I would not go to Carrara, because I couldn't get the marbles I need in twenty years. Then too I have incurred great enmity there as a result of this business, and I would be forced to get tough if I went back there, as we discussed with each other.

I may inform you that the Board of Works [1] has had designs on this matter of the marbles since they got the news from me, and I believe they have already established prices and imposts and permits, and that the notaries, head notaries, commissioners, and subcommissioners have already

---

1 The Board of Works, in charge of construction for the Cathedral of Florence, was anxious to get some marble for the pavement of the Cathedral.

thought of getting the revenues doubled in that village. So give it thought and do what you can to keep this matter from slipping into their hands, for then it would be harder to get it from them than from Carrara. I beg you to answer quickly what you think I should do and to give the Cardinal my greetings. I am here as his agent, so I shall do nothing but what you write me, because I shall take it to be his intention.

When I write you, if I shouldn't write as correctly as one ought, and if I don't hit upon the main verb sometimes, please excuse me, because I have a jingling in my ears which doesn't let me think what I would like.

Yours, Michelangelo, sculptor, in Florence

30

(T O   H I S   B R O T H E R   B U O N A R R O T O   I N
F L O R E N C E ;   P I E T R A S A N T A ,   A P R I L   1 8 ,   1 5 1 8)
Buonarroto: I learn from your last that the agreement [1] is not yet concluded; it makes me suffer acutely, so that I am sending one of my boys there on purpose, just for this, to stay and see all Thursday whether the agreement is made, and to leave Friday morning and come and give me the answer; and if the agreement is concluded as I asked, I shall follow along with the project; if it is not made all day Thursday, when you write me, I shall nevertheless not deduce that Jacopo Salviati [2] doesn't want to do it, but that he cannot, and I shall mount horse at once and go to find Cardinal Medici and the Pope and tell them my situation, and leave the project and go back to Carrara, which they

---

[1] To make a road from the quarries. The agreement was voted April 22 by the Cathedral Board of Works and the Wool Guild.
[2] Brother-in-law of the Pope and prominent in Florentine affairs, he was helpful to Michelangelo.

pray me to do as one prays to Christ. These stonecutters I
brought from down there [Florence] don't understand the
first thing about quarries or marbles either. They have al-
ready cost me more than a hundred and thirty ducats and
they have not yet quarried me a slab of marble that is any
good, and they go about faking that they have found great
things and try to work for the Board of Works and others
with the money they've received from me. I don't know
what pull they have, but the Pope will hear the whole
thing. Since I have been here, I have thrown away about
three hundred ducats and haven't yet seen anything for
myself. I have taken on the bringing of the dead to life in
wanting to tame these mountains and bring skill into this
countryside, for if the Wool Guild gave me a hundred
ducats a month, besides the marbles, to do what I do, it
would not be doing so badly, not to mention the fact of
their not concluding the agreement with me. So give my
greetings to Jacopo Salviati and write by my boy how the
business goes, so I can take action at once, for it eats me up
to stay here in suspense.

Michelangelo in Pietrasanta

The boats I hired in Pisa never arrived. I think I have been
hoodwinked, and that is how everything goes with me. A
thousand curses on the day and hour I left Carrara! That is
the reason for my ruin—but I shall return there soon. To-
day it is a sin to do good. Give my greetings to Giovanni
da Ricasoli.

31

(TO THE CARDINAL DE' MEDICI IN ROME;
FLORENCE, JULY 15, 1518)

Most Reverend Monsignor: Hoping this year to have some
quantity of marbles for the work on San Lorenzo in Flor-

ence, and not finding suitable rooms for working them in San Lorenzo or nearby outside, I took steps to provide one by buying a piece of land at Santa Caterina from the Cathedral Chapter, which land cost me about three hundred broad ducats in gold, and I have been after the aforesaid Chapter two months to get the said land. They have made me pay sixty ducats more for it than it is worth, showing that they know they are doing wrong, but they say they cannot deviate from what is stated in the bull on selling that they have from the Pope. Now if the Pope makes bulls to license stealing, I beg your most reverend lordship to have still another made for me, because I have more need than they, and if this isn't usually done, I beg you to have them do justice by me in this case, that is, this land that I have taken is not nearly enough for what I need; the Chapter has a certain quantity lying behind it, and so I pray your lordship to have another piece given to me, in which I could recover what they have grabbed from me besides what I bought; and if they have something due them, I want nothing from them.

As for the work, the beginnings are difficult . . .[1]

32

(TO PIETRO URBANO IN THE HOUSE OF MICHELANGELO THE SCULPTOR IN FLORENCE; SERAVEZZA, APRIL 20, 1519)

Pietro: Things have gone very badly, and what has happened is that Saturday morning I started out to have a column hoisted very neatly, and nothing was missing, and after I had hoisted it a hundred feet, one link of the chain

---

[1] This letter was not finished.

that was on the column broke and it went into the river in a hundred pieces. This link Donato had had made by his friend Lazzero the blacksmith, and as far as bearing a load goes, it would have held four columns if it had been sound, and to look at from the outside it seemed past all doubt. After it broke we saw the fraud, for it was not solid inside, and there was no more thickness of iron to hold it than a knife handle, so I am amazed it held as far as it did. All of us who were around were in great danger of life and a wonderful stone was spoiled. Last Carnival I left Donato in charge of these irons, to go to the smithy and choose good and sweet iron; you see how he has treated me. And the casings of the winches that he had made for me were all crushed too in their links in hoisting this column, and almost broken, and they are twice as big as the ones of the Board, so that they would hold an infinite weight if they were good iron. But the iron is raw and bad and worse could not be done, and this is what Donato has fixed up with his friend and sent to the smithy, and he has served me as you see. One must have patience. I shall be here these holidays and begin to work, if it please God. Give my greetings to Francesco Scarfi.

Twentieth of April

Michelangelo in Seravezza

33

(TO CARDINAL BERNARDO DOVIZI IN ROME; FLORENCE, JUNE 1520)

Monsignore: I beg your most reverend lordship, not as a friend or servant, since I do not deserve to be either the one or the other, but as a base, poor, crazy man, that you permit Bastiano [1] the Venetian painter to have some part of the work in the Palace, since Raphael is dead; and if your reverend lordship feels you would be throwing away your favors on somebody like me, I think one can on rare occasions find some enjoyment even in doing a service to madmen, just as one does with onions as a change of diet when one is bored with capons. You make use of worthwhile men daily; may your lordship please to try me in this, and the favor would be very great; and the aforesaid Bastiano is a very good man, and even if it would be thrown away on me, it wouldn't be on Bastiano, for I am sure he would do your lordship honor.

34

(TO HIS FATHER IN SETTIGNANO;
FLORENCE, JUNE 1523)

Lodovico: I shall not answer yours, except for such points as I feel are necessary; the others I thumb my nose at. You say you can't draw your allowance from the Funds because I have had the Funds put in my account. This is not true, and I have to answer you on this so you will know you have been deceived by someone you trust, who may have taken it out and used it himself and given you this account for his own convenience. I have not had the Funds put in my account, and in fact I couldn't do it if I wished; but it is true that, in the presence of Raffaello da Gagliano, the notary said to me: "I wouldn't like your brothers to make some contract about these Funds so that after your father's

---

[1] Sebastiano del Piombo worked closely with Michelangelo, perhaps using his drawings to produce paintings. This letter was given to him to present, and provoked much amusement but no commission.

death you wouldn't get anything"; and he took me to the Funds and had me spend fifteen large ducats and attach a condition that nobody could sell it as long as you lived, and you are the beneficiary during your lifetime, as is stated in the contract you know about.[1]

I have explained the contract to you, in fact I have unmade it to suit you, since you are not happy with it. I have explained about the account in the Funds and you can see it when it suits you; I have always made and unmade as you desired; I no longer know what you want of me. If I bother you by living, you have found the way to take care of that, and you'll get back the key of the treasure you say I have; and you'll be doing the right thing, for all Florence knows you were such a rich man and I have always stolen from you and deserve punishment; you'll get a lot of praise for that. Yell out, and say what you want about me, but don't write me any more, because you keep me from working, for I still have to charge off what you have had from me for the last twenty-five years. I don't like to say it to you, but I can't keep from saying it. Take care of yourself, and watch out for those you have to watch out for, for one does not die more than once, and nobody returns to put right the things done wrong. You have waited unto death to do things like this! God help you.

Michelangelo

---

1 Lodovico was disturbed because a contract had been drawn up on June 22 concerning the money which had been the dowry of his deceased second wife. Under this contract the principal could not be alienated by anyone during Lodovico's lifetime, and thereafter it would be at the disposition of Michelangelo. Raffaello da Gagliano was perhaps a relative of the wife. The whole arrangement had probably been made as a painless way of reimbursing some of Michelangelo's advances to his father and brothers.

(TO MASTER GIOVAN FRANCESCO FATTUCCI
IN ROME; FLORENCE, 1523)

Master Giovanni Francesco: It is now about two years since
I came back from Carrara from letting out bids for quarry-
ing the marble for the tombs for the Cardinal, and when I
went to talk to him about it, he said to me I should some-
how get myself in a good frame of mind to make the afore-
said tombs quickly; I sent him in writing all the methods
for doing it, as you know, who read them; that is, that I
would do it on fixed contract, and by the month and day,
and as a gift, as pleased his lordship, because I wanted to
do them. I was not accepted in any way whatever. Then
when the Cardinal took it up again, I offered to make him
models in wood of the same size the tombs are to be, and
put all the figures in them with clay and wool shearings, of
the size and degree of finish they would have to be, and I
showed him this would be a quick way and not expensive
to do, and that was when we wanted to buy the Caccini
orchard. No outcome, as you know. Then when the Car-
dinal was going to Lombardy, I went to call on him as soon
as I heard it, because I wished to serve him. He told me I
should rush the marbles and find men and do as much as
I could, so that he would find something done without ask-
ing him for anything further, and that if he lived he would
do the façade too, and that he was leaving the order for all
the money that would be needed with Domenico Buonin-
segni. When the Cardinal had left, I wrote Domenico
Buoninsegni all these things he had said to me and told
him how I was prepared to do everything the Cardinal de-
sired, and of this I kept a copy and wrote it with witnesses,
so that everyone could tell it wasn't all my doing. Do-
menico came to call on me at once and told me he had no

commission whatever and that if I wanted anything I should write the Cardinal. I told him I did not want anything. At last, on the Cardinal's return, Figiovanni told me he had asked for me. I went there at once, surmising he wanted to talk about the tombs; he said to me: "We really do want there to be something good in these tombs, that is, something by your hand." And he did not say he wanted me to make them. I took my leave and said I would come back to talk to him when the marbles were there.

Now you know how in Rome the Pope [1] has been informed about this tomb of Julius, and how a *motu proprio* has been issued for him to sign to proceed against me and to ask back from me whatever I have received for the aforesaid work, and damages and interest, and you know how the Pope said this was to be done if Michelangelo did not want to make the tomb. So I shall have to do it if I don't want to get into trouble, as you see it is ordained. And now if the Cardinal Medici again wants me to do the tombs of San Lorenzo, as you tell me, you see I cannot, if he doesn't free me from this Rome business; and if he does free me, I promise to work for him at no cost whatever for my whole life; not that I ask to be liberated so as not to do the tomb of Julius, for I do it willingly, but to serve him, and if he doesn't want to free me and wants something from my hand in the said tombs, I shall try my best, while I am working on the tomb of Julius, to take time to do something that may please him.

---

1 Adrian VI was Pope briefly between Leo X and Clement VII.

36

Master Giovan Francesco: You inquire of me in one of yours how my affairs stand as to Pope Julius. I tell you, if I could ask for damages and interest, I'd more likely expect to have something to gain than something to give. Because when he sent for me in Florence, which I think was the second year of his pontificate, I had taken on half of the Council Chamber of Florence, I mean to paint it, for which I was getting three thousand ducats, and the cartoon [1] was already done, as is known to all Florence, so that I felt they were half earned. And of the twelve apostles that I still had to do for the Cathedral one was roughly cut, as is still to be seen, and I had already acquired the larger part of the blocks of marble. And when Pope Julius took me away from here I got nothing from either the one or the other. Then when I was in Rome with the aforesaid Pope Julius and he commissioned his tomb from me, into which a thousand ducats' worth of marble went, he had me paid and sent me to Carrara for it, where I stayed eight months getting the marble rough cut, and brought nearly all of it on to St. Peter's Square, and part stayed at Ripa. When I had finished paying for the transport of the aforesaid marble, and having used up the money I had received for the aforesaid work, I furnished the house I had on St. Peter's Square with beds and household goods on my own, in the expectation of the tomb, and had apprentices who are still living come from Florence to work, and gave them money of my own in advance. At this time Pope Julius changed his notions and no longer wanted it done, and I,

---

[1] *The Battle of Pisa.* See Introduction.

not knowing this, going to ask him for money, was driven out of the room, and because of this slight I left Rome at once, and what I had in the house was injured and the aforesaid marble I had brought stayed in St. Peter's Square up to the election of Pope Leo, and things went badly in every direction. Among the other things that I can prove, two pieces each of nine feet were taken from me, from Ripa, by Agostino Chigi, which had cost me more than fifty gold ducats, and they could be reimbursed because there are witnesses. But to return to the marble: from the time I went for it and that I stayed at Carrara, until I was driven out of the Palace, more than a year went by, for which time I never got anything, and invested several tens of ducats.

Then, the first time Pope Julius went to Bologna, I had perforce to go there with my neck in a halter to ask his pardon, whereupon he had me make the figure of himself in bronze, which was fourteen feet high seated. When he asked me how much it would cost, I answered him I thought it could be cast for a thousand ducats, but it was not my art, and I did not want to commit myself; he answered: "Go on, work and cast it as many times as is needed until it comes out, and we will give you what will make you happy." To make it short, it was cast twice, and at the end of the two years I stayed there I found myself four and a half ducats ahead. And in recompense for this time I never had anything more, and all I spent was from the thousand ducats I said it would take to cast it, which were paid out to me on several occasions by Master Antonio Maria da Legiame, a Bolognese.

When the figure was set up on the façade of San Petronio and I returned to Rome, Pope Julius still did not want me to make the tomb, and having put me to painting the Sistine Ceiling, we made a contract for three thousand ducats. And the first design for the aforesaid work was twelve apostles in the lunettes, and the remainder a certain division into parts filled with ornaments in the usual way.

Then when I had begun the aforesaid work, I felt it would turn out a poor thing, and told the Pope how I felt it would turn out a poor thing in doing the apostles only. He asked me why; I told him, because they were poor too. Then he gave me a new commission to do whatever I wished, and he would make me happy, and I should paint down to the stories painted below. At this time, when the vault was almost finished, the Pope went back to Bologna, so that I went there twice for the money I was to have and did nothing, and lost all that time until I returned to Rome. When I got back to Rome, I set myself to making cartoons for the aforesaid work, that is, for the heads and faces around the aforesaid Chapel of Sixtus, hoping to get money and finish the work. I could never obtain anything, and one day, complaining to Master Bernardo da Bibbiena and to Attalante [1] how I couldn't stay in Rome any longer and would have to go in God's name, Master Bernardo told Attalante to remind him, because he wanted to have money given to me no matter what. And he had two thousand cameral ducats given to me, which, with the first thousand for the blocks of marble, are the ones they are charging to my account for the tomb; and I considered that more was due to me for the time lost and the works done. And out of the aforesaid money, since Master Bernardo and Attalante had restored me to life, I gave one a hundred ducats and the other fifty.

---

[1] Bibbiena, later a Cardinal, was a high functionary in the area of works and maintenance; Attalante was a supervisor of the construction of St. Peter's.

Then came the death of Pope Julius, and at one time in the early days of Leo, Cardinal Aginensis [1] wished to have his tomb enlarged, that is, make a bigger work than the design I had made before, and so a contract was made. And when I did not want the three thousand ducats I had received put against the charges for the tomb, proving that much more was due me, Aginensis told me I was a cheat.

37

(T O   P O P E   C L E M E N T   V I I   I N   R O M E ;
F L O R E N C E ,   1 5 2 4)

Most Blessed Father: Because go-betweens are oftentimes the cause of great disputes, I have therefore made bold without any such to write your Holiness about the tombs here at San Lorenzo. I say I don't know which is better, the harm that helps or the good that hurts. I am certain, mad and evil as I am, that if I had been allowed to go on as I had begun, all the marbles for the aforesaid work would be in Florence today, properly rough-cut and with less expense than there has been up to now, and would be a marvelous thing, like the others I have brought there.

Now I see the affair going on and on and don't know how it will end. I therefore offer your Holiness my excuses in case something should happen that doesn't please you; since I have no authority, I don't feel I am to blame for it, and I beg you, if you want me to do something, not to put men over my head in my own art, but have trust in me and give me a free hand, and you will see what I will do and what account of myself I will render to you.

Turning to the lantern of the chapel of the aforesaid

---

[1] Cardinal Lionardo Grosso della Rovere, a nephew of Julius II.

San Lorenzo here, Stefano has finished putting it up and unveiled it, and it pleased everyone without exception, and so I hope it will your Holiness when you see it. We are making the ball that goes there about two feet high, and it occurred to me to vary it from the others by making it polygonal, and so it is being done.

Your Holiness' servant
Michelangelo, sculptor, in Florence

38

(TO GIOVAN FRANCESCO FATTUCCI
IN ROME; FLORENCE, JULY 1524)

Master Giovan Francesco: In accordance with your last, I went to find Spina to find out whether he had an order to pay for the Library as well as the tombs, and seeing he doesn't, I have not begun the aforesaid work, as you instruct me, because it can't be done without money, and if it is to be done anyway, I beg you to arrange there to have Spina paid here, because no man more suitable could be found, or one who would do such a thing with more love and grace.

As for beginning to work, it is necessary to wait for the marbles to come, and I don't think they will ever come, considering how it's been managed! I would have things to write that would stagger you, but I wouldn't be believed; enough that it's my ruin, because if I were further ahead with my work than I am, perhaps the Pope would straighten out my business,[1] and I would be quit of all my troubles, but he who straightens has a far harder job than he who spoils. Yesterday I came across someone who told

---

[1] The tomb of Pope Julius.

me I'd better go and pay, otherwise I'd be subject to penalties at the end of this month. I did not think there were other penalties than either hell or a fine of two ducats, even if I set up a factory in the silk trade or the goldbeater's and put the balance out to usury. We have paid taxes in Florence for three hundred years; if only I had once been a client of the Proconsul! [1] And still payment must be made. Everything will be taken from me, since I have no means to pay, and I shall come there. If the affair had been straightened out for me, I would have sold something and invested in the Funds and thus paid the taxes, and could still stay in Florence.

39

(TO GIOVANNI SPINA;
FLORENCE, AUGUST 29, 1524)

Giovanni: After I left you yesterday, I kept thinking over my affairs, and seeing how much the Pope has this work on San Lorenzo at heart and how much his Holiness presses me, and since he has spontaneously offered a good salary to me, so that it will be easier for me to serve him more speedily, and seeing that not to take it delays me, and that I would have no excuse at all for not serving him, I have changed my mind, and where up to now I did not ask for it, I now do ask for it, with the thought that it is much better for a number of reasons that there is no point in writing, and most of all in order to return to the house at San Lorenzo that you have taken and settle down there like a respectable man, for not to return there causes talk and does me a good deal of damage. So I would like you to give

---

1 The Rector of the Guild of Judges and Notaries.

me that amount of salary that is due me from the day it was ordered for me up to now, and if you have authority to do it, please say so to Antonio Mini who is working for me, the bearer of this, and when you want me to come for it.

Copy made on the day of St. John's beheading, 1524.

40

(TO GIOVANNI SPINA IN FLORENCE; FLORENCE, APRIL 19, 1525)

Giovanni: As to the tomb of Pope Julius, I feel that a power of attorney should not be sent, because I don't want to go to law. No lawsuit can be brought against me if I confess to being in the wrong. I consider that I have gone to law and lost and have to pay up, and thus I am disposed to do if I can. So if the Pope wants to help me in this matter, which would be a very great pleasure to me, seeing that I cannot finish the aforesaid tomb of Julius either because of old age or poor bodily health, he as the middleman might show a desire for me to refund what I have received for making it, so that I can be rid of this charge, and for the relatives of the aforesaid Pope Julius to be able with this repayment to have it made by whomsoever they wish; and thus his Holiness our Lord can help me considerably, and also in this: that I may be required to pay back as little as possible while still not being unreasonable, getting some of my points accepted, such as the one about the Pope at Bologna and time lost otherwise without any payment, as Master Giovan Francesco [Fattucci] knows, who is informed about it all. And as soon as it is made plain what I have to pay back, I shall take stock of what I have, and sell and do things in such a way that I shall make the re-

payment and be able to think about the Pope's business,
and work; for as things stand I am not living, much less
working. And there could be no solution adopted that
would be surer for me or more precious, or that would
lighten my mind more, and it can be done with love and
without going to law. And I pray God it will be the Pope's
will to straighten it out in this way, because I don't feel it
is anyone's responsibility. And so, please, write to Master
Jacopo, and write in the way you know best, so that the
matter will go forward and I can work.

Copy of a memorandum I made for Giovanni Spina, for
him to write to Rome.

April 19, 1525
                    Michelangelo, sculptor, in Florence

41

(TO SEBASTIANO DEL PIOMBO IN ROME;
FLORENCE, MAY 1525)

Dearest Sebastiano: Last night our friend Captain Cuio
and certain other gentlemen, in their courtesy, wished me
to go with them to dinner, from which I had the greatest
pleasure, because I came out of my melancholy a bit, or
rather out of my madness, and I not only enjoyed the din-
ner, which was very pleasant, but also, and much more
than that, the discussions that took place. And then in the
discussions my pleasure increased still more hearing your
name mentioned by the aforesaid Captain Cuio, and that
was not all; indeed, I was then made still more, in fact in-
finitely happy about the art when I heard the aforesaid
Captain say you were unique in the world and so held to
be in Rome. So if there could have been any more happi-
ness I would have had still more. Hence, seeing my judg-

ment is not false, don't deny to me any more that you are unique when I write you so, because I have too many witnesses, and there is a picture which, by the grace of God, confirms my opinion to all who see the light.

42

(TO MASTER GIOVAN FRANCESCO FATTUCCI IN ROME; FLORENCE, SEPTEMBER 4, 1525)

Master Giovan Francesco: I have written there [to Rome] on previous occasions that since I have to serve Pope Clement on matters that will take a long time to finish, and since I am old, I have no hope of doing anything else, and therefore since I cannot do the tomb of Julius, if I have to indemnify for what I have received, I wish to do so not in labor but rather in money, since I wouldn't have time. I don't know how else to answer you, because I am not up with the facts and don't understand the details in which you are involved. As for doing the tomb of Julius against the wall like that of Pius, I like it, and it is a shorter job than any other method. Nothing else occurs to me except to tell you this: that you should leave my business as it stands, and your own too, and come back, because I understand the plague is returning with great violence, and I would rather have you alive than my business settled; so come back. If I die before the Pope, I shall not need to settle anything any more; if I live, I am sure the Pope will settle it, if not now then another time; so come back. I spent yesterday evening with your mother and advised her, in the presence of Granacci and Giovanni the turner, that she should make you come back.

September 4, 1525

Your Michelangelo in Florence

43

Master Giovan Francesco: If I had as much strength as I have happiness from your last, I believe I could carry out all the things you write me, and swiftly; but since I do not have so much, I shall do what I can.

As to the colossus eighty feet high that you inform me of, which has to go or, rather, is to be put on the corner of the loggia of the Medici garden opposite Master Luigi della Stufa's corner, I have thought about it, and not a little, as you tell me; and it seems to me it doesn't go well on the aforesaid corner, because it would take up too much of the street; but on the other, where the barber shop is, it would turn out much better in my opinion, because it has the square in front and wouldn't disturb the street so much. And since maybe removing the aforesaid shop will not be tolerated, for the sake of the income, I thought the aforesaid figure might be made seated, and the seat might be made high enough so the barber shop would go underneath, by making the aforesaid work hollow inside, since it is most appropriate to make it in pieces, and the rent would not be lost. And also, since the aforesaid shop ought to have a way to expel the smoke, as it does now, I feel the aforesaid statue should have a horn of plenty in its hand, hollow inside, which would serve it for a chimney. Then, since I would have the head of the figure hollow inside like the other members, I think some use ought to be got out of that too, since there is a shopkeeper here on the square, a great friend of mine, who has told me in secret he would make a fine dovecote inside. Then too another notion occurs to me that would be much better, but the figure would have to be made much bigger, and it could be done, since a tower is made up of pieces, and this is that the head could serve as a bell tower for San Lorenzo, which badly needs one, and if the bells were stowed inside and the sound came out of the mouth, the aforesaid colossus would seem to be crying mercy, and especially on feast days when the ringing is more frequent and with bigger bells.

As for getting the marble blocks brought for the outside of the said statue, and to keep anybody from knowing, I feel they should be brought at night and well shrouded, so they won't be seen. There will be a little danger at the gate, and for this we can take measures; at worst there is always the Sangallo gate, which keeps ajar until daylight.[1]

As for doing or not doing the things that are to be done, which you say must be suspended, it is better to let them be done by whoever has to do them, for I shall have so much to do I don't care to do more. For me this will be enough, so long as it is something honorable.

I'm not answering you on all matters, since Spina is coming to Rome soon and will do better by word of mouth than I with the pen, and more in detail.

Your Michelangelo, sculptor, in Florence

44

(MASTER GIOVAN FRANCESCO IN ROME; FLORENCE, OCTOBER 24, 1525)

Master Giovan Francesco: To your last; the four figures that were begun are not finished yet, and there is still a

---

[1] A papal functionary answered this on December 23 with the remark, "About the statue to be made, his Holiness would have you to understand it is the truth and not a joke, and he wishes it to be made." But nothing more came of it.

lot to be done on them. The other four, for rivers, are not
begun, because the marbles are not here, and yet they have
arrived. I do not write you how because it is not to the
point. On the matter of Julius, I am glad to make a tomb
like that of Pius in St. Peter's, as you wrote me, and I shall
have it done here little by little, one thing now and one
later, and pay for it from my own pocket, provided that I
have the salary and keep the house, as you wrote me, that
is, the house where I lived in Rome with the marbles and
the things that are in it, that is to say, provided I shall not
have to give them, I mean the heirs of Pope Julius, any-
thing in order to be freed from his tomb out of what I have
received up to now, except the aforesaid tomb, like that of
Pius in St. Peter's; and a reasonable time may be set for
doing it, and I shall make the figures with my own hand;
and as long as my salary is given me as mentioned, I shall
not cease to work for Pope Clement with such power as I
have, which is little because I am old; and this also, that
I am not to be treated to the sneers I see being directed at
me, because they have a great effect on me and have not let
me do anything I wanted for some months past; for one
cannot work one thing with one's hand and another with
one's brain, especially in marble. Here it is said these things
are done to spur me on, and I say to you it's bad spurs that
make you turn backward. I have not had my salary for a
year past, and I'm fighting poverty; I'm very much alone
with my worries, which are many, and which keep me
busier than my art, because I can't keep anybody to look
after me, since I don't have the means.

This is the copy of the letter that Michelangelo, sculp-
tor, has today this October 24, 1525, sent to Pope Clement,
and I, Antonio di Bernardo Mini, have made this copy
with my own hand.

45

(TO MASTER GIOVAN FRANCESCO FATTUCCI
IN ROME; FLORENCE, APRIL 1526)

Master Giovan Francesco: This coming week I shall have the sacristy figures that are rough-hewn covered up, because I want to leave the sacristy free for these marble cutters, since I want them to begin to install the other tomb opposite the one that is installed, which is completely cut, or almost. And during this time that they are installing it, I thought the vault might be made, and I thought with a lot of hands it would be done in two or three months; I am not an expert. After this coming week our Lord can send Master Giovanni da Udine at his convenience, if he thinks it is to be done now, since I shall be ready.

As regards the entrance hall, this week four columns have been installed, and one was previously. The tabernacles will be a little behind; but still in four months from now I think it will be finished. The ceiling would be begun now but the linden wood is still not good; they will hurry the seasoning as much as possible.

I work as much as possible, and in two weeks I shall have the other Captain begun; then of the important things only the four rivers will be left. The four figures on the sarcophagi, the four figures on the ground that are the rivers, the two Captains,[1] and Our Lady that goes on the tomb at the head of the chapel are the figures I would wish to make with my own hand; of these I have begun six, and I have energy enough to do them in a reasonable time and meanwhile have the others done that are not so important. Nothing else occurs to me; give my greetings to Giovanni Spina and ask him to write a little to Figiovanni and ask

---

[1] The famous seated statues of Lorenzo and Giuliano de' Medici.

him not to pull off the carters and send them to Pescia, because we shall be left without stone, and also not to bewitch the stonecutters so as to make them like him, by saying to them: "Those others have little consideration for you, making you work until evening, now that the night comes at the second hour [after sunset]."

It's hard for us to make one of them work with a hundred eyes, and even that one is spoiled by somebody being soft-hearted. Patience! May God not make displeasing to me what is not displeasing to him.

46

(TO MASTER GIOVAN FRANCESCO FATTUCCI IN ROME; FLORENCE, NOVEMBER 1, 1526)

Master Giovan Francesco: I know Spina has written there very warmly in the last few days about my affairs in the matter of Julius. If he did wrong, considering the times in which we are, it was I who urgently begged him to write. Perhaps suffering has made me tactless. In recent days I had news of what is being said there of my affairs, which made me very fearful, and that was of the ill will that the relatives of Julius have toward me and not without reason, and how a lawsuit is under way and they are asking damages and interest from me in a fashion that a hundred of my condition could not meet. This has put me in great distress and makes me consider what I would do if the Pope failed me, for I could not live in this world. And this was the reason why I had the letter written, as mentioned. Now I don't want a thing except what the Pope may please; I know he doesn't want me ruined or attacked. I have seen the building activity slowing down here and I see expenditures are being publicly reduced, and that a rented house for me at

San Lorenzo and my salary are both being kept, which is no little expense. If it worked out well to cut these too and give me permission to begin something for the aforesaid tomb of Julius either here or there, I would be very glad, because I long more to get out of this obligation than to go on living. Nonetheless, I am not ever going to depart from the Pope's wish, so long as I understand it. So I beg you, when you have learned my attitude, write me the Pope's wish, and I shall not depart from it, and I beg you get it from him and write it to me on his behalf, so I can obey better and with more love, and also so that I could one day justify myself with your letters if the point should come up.

Nothing else occurs to me. If I don't know how to write what you will know how to understand, don't be surprised, for I have completely lost my mind. You know my attitude; you will know what is to be obeyed. Answer, I beg you.

November 1, 1526

> *Yours, Michelangelo, sculptor, at San Lorenzo,*
> *Florence*

47

(TO MY DEAR FRIEND BATTISTA DELLA PALLA IN FLORENCE; VENICE, SEPTEMBER 25, 1529)

My very dear friend Battista: I left there, as I think you know, to go to France, and when I got to Venice I inquired about the route and was told that going from here one must pass through German territory and that it is difficult and dangerous to pass. So I thought I would find out from you, if you will, whether you still have in mind to go, and

request you, and so I do request you, to let me know, and
where you want me to wait for you, and we will go to-
gether. I left without saying a word to any of my friends
and in great confusion, and although, as you know, I
wanted in any case to go to France and had asked permis-
sion several times but had not received it, that was not
however because I had not made up my mind to see the
war end first. But Tuesday morning, September 21, some-
one came out from the gate of San Niccolo where I was at
the bastions and spoke in my ear that I shouldn't stay any
longer if I wanted to save my life; and he came with me to
my house and dined there, and brought me horses, and
never left me until I was out of Florence, showing me that
it was my best course. Whether it was God or the Devil I
don't know.

I beg you to answer the first part of the letter as soon as
you can, because I am eager to go. And if you no longer
have a fancy to go, still I beg you to inform me, so I can
arrange to go by myself as best I can.

Yours, Michelangelo Buonarroti

48

(TO SEBASTIANO DEL PIOMBO IN ROME;
ROME, JUNE 26, 1531)

My dear Sebastiano: I bother you too much; bear it in
peace, and think you will have more glory in raising the
dead than in making figures that seem alive. About the
tomb of Julius I have thought many times, as you write
me I should, and it seems to me there are two ways to get
free of it; one is to do it, and the other is to give them the
money so they may have it done on their own; and of these
two ways neither is to be selected except the one that

pleases the Pope. My doing it, according to me, will not please the Pope, because I could not attend to his affairs, so it would be a question of persuading them—I mean those in charge of the matter for Julius—to take the money and have it done themselves. I would give drawings and models and whatever they wanted, with the blocks of marble that are carved. Adding two thousand ducats, I believe a fine tomb would be produced, and there are young men who would do it better than I would. If this last way were chosen, of giving them the money to have it done, I could pay them a thousand gold ducats now, and somehow the other thousand later, so long as they decide on something that pleases the Pope, and when they are all ready to put this last into effect, I'll write by what means the other thousand ducats can be raised, which I think will not displease them.

I do not write you about my condition in detail, because there is no point; only I tell you this, that three thousand ducats I took to Venice became, when I got back to Florence, fifty, and the City took about fifteen hundred from me.[1] So I can do no more, but ways will be found; and so I hope, seeing the favor the Pope promises me. Sebastiano, dear companion, I stand firm on these arrangements and beg you to get to the bottom of it.

49

(TO HIS BROTHER GIOVANSIMONE
IN SETTIGNANO; FLORENCE, 1533)
Giovansimone: Mona Margarita did not understand properly; in talking the other day of you and Gismondo, with

---

[1] As a fine for leaving the city without permission.

Master Giovan Francesco present, I said I had always done more for you than for myself and suffered many discomforts so you would not suffer them, and you had never done anything but speak evil all over Florence. This is what I said, and for your sake I would it were not true! For you have got yourselves the reputation of beasts. As for staying there, I am delighted to have you stay there and take your ease and attend to getting well, for I shall never fail in what I can, since I consider my obligations and not your words. I would be glad if you would make arrangements to sleep there, so that Mona Margarita could stay there too; and since my father at his death commended her to me, I shall never forget her.

50

(TO FEBO DI POGGIO;[1]
FLORENCE, DECEMBER 1533)

Febo: Although you feel the greatest hate for me, I don't know why; I don't really think it's due to the love I feel for you, but rather to other people's words, which you shouldn't believe, since you have tested me; however, I can't resist writing you this. I leave tomorrow and go to Pescia to find the Cardinal di Cesis and Master Baldassare; I shall go as far as Pisa with them, then to Rome, and I shall not come back here again, and I am letting you know that as long as I live I shall always be at your service with faith and love, more than any other friend you have in the world.

I pray God He will open your eyes in another way, so

---

1 Who Febo di Poggio was is not known. His reply to this letter asks Michelangelo for money and says: "I could not be angry with you, since I regard you in the place of a father."

you will realize that he who wishes your good more than his own health knows how to love, and not to hate as an enemy.

51

(TO MASTER TOMMASO CAVALIERI
IN ROME; FLORENCE, 1533)

I started to write to your lordship, very inconsiderately, and in my presumption I was the first to make a move, as if I had to do it as owing an answer to one from you; and later I realized my error all the more, when I read and savored yours, through your courtesy; and you seem to me so far from being only just born, as you write me in it, that you have been in the world a thousand other times, and I label myself as not born or else born dead, and I would have said, to the distress of earth and Heaven, were it not that in yours I had seen and believed that your lordship willingly accepted some of my works, which made me no less greatly marvel than delight. And if it is really true that you feel within as you write me outwardly, as to your judging my works, if it should happen that one of them as I wish should please you, I shall much sooner call it lucky than good. Not to bore you, I shall write no further. Many things fitting for an answer are left in my pen, but our friend Pierantonio, who I know will be able and want to supply what I lack, will finish orally.

It would be permissible to name to the one receiving them the things that a man gives, but out of nicety it will not be done here.

52

(TO MASTER TOMMASO CAVALIERI
IN ROME; FLORENCE, 1533)

My dear lord: If I had not believed that I had made you sure of the very great, rather, the immeasurable, love I bear you, I would not have thought it strange or wondered at the great suspicion you show in yours that you had of my not writing you, that I might forget you. But it is nothing new or to be amazed about, since everything else goes by contraries, that this should go backwards too, because what your lordship says to me, I should have to say to you; but perhaps you do it to tempt me or to rekindle a new and greater fire, if a greater can be; but be it as it will, I know well that I can forget your name in the same hour when I forget the food I live on; rather, I can sooner forget the food I live on, which only nourishes my body unhappily, than your name, which nourishes body and soul, filling both with such sweetness, that I can feel neither pain nor fear of death as long as memory preserves it to me. Think, if the eye too had its part as well, in what state I would be.

53

(TO MASTER PIETRO ARETINO[1]
IN VENICE; ROME, SEPTEMBER 1537)

Lord Master Pietro, my lord and brother: In receiving your letter I felt joy and sorrow together; I was overjoyed in its coming from you, who are unique in the world in talent, and still I was very sad, because since I have finished a large part of the composition, I cannot put your conception

---

1 This notorious pamphleteer and blackmailer had proposed a plan for the composition of *The Last Judgment.*

into effect, which is put forward in such a way that, if the
Day of Judgment had taken place and you had seen it in
actuality, your words would not have reported it better.
Now to answer as to your writing about me, I may state
that I would not only be glad, but beg you to do it, since
kings and emperors consider it the highest honor to be
named by your pen. In the meantime if I have anything
that takes your fancy, I offer it to you with all my heart.
And finally, don't alter your attitude that you don't want
to travel to Rome, just to see the painting I am doing; that
would be too much. Greetings.

Michelangelo Buonarroti

54

(TO HIS NEPHEW LIONARDO BUONARROTI
IN FLORENCE; ROME, JULY 1540)

Lionardo: I received three shirts with your letter and was
much amazed that you sent them to me, since they are so
coarse that there is not a single peasant here who wouldn't
be ashamed to wear them, and even if they had been fine,
I wouldn't have wanted you to send them to me, because
when I need them I shall send the money to buy some.
About the farm at Pozzolatico, in two or three weeks I shall
have Bonifazio Fazi there paid seven hundred ducats to
buy it back, but first it must be seen what sort of security
Michele [1] will give you, so that your sister can get back the
dowry she has given in case anything should happen. So
talk about it a little with Gismondo and answer me, be-
cause if I don't find the seven hundred ducats are secure,

---

[1] Husband of Lionardo's sister. For dowry Michelangelo gave her a
farm, which he is now buying back.

I shall not buy it back. Nothing else occurs to me. Encourage Mona Margarita to be of good cheer; and as for you, treat her well in word and deed, and be a good fellow; otherwise I am letting you know you will enjoy nothing of mine.

55

(TO MASTER NICCOLO MARTELLI
IN FLORENCE; ROME, JANUARY 20, 1542)
Master Niccolo: I have a letter of yours from Master Vincenzo Perini, with two sonnets and a madrigal. The letter and the sonnet addressed to me are a miraculous thing, so much so that no one could be so correct as to find anything in them to correct. It is true they give me such praises that if I had Heaven in my breast many less would be enough. I see you have imagined that I am what God wished I would be. I am a poor man of little worth, who keeps laboring in the art God gave me, to prolong my life as far as I can; and such as I am, I am your servant and that of the whole house of Martelli, and I thank you for the letter and the sonnets, but not to the extent that I am in your debt, since I am unequal to such high courtesy.
Rome, January 20, 1542
Michelangelo Buonarroti

56

(TO MASTER LUIGI DEL RICCIO,
OCTOBER 1542)
Master Luigi, dear friend: I am much urged by Master Pier Giovanni[1] to begin to paint; I don't think I shall be

---

[1] The Bishop of Forli, nicknamed by Michelangelo My Lord Busybody.

able to for four or six days yet, because the plaster is not dry enough to allow starting. But there is another thing that bothers me more than the plaster, and which keeps me from living, let alone painting, and that is the endorsement that doesn't come, and I know I am only being given fine words to the point where I am in great despair. I have drawn a thousand and four hundred scudi out of my heart, which I could have used to work for seven years and have made two tombs, not one merely, and I did this so as to be able to be at peace and serve the Pope with all my heart. Now I find myself without the money and with more disputes and troubles than ever. What I did about the aforesaid money I did with the consent of the Duke [of Urbino] and with a contract that would set me free, and now I have paid the money the endorsement does not come, so you can see clearly what this matter means, without putting it down in writing. Enough; for the trust of thirty-six years and for giving myself freely to others I deserve nothing else; painting and sculpture, labor and trust have ruined me, and it's still going from bad to worse. It would have been better if in my early years I had set myself to making matches, for then I would not be suffering so! I write this to your lordship so that as one who wishes me well and has managed the matter and knows the truth, you will make it clear to the Pope, so he may be aware that I cannot live, let alone paint; and if I raised hopes of getting started, I did so with the hope of the aforesaid endorsement, which should have been here a month ago. I don't want to live under this burden any more, nor be vituperated daily as a cheat by those who have taken my life and honor from me. Only death or the Pope can free me from it.

Your Michelangelo Buonarroti

57

Monsignor: Your Lordship sends to tell me that I should
paint and have no doubts. I answer that painting is done
with the brain, not the hands; and one who cannot
have his brains about him dishonors himself, so until my
affairs are straight I can do nothing that is good. The en-
dorsement of the last contract doesn't come, and because
the other, made under Clement, is in force, I am stoned
every day as if I had crucified Christ. I say that I did not
understand that the aforesaid contract was read in the
presence of Clement in the same form as the copy I re-
ceived afterwards; and this was because when Clement sent
me to Florence the same day, the Ambassador Gianmaria
da Modena was with the notary and had it written out in
the way he wanted, so that when I got back and received
it, I found a thousand ducats more in it than there was
left, I found the house where I live included in it, and a
hundred other barbs fit to ruin me, and that Clement
would never have stood for; and Fra Sebastiano can be wit-
ness, who wanted me to let the Pope know about it and get
the notary hung; I did not wish that, because I was not
committed to do anything I could not have done if I had
been allowed. I swear I have no knowledge of having had
the money the aforesaid contract states, and that Gian-
maria said he found I had had. But assume I had had it,
since I admitted it, and cannot get out of the contract, and
that I had more money besides, if more is found; and let
a heap be made of all those things, and then see what I

---

[1] This eloquent plea was sent to one of the Cardinals.

have done for Pope Julius in Bologna, Florence, and Rome, in bronze, marble, and painting, and all the time I stayed with him, which was as long as he was Pope, and see what I deserve. I say that in good conscience, according to the salary Pope Paul gives me, I should be getting five thousand scudi from the heirs of Pope Julius. I say this besides, that if I got the price I did for my labors for Pope Julius, it is my fault for not having known how to manage myself, for if it were not for what Pope Paul has given me, I would die of hunger today. And according to these ambassadors, it seems I have enriched myself and robbed the altar, and they make a great noise; and I would know how to make them quiet but I'm not up to it. Gianmaria, the Ambassador in the old Duke's time, told me, after the above contract was made in Clement's presence, when I got back from Florence and began to work on the tomb of Julius, that if I wanted to do the Duke a great pleasure, I should go away in God's name, for he felt no concern over the tomb, but was much annoyed that I served Pope Paul. Then I realized he was the one who had put the house in the contract, to make me go away and get so violently angry about it, in the way we see with those who, for their masters, set traps and shame their enemies. This man who has come now first hunted out what I had in Florence, as if he wanted to see in what stage the tomb was. I find I have lost all my youth bound to this tomb, defending it as much as I could with Pope Leo and Clement, and my too great trust that I didn't want to admit has ruined me. So my fortune wills it! I see many lying in bed with two and three thousand scudi of income, and I with the greatest labor figure out how to grow poor.

But to get back to the painting, I can deny nothing to Pope Paul; I shall paint while I'm unhappy and make unhappy things. I have written this to your lordship so that when it happens, you can the better tell the Pope the truth, and I should be very glad too for the Pope to know it, to know of what stuff this war is made that is waged against me. Let him who has understanding understand.

Your lordship's servant Michelangelo

Further things to say come to mind; and that is, that this Ambassador says I lent Pope Julius' money at usury and got rich from it, as if Pope Julius had counted me out eight thousand ducats in advance. The money I had for the tomb signifies the expenses incurred for the aforesaid tomb at that time; it will be seen that it is near the sum that the contract made in Clement's time would give, because in the first year of Julius I stayed in Carrara eight months to excavate marble and bring it to St. Peter's Square, where I had the rooms behind Santa Caterina; then Pope Julius no longer wanted to make the tomb during his lifetime and set me to painting; then he kept me two years in Bologna to make the bronze pope that was destroyed; then I returned to Rome and stayed with him until his death, keeping my house always open, without help or salary, always living on the tomb money, because I had no other income. Then after the aforesaid death of Julius, Aginensis wanted to continue the aforesaid tomb, but as a larger thing, so I brought the marbles to Macello de' Corvi and had that part carved which is installed in San Pietro in Vincoli, and made the figures I have in my house. At this time, since Pope Leo did not want me to make the aforesaid tomb, he pretended to want to make the façade of San Lorenzo in Florence and asked Aginensis for me, with the result that he gave me permission perforce, on condition I would make the aforesaid tomb of Pope Julius while in Florence. Then, while I was in Florence for the aforesaid façade of San

Lorenzo, since I had no marbles there for the tomb of Julius, I returned to Carrara and stayed there thirteen months, and brought all the marbles for the aforesaid tomb to Florence and built a room there to make it, and began to work. At this time Aginensis sent Master Francesco Palavicini, who is now the Bishop of Aleria, to press me on, and he saw the room and all the aforesaid marbles and figures roughed out for the aforesaid tomb, which are still there today. Seeing this, that is, that I was working for the aforesaid tomb, the Medici who was living in Florence, who was afterwards Pope Clement, did not let me continue; and thus I was left in frustration until Medici became Clement, whereupon in his presence there was made the last contract for the aforesaid tomb up to this present one, in which it was set down that I had received the eight thousand ducats they say I have lent at usury. And I want to confess a sin to your lordship, that, being at Carrara when I stayed there thirteen months for the aforesaid tomb and lacking money, I spent a thousand ducats for the marbles of the aforesaid work that Pope Leo had sent me for the façade of San Lorenzo, or rather to keep me busy; and I wrote him inventing some difficulties, and this I did for the love I bore that work, for which I am paid by being told I am a thief and usurer by ignoramuses who were not even alive then.

I write your lordship this story because I want very much to justify myself with you, almost as much as with the Pope, to whom such evil things are spoken of me, Master Piergiovanni writes me, that he has to defend me, he says; and again, when your lordship sees it possible to say a word in my defense, do so, because I write the truth; among men, I do not say God, I consider myself a decent man, because I never deceived anyone; and again because, sometimes, to defend oneself from good-for-nothings one must turn mad, as you see.

I beg your lordship, when you have extra time, read this story, and keep it for me, and know that there are still witnesses of a great part of what is written. Again, if the Pope should see it, I would be very much pleased, and for all the world to see it, because I write the truth and far less than the actual facts, and I am not a usurious thief, but a Florentine citizen, noble, and son of an honest man, and not from Cagli.[1]

After I had written, I had a delegation from the Ambassador of Urbino, saying that if I want the endorsement to come, I should clear my conscience. I say he has manufactured a Michelangelo in his heart out of that same stuff he has in it.

Continuing still further about the tomb of Pope Julius, I say that after he changed his mind, that is, from making it in his lifetime, as was said, and certain boatloads of marble came to the shore, which I had ordered some time before at Carrara, not being able to get money from the Pope because he had decided not to go on with the work, I had to pay for the shipment either a hundred and fifty or two hundred ducats which I borrowed from Baldassare Balducci, that is, the bank of Master Jacopo Gallo, to pay the freightage of the aforesaid marbles; and since stonemasons came from Florence at that time, whom I had sent for because of the aforesaid tomb, of whom some are still living, and since I had furnished the house that Julius had given me behind Santa Caterina with beds and other furnishings for the blockcutters and for other things for the said tomb, I felt much at a loss without money, and, press-

---

1 A very small town; that is, I am a city man who knows what's what.

ing the Pope to continue as much as I could, he, one morn-
ing when I was about to talk with him about the matter,
he had me turned away by a groom. When a Bishop from
Lucca who saw this act said to the groom, "Don't you
know this man?" the groom said to me, "Pardon me, sir,
I have orders to do this." I went off to my house and wrote
this: "Most Blessed Father: I have this morning been
driven out of the Palace on behalf of your Holiness,
whence I wish you to understand that from now on, if you
want me, you will seek me elsewhere than in Rome." And
I sent this letter to Master Agostino the steward, to give to
the Pope, and I called into the house one Cosimo, a car-
penter, who lived with me and did my work around the
house, and a stonecutter, who is alive today, and told them,
"Go for a Jew, and sell what is in this house, and come
away to Florence," and I went and took the post horses,
and went off toward Florence. The Pope, having received
my letter, sent five men-at-arms after me, who reached me
at Poggibonsi about three hours after sunset and presented
me with a letter from the Pope, which said, "At once, when
you have seen these presents, under pain of our displeasure,
you are to return to Rome." The aforesaid men-at-arms
wanted me to answer to show they had found me. I an-
swered the Pope that any time he would keep to what he
was obligated I would return; otherwise he should never
hope to have me. And then, when I was living in Florence,
the Pope sent three briefs to the City Council. At last the
Council sent for me and said, "We don't want to make
war against Pope Julius for you; you have to go away, and
if you want to go back to him, we will give you letters of
such authority that if he should do you any harm, he would
be doing it to this Council." And thus indeed it did, and I
went back to the Pope, and what followed would be long

to tell. Enough; this affair did me more than a thousand
ducats' damage, because when I left Rome it made a lot
of noise, with shame to the Pope, and nearly all the marbles
I had on St. Peter's Square were stolen from me, and espe-
cially the small pieces, so I had to redo them, to such a
point that I say and affirm that either for damages or in-
terest five thousand ducats is due me from the heirs of
Pope Julius; and in the meantime those who have taken
all my youth and honor and property from me call me
thief! And again, as I wrote before, the Ambassador of
Urbino sends to tell me that I should first clear my con-
science, and then the endorsement from the Duke will
come. He didn't talk that way before he made me deposit
fourteen hundred ducats. In these things I write I may be
mistaken in the dates only from the beginning on; every
other thing is true, and more than I write.

I beg your lordship for the love of God and the truth
read these things, so that if it arose you could defend me
to the Pope against those who speak ill of me without
knowledge of anything and have put into the Duke's head
that I am a great rascal, with their false reports. All the dis-
agreements that arose between Pope Julius and me were
due to the envy of Bramante and Raphael of Urbino, and
this was the cause of his not continuing his tomb in his
lifetime, in order to ruin me; and Raphael had good reason
for it, for what he had in art he had from me.

58

(TO HIS NEPHEW LIONARDO;
ROME, JULY 1544)

Lionardo: I have been ill, and you, at the instigation of
Master Giovan Francesco, have come to put an end to me

and see if I leave anything.[1] Isn't there enough of mine in
Florence to suffice you? You can't deny you are like your
father, who drove me out of my house in Florence. Know
that I have made a will in such a way that of what I have
in Rome you are not to think any more. So go in God's
name and don't turn up in front of me, and don't write me
ever again, and do as the priest does.

Michelangelo

59

(TO HIS BROTHERS GIOVANSIMONE AND
GISMONDO; ROME, DECEMBER 6, 1544)

For some time I have been thinking of investing up to a
thousand ducats little by little in a wool business for
Lionardo, if he behaves properly, with this condition, that
he cannot without your permission withdraw it or do any-
thing different with it; and I have a banker's order to start
in this sense with two hundred scudi, which I shall now
have paid there, if you answer that I should do it; and if
you feel I should do it, you must be careful it is not put in
danger, because I didn't find it on the street. Answer me
what you feel should be done; you are able to judge Lio-
nardo's conduct better than I, and whether we should be-
come involved.

Michelangelo Buonarroti in Rome

60

(TO MASTER SALVESTRO DA MONTAUTO
IN ROME; ROME, FEBRUARY 3, 1545)

*My Lords, Master Salvestro and Company, in Rome, as on
the reverse of the sheet:* As you know, I being kept busy in

---

[1] Lionardo hastened to Rome when he learned that Michelangelo was
ill.

the service of our lord Pope Paul III to paint his new chapel, and so unable to finish the tomb of Pope Julius II in San Pietro in Vincoli; and the above-mentioned Holiness, our lord, having interposed with the consent and by an agreement made with the Lord Hieronimo Tiranno, Ambassador of the most illustrious Lord Duke of Urbino, which agreement his excellency thereafter endorsed, I deposited with you various sums of money to finish the said work, of which Raffaello da Montelupo was to have four hundred and forty-five scudi of ten julii per scudo as the balance of five hundred and fifty similar scudi, and this to finish five marble statues begun and roughed out by me and commissioned from him by the above-mentioned Ambassador of the Duke of Urbino, that is, an Our Lady with the Child in her arms, a Sybil, a Prophet, an Active Life, a Contemplative Life, all of which appears in the contract drawn by Master Bartolomeo Capello, notary of the chamber, under date of August 21, 1542. Of which five statues, our lord upon my request and for my satisfaction having conceded a little time to me, I finished two with my hand, that is, the Contemplative and Active Life, for the same price that the said Raffaello was to do them and the same money that he was to have. And since then the said Raffaello has finished the other three and installed them as may be seen in the tomb itself. Wherefore you will pay him at his pleasure a hundred and seventy scudi in coin at ten julii per scudo which remain in your hands from the above sum, taking a final receipt from him by the hand of the same notary, for which he is to consider himself satisfied and entirely paid for the said work; and deduct them from the sum that remains in your hands. And good health.
Rome, February 3, 1545 from the Birth of Christ.
Your Michelangelo Buonarroti in Rome

61

(TO HIS NEPHEW LIONARDO
IN FLORENCE; ROME, 1545)

Lionardo: I wrote you last Saturday that I would have pre-ferred two flasks of trebbiano to the eight shirts you sent me. Now I am notifying you that I have received a quan-tity of trebbiano, that is, forty-four flasks, of which I have sent six to the Pope and so much to other friends that I have allocated almost all of them, because I can't drink it; and although I did so write you, that doesn't mean I want you to send me one thing more than another. It's enough for me for you to be an honest man and do honor to your-self and the rest of us.

Michelangelo in Rome

62

(TO VITTORIA COLONNA, MARCHIONESS
OF PESCARA, IN ROME; ROME, 1545)

Lady: Before I took the things your ladyship has repeat-edly desired to give me, I wished to make something for you with my hand, so as to receive them as little un-worthily as I could; then, having realized and seen that the grace of God is not to be bought and it is a great sin to keep you in suspense, I avow my fault and willingly accept the aforesaid things; and when I have them I shall feel I am in Heaven, not because I have them in my house, but because I am in theirs, whereof I shall be left more obliged to your ladyship, if I can be more than I am.

The bearer of this will be Urbino who works for me, to whom your ladyship can say when you wish me to come and see the head you promised to show me. And greetings.

Michelangelo Buonarroti

63

(TO VITTORIA COLONNA; ROME, 1545)

Lady Marchioness: Since I am in Rome, I do not feel that
the Crucifix should be left to Master Tommaso and he
should be made the go-between between your ladyship and
me your servant, so that I can do you a service, and espe-
cially since I have wished to do more for you than for any
man I ever knew in the world; but the great busyness in
which I have been and am has not allowed me to let your
ladyship know this, and since I know you know that love
wants no master, and that he who loves does not sleep, go-
betweens were still less suitable; and though it might seem
I did not remember, I was doing something I did not speak
of, in order to effect something you did not expect. My
plan has been ruined: "Who soon forgets such trust does
evilly."

Your ladyship's servant
Michelangelo Buonarroti in Rome

64

(TO HIS NEPHEW LIONARDO IN FLORENCE;
ROME, FEBRUARY 6, 1546)

Lionardo: You were very quick to notify me about the
Corboli property; I didn't suppose you were still in Flor-
ence. Are you afraid I may change my mind, as perhaps
you have been prompted? And I tell you, I want to go slow,
because I have earned the money by a labor here that no
one can know that was born clothed and shod like you.

As to your having come to Rome in such a hurry, I don't
know whether you would have come if I had been in misery
and lacking for bread; enough for you to throw away the
money you haven't earned. You are so anxious not to lose

this inheritance! And you say it was your duty to come here for the love you bear me; the termite's love! If you bore love toward me you would have written at this point: "Michelangelo, spend the three thousand ducats there for yourself, since you have given us so much it's enough for us; we prefer your life to your property."

You have lived on what was mine for forty years now, and I have never had a good word from you, not to mention anything else.

It is true last year you were so rebuked and scolded that for shame you sent me a quantity of trebbiano. Would you hadn't even sent it!

I don't write you this because I don't want to buy; I want to buy to give myself an income, because I can't work any longer, but I want to go slow, so as not to buy any troubles, so don't hurry.

Michelangelo in Rome

When something is said or asked of you there on my behalf, if you don't see a line in my handwriting don't believe anybody.

The thousand ducats or scudi I sent you, if you think over what can happen to shops on account of wicked employees or other things, you will sooner buy the property, because it's a more stable thing. But anyway, consult together and do what you feel best.

65

(TO THE MOST CHRISTIAN KING
OF FRANCE; ROME, APRIL 26, 1546)

Sacred Majesty: I know not which is greater, the grace or the wonder that your Majesty has deigned to write to one of my station, and still more to ask him for things of his, unworthy of your Majesty's name, not to mention anything else; but since it is so, your Majesty should know that I have desired to serve you for a long time, but have not done so because I have had no time that was suitable, nor, for that matter, any at all in Italy, for my art. Now I find myself old and busy for a few months with Pope Paul's affairs, but if after this activity I am left some space of life, I shall try to put into effect what I have desired, as I said, to do for your Majesty for a long time, that is, one thing in marble, one in bronze, one in painting. And if death interrupts this wish of mine, and if one can paint or carve in the other life, I shall not fail there, where there is no more growing old. And I pray God He will give your Majesty a long and happy life.

Rome, April 26, 1546
> *Your most Christian Majesty's most humble servant*
> *Michelangelo Buonarroti*

66

(TO HIS NEPHEW LIONARDO IN FLORENCE; ROME, JUNE 5, 1546)

Lionardo: I have had the memorandum of the power of attorney copied without change, and I make you my attorney and send it to you. Have it looked over yourself, and if it is according to your wish that is enough for me, for my mind is on things other than powers of attorney; and don't write me any more, for whenever I have one of your letters I get a headache, it's such work to read it! I don't know where you learned to write. I believe if you had to write to the world's greatest ass, you'd write more carefully. So don't add bothers to those I have, for I have enough to suffice me. You have the power of attorney to show and to be examined, and if you don't have that done the loss will be yours.

Michelangelo in Rome

67

(TO LIONARDO; ROME, DECEMBER 1 5 4 6)
Lionardo: About a year ago a manuscript book of Floren-
tine chronicles came into my hands, where I found that
about two hundred years ago, if I recall correctly, a
Buonarroto Simoni was a member of the Council several
times, then a Simone Buonarroti, then a Michele son of
Buonarroto Simoni, then a Francesco Buonarroti. I didn't
find Lionardo, who was a member of the Council, the
father of Lodovico our father, because it didn't get down
that far. So I feel you should write yourself Lionardo son
of Buonarroto Buonarroti Simoni. There is no need to an-
swer the rest of yours, because you still haven't understood
anything of the matter I wrote you about, nor about the
house.

Michelangelo in Rome

68

(TO LIONARDO; ROME, 1 5 4 7)
Lionardo: I wrote you about getting married and informed
you about three girls who had been spoken of to me here;
one is a daughter of Alamanno de' Medici, one the daugh-
ter of Domenico Gugni, and the other the daughter of
Cherubin Fortini. I do not know any of these men, so I can
tell you neither good nor ill, nor advise you about one more
than another. But if Michele Guicciardini would take a
little trouble, he could find out how matters are and give us

information, and likewise if I hear anything else. So ask him to do it on my behalf and give him my greetings. As for buying a house, I feel that it's a necessity before you get married, because there's no room where you are. But when you write me, do it so I can understand the letters, if you want me to answer as to my opinion. Master Giovan Francesco could also give some good advice on these matters, because he is old and experienced; give him my greetings. But the need above all is for the counsel of God, because it's a great step, and I remind you that between husband and wife there should always be at least ten years' difference, and to take care that besides being good she is healthy. I have nothing else to say.

Michelangelo in Rome

69

(TO LIONARDO; ROME, AUGUST 1547)

Lionardo: With your letter I got the receipt for the five hundred and fifty gold scudi in gold, as I paid them to Bettino here. You write me that you will give that woman four of them for the love of God, which pleases me; the rest, up to fifty, I also want to be given for the love of God, part for the soul of Buonarroto your father and part for mine. So see to it that you find out about some needy citizen who has daughters to be married or to enter a convent, and give them to him, but secretly, and take care not to be tricked, and have a receipt made and send it to me, because I speak of citizens and I know those who are in need are ashamed to go about begging. As for getting married, I tell you I can't recommend one more than another, because it is such a long time since I was there that I can't know in what condition the citizens are, so you must think of it for yourself, and when you have found something that pleases you I shall be very glad to give you advice.

You sent me a brass yard measure, as if I were a mason or carpenter who would have to carry it around with him. I was ashamed to have it in the house and gave it away.

Francesca writes me she is not well, and has four children, and has many problems because of not being in good health. I am very grieved to hear it; as for the other things, I don't think she is lacking for anything. As for the problems, I believe I have many more than she, and old age on top of them, and have no time to entertain relatives; so comfort her on my behalf to have patience, and give Guicciardino my greetings.

I advise you to spend the money I sent you on something sound, property or something else, because it is very dangerous to keep it, now especially. So be sure to sleep with your eyes open.

Michelangelo Buonarroti in Rome

70

(TO LIONARDO; ROME, MARCH 1548)

Lionardo: I am very pleased that you informed me of the decree of banishment, because, though I have been careful up to now not to talk or have any dealings with the exiles, I shall be much more careful for the future.[1] As for having been sick in the house of the Strozzi, I consider that I was not in their house but in the room of Master Luigi del Riccio, who was my good friend, and since Bartolomeo Angelini died I have not found a better man than him to do my business, or more faithful; and since he died I have

---

[1] A strict law of exile had been decreed by Cosimo de' Medici.

not frequented the aforesaid house any more, as all Rome can bear witness, as it can to what sort of life mine is, because I always live alone, go about little and do not speak to anyone, and especially Florentines; and if I am greeted on the street, I cannot do other than respond with fair words, and pass along; and if I had information on who the exiles are, I would not answer in any way whatever; and, as I have said, from now on I shall be very careful, and especially since I have so many other worries that it's a labor to live.[1]

As for setting up a shop, do what you feel is good, because it's not my profession and I can't give good advice; only I tell you this, that if you use the money you have badly, you won't get it back again.

Michelangelo in Rome

---

[1] Michelangelo's alarm here prevents him from telling the whole truth. The Florentine exiles favored the old republic and were opposed to the establishment of the dukedom. Michelangelo had worked for the republic during its last stand, the siege in 1529, as a fortification engineer, but had fled to Venice under mysterious circumstances (letter 47); this illustrates his ambiguous position. Later, the leaders of the Florentine exiles in Rome were the Strozzi banking family and the Cardinals Ridolfi and Salviati, all cousins whose mothers were Medici of the older, extinct branch. Michelangelo had close connections with all of them. His close friend Luigi del Riccio was an employee of the Strozzi banking house, and his other friend Donato Giannotti was secretary to Cardinal Ridolfi. For Ridolfi Michelangelo carved the *Brutus*, unquestionably a symbol of republican revolt against tyrants, remarkable as the only secular work of his later years. After staying at the Strozzi house during his illness, in spite of what he says here, he made a gift to the Strozzi of his two marble *Slaves*, now in the Louvre, an extraordinary contrast with his reluctance to provide works for various kings. He also visited Riccio at the Strozzi country estate at Lunghezza (see note to poem 169). His offer to produce a painting for Cardinal Salviati may have produced the portrait of the Cardinal by Michelangelo's friend Sebastiano del Piombo. On the other hand, he insisted in conversation with Giannotti that Dante had been right in consigning Brutus to the deepest circle of Hell.

71

Lionardo: I got the crate of pears, which came to eighty-six; I sent the Pope thirty-three; he thought they were fine and liked them very much. As for the crate of cheese, the Customs Bureau says that carter is a wretch and didn't take them to the customs, so I shall do to him as he deserves whenever I know he is in Rome, not on account of the cheese but to give him a lesson in having so little respect for men. I have been very ill these last days from not being able to urinate, because I am extremely susceptible there; but now I am better; I write you so that some buzzing bee won't write you a thousand lies to make you jump. Tell the priest not to address me any more "to Michelangelo, sculptor," because I am known here in no way but as Michelangelo Buonarroti, and if a Florentine citizen wants an altarpiece painted he must find a painter, for I was never a painter or sculptor like the ones who keep a shop. I have always avoided that for the honor of my father and brothers, although I have served three popes, which has been perforce. Nothing else occurs to me. By my last previous one you will have got my opinion about the woman. Regarding those lines I have written about the priest, don't tell him anything, because I want to give the impression of not having had his letter.

Michelangelo Buonarroti in Rome

72

Lionardo: Your last letter, since I couldn't and didn't know how to read it, I threw on the fire, so I can't answer you about anything in it. I have written you several times that every time I have a letter of yours I get a headache before I figure out how to read it. So I tell you from now on, don't write me any more, and if you have to let me know anything, get hold of someone who knows how to write, since I use my head for something else besides shuddering over your letters. Master Giovan Francesco writes me that you would like to come to Rome for some days; I am surprised you can leave, having gone into the partnership you wrote me about. So be careful not to throw away the money I sent you, and likewise Gismondo must be careful of it too, because he who hasn't earned it doesn't understand it; and we see from experience that the majority of those born to riches throw them away and die ruined. So open your eyes and think, and realize in what wretchedness and toil I live, old as I am. In the last few days a Florentine citizen has come to talk to me of a daughter of the Ginori family, about whom, he tells me, you have been talked to there, and that she pleases you. I don't believe it is true, and also I don't know how to advise you because I have no information. But I am not pleased that you should marry one whom, if her father had a suitable dowry to give, he would not give to you. I would wish that whoever wants to give you a wife should want to give her to you, not to your property. I feel that not seeking a large dowry for taking a wife should be your initiative, rather than for others to want to give you a wife because she has no dowry. However, you have to desire only health of soul and body, nobility of blood, and her character and the relatives she has, which are quite important.

I have nothing else to tell. Give my greetings to Master Giovan Francesco.

Michelangelo Buonarroti in Rome

73

(TO LIONARDO; FLORENCE,
FEBRUARY 1, 1549)

Lionardo: In my last I sent you a list of eligible girls, which was sent me from there, I believe by some broker, and he must be a man of little judgment, since he should have considered what sort of information I could have on the families of Florence after I have been living in Rome sixteen or seventeen years.

So I tell you, if you want to get married do not be at my beck, because I cannot advise you of the best; but I do tell you not to go after money, but only virtue and good reputation.

I believe there are many poor and noble families in Florence with whom it would be a charity to become allied, even if there were no dowry, because there would also be no pride. You need one who will stay with you and whom you can command, and who will not put on airs and go to banquets and weddings every day; for where a court is it is easy to become a whore, and especially for one without relatives. And to say it seems you want to become ennobled shows a lack of respect, because it is known we are ancient Florentine citizens and as noble as any other house; so put your trust in God and pray Him to give you what you need, and I shall be very glad if when you find something you feel is suitable, you let me know before you close the alliance.

As for the house you wrote me about, I answered you that it was praised to me and you shouldn't bother about a hundred scudi.

You also informed me about the farm at Monte Spertoli; I answered you that I had lost the desire for it, not because that was true, but for another reason. Now I tell you that if you find a good thing, and I can enjoy the income, let me know, because if it's a sure thing, I'll take it; and as to the house, if you take it, let me know what money I have to send; and what has to be done do quickly, because time is short.

I have been advised against what I wrote you about Santa Maria Nuova, so do not think of it.

February 1, 1549

74

(TO LIONARDO; ROME,
FEBRUARY 21, 1549)

Lionardo: I have written you several times, in connection with getting married, that you should not believe any man who might speak to you on my behalf, if you don't see my letters. I answer you again, because it is more than a year since Bartolomeo Bettini began trying to give me a niece of his. I have always given him back words. Now again he has made a strong attempt by means of a friend of mine. I answered that I knew you were leaning toward one you like and have almost signified your intention, and that I don't want to dissuade you. I am telling you so that you will know how to answer, because I think he will have you spoken to warmly there. Don't let yourself be hooked by the bait, because the offers are considerable, and you would end up in a way that isn't at all what you need. Bartolomeo is an honest man and loyal and respectable, but he is not our equal, and you have a sister who is married into the house of the Guicciardini. I don't believe I need to tell you anything else, because I know you know honor is worth more than property. I have nothing else to tell you. Give my greetings to Guicciardino and Francesca and tell her on my behalf to be calm, because she has many companions in her troubles and especially today, when the best suffer most.

February 21, 1549

Michelangelo Buonarroti in Rome

75

(TO LIONARDO; ROME, MARCH 15, 1549)

Lionardo: What I wrote you in my last there is no point in repeating in another form. As for my illness in which I am unable to urinate, I have been very badly off since then, groaning day and night without sleep or any rest, and as far as the doctors judge they say I have the stone. I am still not sure of it, but I am dosing myself for the aforesaid illness and am given good hope. Nevertheless, since I am old and have such a cruel illness, I should not feel assured. I am advised to go to the bath of Viterbo, and one cannot go there until the first of May, so in the meantime I shall be temporizing as best I can, and perhaps I shall be fortunate enough so that this illness will not last, or find a good remedy; yet I have need of the help of God. So tell Francesca to say prayers, and tell her that if she knew how I had been, she would see she is not without company in her misery. Otherwise I am physically almost as I was at thirty. This illness has come over me because of my great discomforts and not valuing my life very much. Patience! Perhaps it will go better than I guess, with God's help, and if otherwise I shall let you know, because I want to settle my affairs of body and soul, and for that it will be necessary for you to be present, and when I think it is time I shall let you know, and don't move on account of anybody else's words without my letters. If it is the stone, the doctors tell me it is at the beginning and small, and so they give me good hopes, as mentioned.

If you are informed of any extreme poverty in some noble house, for I think such is to be found, let me know, and who it is, and I shall send you something up to fifty scudi to give them for the good of my soul. This would not lessen at all what I have ordered to leave to you, so do it without fail.

March 15, 1549

Michelangelo Buonarroti in Rome

76

(TO LIONARDO; ROME, APRIL 5, 1549)

Lionardo: Last week I sent Bettino fifty gold scudi in gold by Urbino, which should be paid to you there. I suppose you will have received them and will do what I wrote you, either for the Cerretani or others, where you see the need, and will let me know. As for settling my affairs and what I wrote you, I didn't mean any more than that, being old and sick, I felt I should make my will. And the will is this, to leave to Gismondo and to you what I have, in this way, that Gismondo my brother is to get as much as you my nephew, and that neither can make a decision about my affairs without the agreement of the other; and if you feel like doing this through a notary, I shall endorse it at any time.

As for my illness, I am a good deal better. We are sure I have the stone, but it is a small thing, and by God's grace and the power of the water I drink it is dissolving little by little, to the point where I hope to be free of it. But still, since I am old, and for many other reasons, I would like very much to settle there what personal property I have here, to serve my needs and then be left to you, and this would be about four thousand scudi; and especially now, when I would like to have everything here in as good order as possible, since I have to go to the baths. Get together with Gismondo and think it over a little and let me know, because it is a matter of concern to you as much as to me.

As to getting married, this morning a friend of mine came to see me and asked me to inform you about a daughter of Lionardo Ginori, born to a mother from the Soderini family. I am letting you know as asked, but I don't know what to say otherwise, since I have no information; so think it over carefully and don't be influenced by anything, and when you have decided, give me an answer so I can answer my friend yes or no.

April 5, 1549

Michelangelo Buonarroti in Rome

I would be very glad if before you got married you bought a nicer and roomier house than the one where you are living, and I would send you the money.

What I write you about the Ginori girl I write you only because I have been asked, not so that you will take one more than another. So do just as the fancy takes you and without being influenced, as I have written you before. For me it is enough to be told in advance, so look around and think about it and do not delay, once your mind is made up.

77

(TO LIONARDO; MAY 25, 1549)

Lionardo: From your last I gather that the Chianti property has come into your hands. You seem to say for two thousand three hundred florins, of seven pounds each. If it

is a good thing, as you say, you have done well not to
bother about the price. I have taken Bartolomeo Bettini
five hundred gold scudi in gold to pay there to you as the
first installment, and on Saturday next I shall send another
five hundred through the Altoviti, and when Urbino is
here, who went to Urbino a few days ago but will be back
in eight or ten days, I shall send you the balance. The gold
scudi in gold that I send you are worth fifteen julii each
here. About the Monte Spertoli property, if it is a good
thing and they are selling it during the minority of the
heir, see to it that it gets into your hands as well, and don't
bother about the price. Nothing else occurs to me. Go for
the aforesaid money and notify me. Enclosed is the order
for payment.

May 25, 1549

78

(TO BENEDETTO VARCHI IN
FLORENCE; ROME, 1 5 4 9)

Master Benedetto: So it may indeed appear that I have
received your little book, as I have, I shall answer some-
thing to the questions it asks me, although I am not well
informed.[1] In my opinion painting is to be considered the
better the more it approaches relief, and relief is to be con-
sidered the worse the more it approaches painting; and
therefore I used to feel that sculpture was the lantern of
painting, and that there was the difference between them
that there is between the sun and moon. Now, since I have
read the point in your little book where you say that, philo-

---

[1] Benedetto Varchi, a Florentine scholar, edited a symposium on the
question of which is the nobler art, painting or sculpture.

sophically speaking, those things that have the same end
are the same thing, I have changed my opinion, and say
that, if greater judgment and difficulty, obstacles and labor,
do not make greater nobility, painting and sculpture are
one identical thing; and since it is so concluded, every
painter ought to do no less sculpture than painting, and
likewise the sculptors as much painting as sculpture. I
mean by sculpture what is done by main force in cutting
off; what is done by adding is similar to painting; enough
that since the one and the other come from the same
faculty, that is, sculpture and painting, they can make
peace together between themselves and leave such disputes
behind, for more time goes into them than into making
figures. As for the man who wrote that painting was more
noble than sculpture, if he had understood the other things
he wrote as well as he did this, my serving maid would
have written them better. Infinite things, never yet said,
ought to be said about these studies, but, as I have said,
they would call for too much time, and I have little, be-
cause I am not only old but almost one of the number of
the dead; so I beg you to accept my excuses. And I greet
you and thank you as much as I can and know how for the
too great honor that you do me, one not suitable for me.

Yours, Michelangelo Buonarroti in Rome

79

(TO MASTER LUCA MARTINI;
ROME, 1549)

Lord Master Luca: I have received one of yours from Mas-
ter Bartolomeo Bettini with a little book, a comment on
a sonnet from my pen. The sonnet does in fact come from
me, but the comment from Heaven, and is truly a mar-

velous thing, which I say not as my opinion but as that of men able to judge, especially of Master Donato Giannotti, who never tires of reading it and who greets you. As to the sonnet, I know it for what it is, but regardless of that I cannot keep from a little access of vanity, since it has been the cause of such a beautiful and learned comment. And since I feel myself become what I am not, in its author's words as in his praises, I beg you to employ such words to him as are suitable to such love, affection, and courtesy. I beg you to do this because I feel myself powerless, and when one has such a good reputation, one shouldn't tempt fortune; it is better to be silent than fall from the heights. I am old, and death has robbed me of the thoughts of youth, and just let anyone who doesn't know what old age is wait until it comes, for he cannot know beforehand. Give my greetings, as I said, to Varchi, as a most devoted admirer of him and of his virtues, and one at his service wherever I may be.

Yours, and at your service in all things possible to me.
Michelangelo Buonarroti in Rome

80

(TO LIONARDO; ROME, JULY 19, 1549)

Lionardo: From your last I learned all the expenses incurred over the Chianti property, which there was no point in, because if, as you write, they are well spent, everything is fine. As for the land bordering the aforesaid property, of which you write me, I answered you that you should get hold of it if there is good security. About Monte Spertoli nothing more has been done. It will be good to buy it if it should come up for sale, since , as you wrote, there is the security that minors have it. In the last few days I have had a letter from that wife of Tessitore's, who says she wanted to get you married to one who is a Capponi on her father's side and a Nicolini on her mother's, and who is in the convent at Candeli; and she has written me a whole long Bible with a little sermon that exhorts me to live well and give alms, and says she has exhorted you to live like a Christian; and she must have told you she is inspired by God to give you the aforesaid girl. I say she would do much better to attend to spinning or weaving than go about distributing such holiness. My feeling is she wants to be another Sister Domenica,[1] so do not trust her. As for getting married, since I feel it is necessary, I cannot advise you about one more than another, because I have no information on the citizens, as you can imagine and as I have written you on other occasions; so you must think for yourself, and seek diligently, and pray God that He be with you indeed, and if you should find one you like, I should be very glad if you would let me know before it is settled.

July 19, 1549

Michelangelo in Rome

81

(TO MASTER GIOVAN FRANCESCO FATTUCCI, PRIEST OF THE CATHEDRAL, VERY DEAR FRIEND IN FLORENCE; ROME, OCTOBER 1549)

Master Giovan Francesco, dear friend: Though we have not written each other anything for some months, our long and good friendship is not forgotten, nor is it that I do not

---

1 A pretended prophetess who at one time had quite a reputation in Florence.

desire your welfare as I always have or do not love you with all my heart, and more for the infinite kindnesses received. About old age, in which we find ourselves equally, I would be very glad to know how yours is treating you, for mine does not make me very happy, so I beg you write me something. You know how we have a new Pope, and who he is; about this all Rome is rejoicing, thank God, and nothing but the greatest good is expected of it, especially for the poor, because of his liberality. About my own affairs I would be very glad, and you would do me a great kindness to let me know how Lionardo's affairs are going, and the truth without ceremony, because he is young and I am anxious for him and the more so since he is alone and without advice. Nothing else occurs to me, except that in recent days Master Tommaso Cavalieri has begged me to thank Varchi on his behalf for a certain wonderful little book of his that has been printed, in which, he says, he speaks very honorably of him and no less of me; and he has given me a sonnet that I did for him about the same time, requesting me to send it to him [Varchi] to expound, which I enclose with this; if you like it, give it to him; if not, give it to the fire, and consider that I am fighting with death and have other matters in my head; yet sometimes one must do such things.[1] I beg you to thank Master Benedetto for doing me such honor in his sonnets, as I have said, and offer him what little I am.

Yours, Michelangelo in Rome

---

[1] In a rough draft this part of the letter read: "These past days, being very unhappy around the house, hunting among some things, a great number of these squibs fell into my hands that I used to send you, of which I send you four that I perhaps sent you another time. You will surely say I am old and mad; and I say, to keep healthy and keep down suffering, nothing is better than madness."

82

(TO MASTER GIOVAN FRANCESCO FATTUCCI
IN FLORENCE; ROME, AUGUST 1, 1550)

Master Giovan Francesco, dear friend: Since I happen to
have to write to Master Giorgio [Vasari] the painter there,
I take advantage of it to put you to a little bother, which is
to give him the letter which is in this, considering him a
friend of yours; and so as not to be too brief in writing you,
having nothing else to write, I send you one of my tales
[poems] that I wrote to the Marchioness of Pescara [Vit-
toria Colonna], who was exceedingly fond of me, and I of
her no less. Death took a great friend [*amico*, the masculine
form] from me. Nothing else occurs to me. I am in my
usual health, bearing the disabilities of old age with pa-
tience. I believe you are doing the same.
August 1, 1550

83

(TO LIONARDO; AUGUST 7, 1550)

Lionardo: Since the receipt of the trebbiano wine and the
shirts I have had no reason to write you; now, it's because it
would be convenient for me to have two briefs of Pope
Paul's, which contain the life salary that his holiness pro-
vides me while I remain in his service in Rome, which
briefs I sent there [to Florence] with other papers in the
box you received, and they must be inside certain tin boxes;
I know you will recognize them; so you can do them up in
a bit of waxed cloth and send them in a little box well done
up with ropes, and if you can see a way that you can send
them by someone trustworthy, so they won't go astray, send
them to me and put whatever valuation on it you like, so
that I get them. I want to show them to the Pope, so he

can see that, according to them, I am his holiness's credi-
tor, I believe, for more than two thousand ducats; not that
such a thing will do me any good, but for my own satisfac-
tion. I think the postman could carry them, since they are
a small thing.

On the matter of getting married there is no more talk,
and everyone tells me I should give you a wife, as if I had
a thousand in a sack. I have no way to give thought to it,
because I have no knowledge of the citizens. I should be
very glad if you were to find one, and you must, but I can
do nothing more, as I have written you several times.

Nothing else occurs to me. Give my greetings to the
priest and my friends.

August 7, 1550

Michelangelo Buonarroti in Rome

84

(TO LIONARDO; ROME, AUGUST 16, 1550)

Lionardo: In your last you write me that Cepperello wants
to sell the farm that borders on ours at Settignano, and as
for that woman who has it for life, the aforesaid Cep-
perello, if he could arrange to sell it now, must arrange for
her to have as much of the price as is proportionate to the
time the said woman lives, even though she will inevitably
keep it until her death. I do not feel this is a thing
that should be done, on account of many accidents that
could happen, which would be dangerous, while we were
not in possession; therefore we should wait until she dies,
and if Cepperello comes to speak to me, I shall tell him my
attitude; but I have no intention of going to hunt him up.

I wrote you about the two briefs as you know; if you see
a way in which you could send them to me by a trust-

worthy person so that I am sure to get them, send them to me; if not, let them stay.

About getting married, you write that you first want to come here to talk to me face to face; I am very badly off as to living arrangements and at great expense, as you will see; I do not say on that account that you ought not to come, but I think it would be best to let half of September go by, and in the meantime maybe I'll find a maid who would be good and clean, though it is difficult because they are all pigs and whores; let me know; I pay ten julii a month; I live poorly, but I pay well.

In the past few days I have been spoken to about a daughter of Altovito Altoviti; she has neither father nor mother and is in the convent of San Martino. I don't know her and don't know what to say about this.

August 16, 1550

Michelangelo Buonarroti in Rome

85

(TO LIONARDO; DECEMBER 20, 1550)

Lionardo: I got the March cheeses, that is, a dozen of them. They are very fine; a part of them shall be for friends and a part for the house. And as I have written you on other occasions, don't send me anything more unless I ask you for it, and especially what costs you money.

About getting married, as is necessary, I have nothing to tell you, except not to consider the dowry, because property is more common than men; you must have an eye only to nobility and health, and to goodness more than anything else. As for beauty, since you are not the handsomest young fellow in Florence, you should not be too much concerned about that, so long as she is not lame or distasteful. There is nothing else to add about this.

Yesterday I had a letter from Master Giovan Francesco asking me if I have anything of the Marchioness of Pescara's. I would like you to tell him that I'll hunt and answer him this coming Saturday, although I don't think I have anything, because when I was sick in bed away from the house, many things were taken away from me. If you should know of any great poverty in some noble citizen, and especially those having daughters in the house, I would be very glad if you would let me know, because I would like to help them for the good of my soul.

December 20, 1550
> *Michelangelo Buonarroti in Rome*

86

(TO LIONARDO; FEBRUARY 2 8, 1 5 5 1)

Lionardo: By your last, about getting married, I gather you haven't got anywhere yet; I don't like it, because it is really necessary to get married, and as I have written you on other occasions, I don't feel that, having what you have and will have, you need to look for a dowry, but only for goodness, health, and nobility; and consider that, if one who is well brought up, good, healthy, and noble, has nothing, you could marry her as an act of charity, and if you did this, you would not be tied up with the ostentation and caprices of women, so that the result would be more peace in the house; and as for feeling a desire to be ennobled, as you wrote me before, that is not a valid point, because it is known that we are ancient Florentine citizens. So think over what I write you, since neither in your lot nor in your person are you worthy of the greatest beauty in Florence. Take care, so that you won't be cheated.

As for the alms I asked you to give there, you replied I should tell you how much I wished to give, as if I were in a position to give some hundreds of scudi. When you were here last, you bought me a piece of cloth, which I thought I understood had cost you between twenty and twenty-five scudi, and these scudi I then thought to give in Florence for the souls of all of us. Since then, and because of the great famine here, they have been changed into bread, and if no other help comes, I even wonder whether we shall all die of hunger.

Nothing else occurs to me. Give my greetings to the priest and when I can, I shall answer what he asked me. *Last of February* 1551

Michelangelo in Rome

87

(TO LIONARDO; MARCH 7, 1551)

Lionardo: I got the pears, ninety-seven of the pole kind, since you baptize them thus. There is nothing else to be said about them. On the matter of getting married, I wrote you my views last Saturday, that is, that you should give no consideration to the dowry, but only to her being of good blood, noble, and well brought up and healthy; I don't know of anything else specific to tell you, since I know as much of Florence as one who has never been there. In these last days I have been told about one of the Alessandri, but I didn't learn any details. If I learn any, I shall inform you in my next.

Master Giovan Francesco asked me about a month ago for something of the Marchioness of Pescara's, if I had anything. I have a little parchment book she gave me about ten years ago, in which there are a hundred and three sonnets, excluding those she sent me from Viterbo on paper, which are forty; these I had bound in the same little book and lent it at that time to many persons, so that they are all in print. I also have many letters which she wrote me from Orvieto and Viterbo. That is what I have of the Marchioness's. So show this to the aforesaid priest, and let me know how he answers.

About the money that I wrote you to give out there as alms, as I think I wrote you on Saturday, I have to convert it into bread because of the shortage there is, so that if some other help doesn't turn up I question whether we may not all die of hunger.

March 7, 1551

Michelangelo in Rome

88

(TO LIONARDO; DECEMBER 19, 1551)

Lionardo: From your last I learned about the shortness of sight,[1] which I feel is no small defect, so I answer you that here I have promised nothing, and since up to now you have promised nothing there, I feel it's a thing not to get mixed up with, since you are certain; because, as you write me, it is hereditary. Now I tell you again what I have written before, that you should look for one who is healthy, and more for the love of God than for a dowry, so long as she is good, and noble, and don't let her poverty disturb you, because then one can live more in peace, and what dowry is suitable I shall give you. Nothing else occurs to

---

1 Of one of the girls under discussion as a wife.

me on this point. I find myself old and with a little capital that I wouldn't want to spend here, so if I found a good house or property there that was a safe thing, for the sum of a thousand and five hundred scudi, I would be for taking it; so look out for one, so that it won't be lost if I were to die here, which may happen any time.

December 19, 1551

> *Michelangelo Buonarroti in Rome*

89

(TO LIONARDO; FEBRUARY 20, 1552)

Lionardo: Talking the other day about that matter with the uncle, he told me he was very much astonished that it was being held up, and he imagined some pinchpenny had interfered, to get at that property or to inherit it; I thought I ought to tell you what was said.

Now, as I write, one of yours has been brought to me, from which I learn of a daughter of Carlo, son of Giovanni Strozzi. I knew Giovanni Strozzi when I was a boy, and he was an honest man; I have nothing else to tell you; I also knew Carlo, and think it may be a good thing.

About the property you inform me of, I don't like them near Florence; I feel it would be more to the point in Chianti, so if something safe were to be found there, I would be for taking it and not bothering about two hundred scudi.

About getting married, I have no way of understanding anything here, since I have no dealings at all with Florentines, and less with others.

I am old, as I wrote you in my last, and in order to remove anyone's vain hopes, if there are such, I am thinking of making a will and leaving what I have there to Gismondo my brother and you my nephew, and that neither can take steps of any kind without the other's consent, and if you remain without legitimate heirs, San Martino is to inherit everything, that is, the income should be given for the love of God to the humble, that is, to poor citizens, or otherwise as is best, as you will advise me.

February twenty, 1552

Michelangelo Buonarroti

90

(TO LIONARDO; JUNE 24, 1552)

Lionardo: I got the trebbiano wine, that is, forty-four flasks, for which I thank you. I think it is very good, but I can enjoy it little, because when I have given my friends a few bottles, what is left turns to vinegar in a few days. So another year, if I am here, it will be enough to send ten flasks, if it can go in someone else's shipment.

In the last few days Bishop Minerbetti was here, and when I met him with Master Giorgio [Vasari] the painter, he asked me about you and about getting married, and we talked it over; he said he had a good wife to give you, and besides she would not have to be taken for the love of God. I did not inquire further, because I felt he was going too fast. Now you write me some member of his family, I don't know who, has talked to you there and encouraged you to get married and told you I want it very much. This you would be able to know yourself from the letters I have written you over and over, and I repeat it again, so that our existence may not come to an end here, even though the world wouldn't be undone, still every creature does its best to conserve its own species. So I want you to get married when you find something suitable, that is, healthy and well brought up, from people of good reputation; and when the qualities that one looks for in such a case are good, not to look for a dowry; and still, if you don't feel like getting married on account of your own health, it is better to try to live than to kill oneself to produce others. I tell you this, finally, because I see this going on a long time, and I wouldn't want you on my urging to do something against your own self, because you would never get any good of it and I would never be happy.

As to my finding you something here that would be suitable, you can imagine that in such a matter I am the last person on earth, because I have no acquaintances, and especially among the Florentines, but I shall be very glad if, when you have something concrete, you let me know before you settle the matter. I have nothing else to tell you. Pray God He will give us a good one.

June 24, 1552

Michelangelo in Rome

91

(TO LIONARDO; ROME, OCTOBER 1552)

Lionardo: I have had great pleasure in learning from yours that the affair satisfies you. But take care, since between the two you saw together you aren't sure which is the one they are talking about, that you aren't given the one in place of the other, as was done to a friend of mine once. So keep your eyes open and don't be in a hurry. As for the dowry, I shall secure it and do what you tell me, but it has been said to me here there is no dowry at all. So go into it with leaden shoes, because one can never turn back, and I would be greatly grieved if you didn't satisfy yourself, whether on account of the dowry or anything else. The family connection pleases me very much, as I wrote you, and since the elements to be desired in such a case are also present, I don't think the dowry should be bothered over if it isn't as you wish. I have told you to keep your eyes open, because you are being pressed, and I feel it shouldn't be thus, they being who they are in every branch, so one must pray over it and have prayers said, so that what is best may happen, since things like this are done only once.

Michelangelo in Rome

92

(TO LIONARDO; ROME, OCTOBER 28, 1552)

Lionardo: Enclosed in this is the answer I make to Michele Guicciardini about your getting married; and I write him that I am prepared to have my property be the security for the dowry, wherever or however you like, and I request him to take a little trouble in this matter; so take the letter to him and he will explain my feelings to you about how the security should be handled, or otherwise if you prefer; and to you I say don't buy a pig in a poke, but see to it that you examine her very carefully with your own eyes, because she could be lame or unhealthy, and then you would never be happy; so be as diligent as you can and ask God to help you. Nothing else occurs to me, and writing is a great bother to me.

October 28, 1552

Michelangelo Buonarroti in Rome

93

(TO LIONARDO; APRIL 22, 1553)

Lionardo: From yours I learn how the discussions have come to fruition that were picked up again about Donato

Ridolfi's daughter, for which God be thanked, and I pray Him that it has happened by His grace. With regard to the security for the dowry, I have had the power of attorney made out in your name, and so I send it to you with this, so that the dowry that you write me of, a thousand and five hundred ducats of seven lire each, can be secured on whatever part of my property you like. I have spoken with Master Lorenzo Ridolfi and said the appropriate words as best I could. Nothing else occurs to me for now. Write me further how the matter works out, and I shall think about sending something, as is usual.

April 22, 1553

Michelangelo Buonarroti

94

(TO LIONARDO; ROME, MAY 20, 1553)

Lionardo: I learn from your last how you have your wife at home and how you are very happy with her, and how you greet me on her behalf, and how you haven't yet given security for the dowry. I have very great pleasure in the satisfaction you have, and I feel God should be thanked continually, as much as man knows how and can. As to securing the dowry, if you don't have it don't secure it, and keep your eyes open, because in these matters of money some argument always comes up. I do not understand these matters, but I feel you should have settled everything before you had the woman at home. As for greeting me on her behalf, thank her and offer her compliments on my behalf such as you will know better how to make orally than I would in writing. I do want it to be realized that she is the wife of a nephew of mine, but I haven't been able to give her a token of it so far, because Urbino wasn't here.

Now he has returned, two days ago, so I am thinking of
making some sort of demonstration. I am told a nice neck-
lace of pearls of price would be appropriate. I have a jew-
eler friend of Urbino's looking for them, and hope to find
some, but don't tell her anything about it yet, and let me
know if you think I should do something else. Nothing else
occurs to me. So take care of your life and take notice and
be observant, for the number of widows is always far
greater than the number of widowers.

May 20, 1553
            Michelangelo Buonarroti in Rome

95

(TO LIONARDO; ROME, JUNE 21, 1553)

Lionardo: I have received the crate of trebbiano you sent
me, that is, forty-four flasks; it is very good, but it is too
much, because I have no one any more to give it to as I
used; so if I am alive this next year, I don't want you to
send me any more.

I have arranged for two rings for Cassandra, a diamond
and a ruby; I don't know by whom to send them. Urbino
has told me that one Lattanzio da San Gimignano, a friend
of yours, is leaving here after St. John's Day, and I thought
of giving them to him to take to you, or else you suggest
someone to me who is trustworthy, so they won't be ex-
changed or go astray. Let me know as quickly as possible
what you feel I should do. When you have them, I would
be glad if you would have them appraised, to see if I have
been cheated, because I am ignorant of such matters.

June 21, 1553
            Michelangelo Buonarroti in Rome

96

(TO GIORGIO VASARI; ROME, APRIL 1554)
Master Giorgio, dear friend: I had the greatest pleasure from yours, seeing you still remember the poor old man, and more that you were there at the triumph you write me of, of seeing another Buonarroto come anew, for which news I thank you all I can and know how; but I do not at all like such pomp, for man ought not to laugh when the whole world weeps; so I feel Lionardo has little judgment, and especially in celebrating the birth of a child with a joy that should be reserved for the death of one who has lived well. Nothing else occurs to me. I thank you heartily for the love you bear me, though I am not worthy of it. Things here are just so-so. On I don't know what day of April 1554.
                 Yours, Michelangelo Buonarroti in Rome

97

(TO VASARI; SEPTEMBER 19, 1554)
Master Giorgio, dear friend: You will surely say I am old and crazy to want to produce sonnets, but since many say I am in my second childhood, I wanted to act the part. From yours I see the love you bear me; know that without doubt I would be very glad to lay down my fragile bones beside my father's, as you entreat me, but if I left here now, I would be the cause of a great disaster in the construction of St. Peter's, of great shame and of great sin. But when the whole arrangement is established in such a way that it can't be changed, I hope to do everything you write, if indeed it is not a sin to discommode several greedy persons who are waiting for me to leave quickly.
September 19, 1554
                 Michelangelo Buonarroti in Rome

98

(TO LIONARDO; ROME, MARCH 1 5 5 5)

Lionardo: From your last I learn of the death of Michel-angelo,[1] which has made me as unhappy as I was overjoyed before; rather, much more. We must be patient and con-sider it is better than if he had died in old age. You do your best to keep on living, for the property that cost so much labor would be left without men.

Cepperello has told Urbino he is going there [to Flor-ence], and that the woman we talked about before, who had the farm for life, is dead; I believe he will come to see you. If he wants to sell it for the proper price with good security, take it and let me know, and I'll send you the money.

Michelangelo Buonarroti in Rome

99

(TO LIONARDO; ROME,
NOVEMBER 3 0, 1 5 5 5)

Lionardo: From yours I learn of my brother Gismondo's death, and not without the greatest pain. We need to have patience, and since he died with all his faculties and all the sacraments which the church ordains, God is to be thanked.

I am in many troubles here, and Urbino is still in bed in a bad way, and I don't know what will come of it; I am as distressed as if he were my son, for he has been very faithful in my service for twenty-five years; and since I am old, I haven't the time to make another one fit in with my

---

1 Lionardo's newborn son.

ways, so it makes me very troubled; so if you have some de-
voted person there, I beg you have prayers said to God for
his health.

November 30, 1555

Michelangelo Buonarroti in Rome

100

(TO LIONARDO; ROME,
DECEMBER 4, 1555)

Lionardo: Regarding the property Gismondo left, of which
you write me, I say everything is to be left to you. See to it
that you follow his will and pray for his soul, for nothing
else can be done for him.

I must tell you that yesterday evening the third of De-
cember, at the fourth hour, Francesco called Urbino passed
from this life, to my greatest distress, and he has left me so
much troubled and afflicted that it would have been
sweeter for me to die along with him, such was the love I
bore him, and he merited no less, because he had become a
fine man, full of faith and loyalty, so that now I feel de-
prived of life through his death and can find no peace for
myself. So I would be very glad to see you, but I don't
know how you can leave there for love of your wife. Let me
know if, after a month or a month and a half, you could
come as far as here, always with the understanding that you
have the Duke's permission. I said your coming should be
with the Duke's permission, for propriety, but I don't be-
lieve it's needed; handle it as you feel is best, and give me
an answer. Write if you can come, and I will write you
when you are to leave, because I want Urbino's wife to
have left the house first.

Michelangelo Buonarroti in Rome

101

Master Bartolomeo, dear friend: It cannot be denied that
Bramante was skillful in architecture, as much as anyone
from the time of the ancients up to now. He established
the first plan of St. Peter's, not full of confusion but clear
and neat, with ample light and isolated on all sides, so that
it did no harm to anything in the Palace and was considered
a beautiful thing, as is still clear today, so that any who
have deviated from Bramante's aforesaid arrangement, as
Sangallo did, have deviated from the truth; and anyone
with unprejudiced eyes can see whether it is so in his
model. In the first place, the circle he puts outside cuts off
all the light from Bramante's plan, and not only this, it has
no light itself, and so many dark hiding places between the
upper and lower parts that it is arranged conveniently for
an infinity of mischief, such as hiding outlaws, coining
false money, getting nuns with child and other mischief,
such that when, in the evening, the aforesaid church would
be locked, it would take twenty-five men to hunt out who-
ever might be lying hidden inside, and finding them would
be hard for them, and that's how it would be. Then there
would be this inconvenience besides, that in circling around
within the addition that the model makes on the outside
of Bramante's aforesaid composition, the Pauline Chapel,
the Seal rooms, the Rota, and many other buildings would
have to be demolished, and I do not think even the Sistine
Chapel would remain intact. As for the part from the circle
outward that has been carried out and which, they say, has
cost a hundred thousand scudi, this is not true, because it
could be done for sixteen thousand, and little would be
lost in tearing it down, since the stones made for it and

the foundations couldn't be more useful, and the building would be improved two hundred thousand scudi worth and three hundred years' time. This is what I feel, without any emotion, because winning would be the greatest loss to me. And if you can get the Pope to understand this, you will give me pleasure, because I don't feel well.

Yours, Michelangelo

If the Sangallo model is followed, even more would follow; only let everything done in my time not get torn down, for it would be a very great piece of harm.

102

(TO MASTER GIORGIO [VASARI],
MOST EXCELLENT PAINTER,
IN FLORENCE; ROME, MAY 11, 1555)

I was assigned to the construction of St. Peter's by force and have served about eight years not only gratis, but to my very great hurt and unhappiness, and now that it's well on the way and there is money to spend and I am about to vault the dome soon, it would be the ruin of the aforesaid construction if I left; it would be the greatest shame throughout Christendom, and the greatest sin to my soul; so, my dear Master Giorgio, I beg you on my behalf to thank the Duke for his very great offers about which you write me, and beg his lordship that, with his kind permission and grace, I may continue here until I can leave with a good name and honor, and without sin. .

May 11, 1555

Yours, Michelangelo Buonarroti in Rome

103

Master Giorgio, dear friend: Just lately one evening a very
fine and proper young man, that is, Master Lionardo the
Duke's chamberlain, came to see me at home and with
great love and affection made me the same offers on his
lordship's behalf as you in your last. I gave him the same
answer I gave you, that is, that for my part I thanked the
Duke for such great offers as much and as well as I could,
and begged his lordship for permission to continue my
work on the construction of St. Peter's here until it is com-
pleted, so that it could not be changed in order to give it
another form, because, if I left sooner, it would be the
cause of a great catastrophe, a great shame, and a great sin,
and this I beg you for the love of God and St. Peter to beg
the Duke, and give his lordship my greetings. My dear
Master Giorgio, I know that you recognize in my writing
that I am at the twenty-fourth hour, and not a thought
arises in me that doesn't have death carved in it; and God
grant I still keep it in impatience for a few years.

June 22, 1555
            Yours, Michelangelo Buonarroti in Rome

104

Master Giorgio, dear friend: I can write only with difficulty,
but still as an answer to yours I shall say something. You
know that Urbino is dead, which for me was a very great
mercy of God, but my heavy hurt and infinite sorrow. The
mercy is that, as in his life he kept me alive, dying he

taught me to die, not against my will but welcoming death. I had him twenty-six years and found him most loyal and faithful, and now that I had made him rich and expected him to be a staff and refuge for my old age, he has been taken from me, and no hope is left me but to see him again in Heaven. And of this God has given a sign through the happiness with which he met death, and he was much more distressed than in his own dying at leaving me alive in this traitorous world, with so many troubles, although the greater part of me has gone with him and nothing is left me but an infinite sorrow. And I greet you and request you, if it does not disturb you, to make my excuses with Master Benvenuto [Cellini] for not answering his, because I am filled with such grief at thoughts like this that I cannot write; and give him my greetings, and I greet you.

February 23, 1556

Yours, Michelangelo Buonarroti in Rome

105

(TO LIONARDO BUONARROTI SIMONI,
VERY DEAR NEPHEW, REQUESTING THE
CORTESI TO GIVE IT TO HIM, IN FLORENCE,
AT ONCE; ROME, OCTOBER 31, 1556)

Lionardo, very dear nephew: Some days ago I received one of yours, which I have not answered sooner, not having any convenient way; and now I shall fill in everything, so you will not be surprised, and so you will understand. More than a month ago, finding that the work on the construction of St. Peter's had slowed down, I decided to go as far as Loreto, as an act of devotion; so, being a little tired when in Spoleto, I stopped a bit to rest, with the result that I couldn't follow up my intention, since a man was

sent specially for me to say I had to return to Rome.[1] So
that, not to disobey, I started back and returned to Rome,
where by God's grace I find myself, and here one lives as
may please God, considering the crisis that's going on, so
I won't exert myself on anything else until there is a good
hope of peace here, which God please there may be. Attend
to keeping healthy, praying God to help us.
Rome, last day of October 1556
                    Yours as a father,
                    Michelangelo Buonarroti in Rome

106

(TO LIONARDO; ROME,
FEBRUARY 13, 1557)

When about two years ago the Duke of Florence's man,
Master Lionardo, came to find me here in Rome, he said
his lordship would have been greatly pleased by my return
to Florence, and made me many offers on his behalf. I an-
swered him that I begged his lordship to allow me sufficient
time to be able to leave the construction of St. Peter's at
such a point that it could not be changed, with another
design different from my arrangement. I then continued on
the aforesaid construction, having heard nothing more, and
it is still not at the aforesaid point, and besides, I am now
required in addition to make a great wooden model with
the dome and the lantern, so as to leave it at the point at
which it is fully finished; and all Rome begs me to do this,
most of all the most reverend Cardinal of Carpi, with the
result that I believe I shall have to stay here not less than

---

1 Michelangelo had fled from Rome for fear of a Spanish army then
approaching.

a year to do it; and this much time I beg the Duke to allow me for the love of Christ and St. Peter, so I can return to Florence without this pressure, and with the intention of not having to go back to Rome. As for the construction being locked up, this is not true, as can be seen, because, among stonecutters, masons, and helpers, sixty men are still working on it, and with hope of continuing.

I would like you to read this letter to the Duke, and beg his lordship on my behalf to give me the grace of the above-mentioned time, which I need before I can return to Florence, because if the arrangement of the aforesaid construction were changed on me, as envy seeks to have it, it would be as if in all this time I had done nothing.

107

(TO CORNELIA, WIDOW OF URBINO; ROME, MARCH 28, 1557)

I had realized you were annoyed with me, but I couldn't find the reason. Now from your last I feel I have understood why. When you sent me the cheeses, you wrote me that you wanted to send me other things too, but the hand-kerchiefs weren't finished yet; and I wrote you, so that you wouldn't go to any expense for me, not to send anything else, but that if you would ask me for anything you would give me the greatest pleasure, since you knew, or, even more, must be quite sure of the love I still bear Urbino though he is dead, and to all that is his. As for coming there to see the children, or sending Michelangelo here,[1] I must write you in what state I find myself. Sending Michelangelo here is not practical, because I live without women

---

[1] Urbino's son, Michelangelo's godchild.

and with no one to look after the house, the child is still too delicate, and something could happen that would make me very unhappy, and then there is also the fact that the Duke of Florence for the past month has been graciously making great efforts to get me to go back to Florence, with very great offers. I have asked him for enough time to settle my affairs here and leave the construction of St. Peter's in good state, with the result that I expect to remain here all this summer, and when my affairs and yours are settled, with regard to the Monte della Fede, to go to Florence this winter for always, because I am old and have no time to come back to Rome again, and I shall be passing your way, and if you want to give me Michelangelo, I shall keep him in Florence with greater love than the children of my nephew Lionardo, teaching him what I know, which his father wished him to learn. Yesterday on March the twenty-seventh I had your last letter.

Michelangelo Buonarroti in Rome

108

(T O   L I O N A R D O   I N   F L O R E N C E ;
R O M E ,   J U N E   1 6 ,   1 5 5 7)

Lionardo: I have received the wool and the silk; when I find someone to take it, I shall send it, and she [Urbino's widow] will send me the money at once. You will let me know about the rest of the money when you have done what I wrote you.

As for how I am, I am ill in body, with all the ills that the old usually have; with the stone, so that I cannot urinate, in my side and in my back, to such an extent that often I cannot climb the stairs; and the worst is I am filled with pains; for if I left the comforts for my troubles that I have here, I wouldn't have three days to live, and yet I do not wish on that account to lose the Duke's favor, nor would I want to fail the construction of St. Peter's here, nor fail myself. I pray God to help and counsel me, and if I got really bad, that is, in a dangerous fever, I would send for you at once. But don't think about it and don't set about coming if you don't have a letter from me to come.

Give my greetings to Master Giorgio, who can help me a great deal if he wishes, because I know the Duke thinks highly of him.
June 16, 1557

Michelangelo Buonarroti in Rome

109

(TO THE MOST ILLUSTRIOUS LORD,
COSIMO DUKE OF FLORENCE;
ROME, MAY 1557)

Lord Duke: About three months ago, or a little less, I informed your lordship that I could not yet leave the construction of St. Peter's without great hurt to it and my own very great shame, and that if I wanted to leave it at the desirable point, where it wouldn't lack what it must have, I would still need a year, and I felt that your lordship was agreeable to giving me this time. Now I have another, again from your lordship, which urges me to return more strongly than I had expected, so that I feel no little pain, because I am in more trouble and labor over the affairs of the construction than ever before; and this is because in the vault of the King of France's chapel, which is an intricate and unusual thing, a certain error has arisen, because I am old and can't go there often, so that I have to undo a great part of what was made, and Bastiano da San

Gimignano can bear witness which chapel this is and of how important it is to the rest of the construction. Once the aforesaid chapel has been put right, I believe it will be finished by the end of this summer; nothing else is left for me to do after that but to leave the model of the whole thing here, as everyone begs of me and Carpi most of all, and then to return to Florence with a mind to rest there in the company of death, with whom I try to make friends day and night, so that he won't treat me worse than other old men.

Now to return to the point, I beg your lordship to allow me the time requested of another year on account of the construction, as I had felt you were agreeable to doing when I wrote last.

Your lordship's least servant
Michelangelo Buonarroti in Rome

110

(TO GIORGIO VASARI; ROME, MAY 1557)

Master Giorgio, dear friend: I call God to witness that I was set to building St. Peter's by Pope Paul ten years ago against my will and with the greatest pressure, and if I had continued to work on the aforesaid construction up to to-day as it was being done then, I would now be where I wanted to be on the aforesaid construction, so as to be able to return to you; but it has slowed up a great deal from failure to work, and is going slowly when it has reached the most laborious and difficult part, so that if I abandoned it now, it would be nothing less than the greatest shame to lose all the reward of the labors I have endured for the love of God in the aforesaid ten years. I have written you this account in answer to yours, and because I have a letter from the Duke that has very much astonished me, that his lordship has deigned to write with such courtesy. I thank God and his excellency as much as I can and know how. I am getting off the point, because I have lost my brains and my memory, and writing is great trouble for me, because it is not my art. The final point is this: to let you know what would result if I abandoned the above said construction and left here. First of all, I would make a number of thieves happy and be the cause of its ruin and maybe of its being closed up forever; also, I have certain obligations here including a house and other things up to the value of some thousands of scudi, and if I leave without permission, I don't know what would become of them; also, I am in bad shape as to keeping alive with the stone in my bladder, kidney stone, and pains in the side, as it is with all old people, and Master Eraldo can bear witness to this, for I owe him my life. And so you will understand I haven't the spirit to come there and then return here, and if I am to come there for good, some time will be needed to arrange my affairs here so that I won't have to think of them any more. I left there so long ago that when I got here Pope Clement was still alive, who died two days later. Master Giorgio, I greet you and beg you to greet the Duke for me, and act for me, because I have no strength any more except for dying, and what I write you of my state here is more than true. The answer I gave the Duke I gave because I was told I should answer, because I hadn't the strength to write to his lordship, and particularly not at once, and if I had felt able to sit a horse, I would have come there at once and returned without its being known here.

Michelangelo Buonarroti

111

(TO LIONARDO; ROME,
DECEMBER 16, 1558)

Lionardo: Bartolomeo Ammanati, head of the Cathedral
Works of Florence, writes and asks advice on behalf of the
Duke about a certain stair that is to be made in the Library
of San Lorenzo. I have made a bit of a sketch of it roughly
in clay, as I feel it can be made, and thought to fit it up in
a box here and give it to whoever he writes he will send
here for it; so speak to him and let him know as quickly
as you can.

In my last I wrote you about a house, because if I can get
free here before I die, I would like to know I have a nest
there for me and my troop alone, and in order to do this I
am thinking of turning what I have here into money, and
if I could do it any sooner with free permission from here
and there, I would do it sooner, for, as I wrote you, I am
not lucky here.

December 16, 1558
                Michelangelo Buonarroti in Rome

112

(TO DUKE COSIMO DE' MEDICI;
ROME, NOVEMBER 1, 1559)

Most illustrious Lord Duke of Florence: The Florentines
have several times before had the strongest wish to set up a
church of St. John here in Rome. Now, hoping in your
lordship's time to have more facilities for it, they have de-
cided on it and put five men in charge, who have asked and
begged me several times for a design for the aforesaid
church. Since I knew that Pope Leo previously got the
aforesaid church started, I answered them that I did not

want to take charge of it without the Duke of Florence's order and permission. Now it happens that I find a most benign and gracious letter from your most illustrious lordship, which I take to be an express command that I take charge of the aforesaid church of the Florentines, indicating that it gives you much pleasure. I have already made several drawings for it, suitable to the site that the above-mentioned commissioners have given me for this work. They, being men of great talent and judgment, have chosen the one that would be most imposing; this will be redrawn and copied more neatly, which I cannot do on account of old age, and then be sent to your most illustrious lordship, and whatever you want will be executed.

It grieves me in these circumstances to be so old and so at odds with life that I can promise little to the aforesaid construction personally; yet while staying in my house I shall make an effort to do what may be asked of me on behalf of your lordship, and God will I may not fail you in anything.

November first, 1559

> *Your excellency's servant*
> *Michelangelo Buonarroti in Rome*

113

(TO CARDINAL RIDOLFO PIO DA CARPI;
ROME, 1560)

Most reverend Monsignor: When a plan has various parts, all those that are alike as to kind and size must be treated in the same way and in one same style, and those opposite them similarly. But when the plan changes form entirely, it is not only permitted, but required, to change the ornaments too from those mentioned, and their opposites similarly; and the parts in the middle are free to be as they wish; as the nose which is in the middle of the face is not tied to either one or the other eye, but one hand is definitely required to be like the other, and one eye like the other, because they are placed at the sides and opposite one another. And so it is certain that members in architecture derive from the members of man. One who has not been or is not a good master of the human figure, and most of all anatomy, cannot understand all this.

Michelangelo Buonarroti

114

(TO THE OVERSEERS OF THE
CONSTRUCTION OF ST. PETER'S;
ROME, 1560)

You are aware I told Balduccio that he should not send his lime if it wasn't good. Now having sent poor stuff, which must be taken back without any question, one may believe that he had made an agreement with whoever accepted it. This is a great favor to those whom I threw out of the aforesaid construction for a similar reason, and whoever accepts bad materials is only making friends with those whom I have made my enemies. I think there must be a new conspiracy. Promises, tips, and presents corrupt justice. So I request you from now on, in the name of that authority I have from the Pope, never to accept anything that is not fit to use, even if it comes from Heaven, so that I may not seem to have favorites, as I have none in fact.

Yours, Michelangelo

115

Most illustrious and most reverend, my much cherished lord and master: Master Francesco Bandini told me yesterday that your most illustrious and most reverend lordship has said that the construction of St. Peter's could not be going worse than it was going, a thing that really grieved me a great deal, because you have not been told the truth; and besides, I desire more than all other men, as I ought, that it should go well. And if I don't deceive myself, I believe I can truthfully assure you that, with regard to the work being done now, it could not be going better. But since perhaps my own interest and my old age can easily deceive me, and thus unwillingly harm or prejudice the above-mentioned construction, I propose to ask permission from his holiness, our lord, as soon as I can, to withdraw, nay rather, to speed up time. I wish to entreat as I am now doing that your most illustrious and most reverend lordship may please to free me from this vexation, which by command of the Popes, as you know, I have willingly been in without payment for seventeen years. In which time one may plainly see how much has been done through my labor on the aforesaid construction. If I can effectively beg your permission to give up the work, you could never do me a greater single kindness. And with all reverence I humbly kiss the hand of your most illustrious and most reverend lordship.

At home, Rome, September 13, 1560

> *Your most illustrious and*
> *most reverend lordship's humble servant*

116

(TO LIONARDO IN FLORENCE;
ROME, AUGUST 21, 1563)

Lionardo: I see from your letter that you are trusting certain envious, paltry fellows, who are writing you many lies, since they cannot twist or rob me. They are a gang of gluttons, and you are so silly you consider them trustworthy on my affairs, as if I were a child. Remove them from your presence, since they are envious scandalmongers and evil livers. As for being miserable because of the way I am being looked after and the other things you write me, I tell you I couldn't be living better, nor more faithfully looked after in everything; as for being robbed by the one I think you mean, I tell you I have people I can trust and be at peace with in the house. So attend to living, and don't think of my affairs, because I know how to watch out for myself if I have to, and am not a child. Keep well.

Rome, August 21, 1563

Michelangelo